Wakefield Press

Whispering Wire

Rosamund Burton was born in Ireland and grew up in England, before returning to Ireland with her family when she was eighteen. She became an actress, performing at Dublin's Gate and Gaiety Theatres, and in the film *Educating Rita* with Julie Walters and Michael Caine. She then worked for the UK's first left-wing think-tank. She moved to Australia in the mid-1990s following her fascination with her mother's stories of growing up in Australia. She writes for a range of newspapers and magazines and lives in Sydney with her husband Steve.

By the same author

*Castles, Follies & Four-Leaf Clovers:
Adventures Along Ireland's
St Declan's Way* (Allen & Unwin 2011)

Whispering Wire

Tracing the Overland Telegraph Line
through the Heart of Australia

ROSAMUND BURTON

Wakefield Press

Wakefield Press
16 Rose Street
Mile End
South Australia 5031
www.wakefieldpress.com.au

First published 2022

Copyright © Rosamund Burton, 2022

All rights reserved. This book is copyright. Apart from
any fair dealing for the purposes of private study, research,
criticism or review, as permitted under the Copyright Act,
no part may be reproduced without written permission.
Enquiries should be addressed to the publisher.

Any errors regarding people mentioned in this book are my own. I have
tried to contact all the people in the book but have been unable to find
some of them. So a couple of names have been changed.

Illustrations by Fleur Winten
Edited by Julia Beaven, Wakefield Press
Typeset by Michael Deves, Wakefield Press

ISBN 978 1 74305 960 9

A catalogue record for this book is available from the National Library of Australia

Wakefield Press thanks Coriole Vineyards for continued support

For Steve

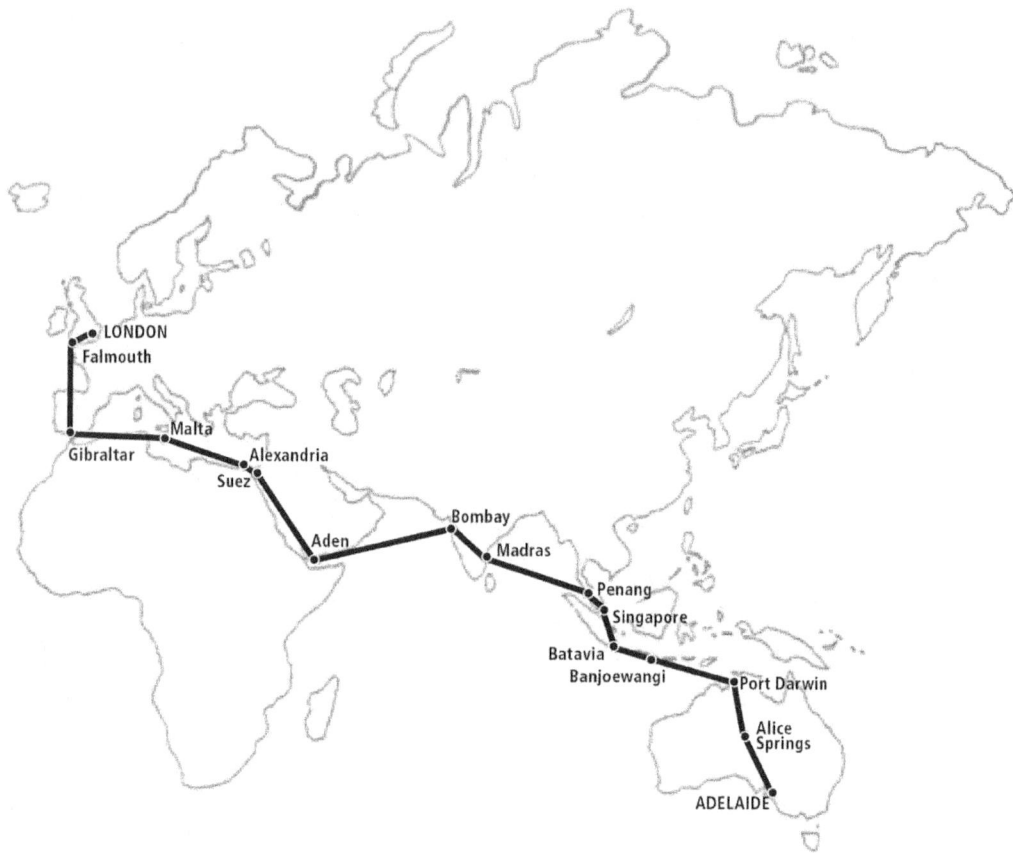

The final section of a submarine cable from England to Port Darwin was laid in November 1871.

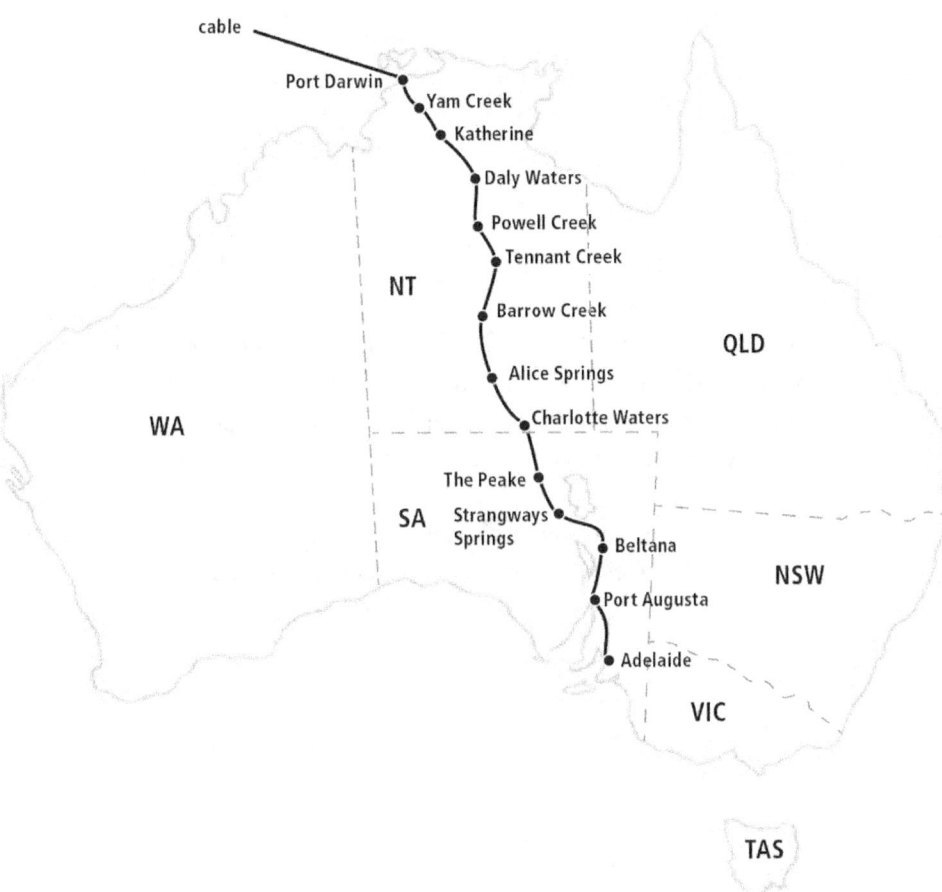

The Overland Telegraph Line was completed in August 1872.

I acknowledge the Traditional Custodians of the Country through which the Overland Telegraph Line runs. I recognise their continuing connection to land, waters and culture. I pay my respects to their Elders past, present and emerging.

Please note that this book includes references to several Aboriginal people who are now deceased.

Contents

Preface		xi
Chapter 1	Planning and Preparing	1
Chapter 2	Adelaide	6
Chapter 3	Old Photographs and Charles and Alice Todd	11
Chapter 4	On Our Way	17
Chapter 5	Tea and Todd	25
Chapter 6	Rain, Maggie Beer and Sir Sidney Kidman	34
Chapter 7	Telegraph Developments and the Hen Party	39
Chapter 8	Rattling Along the Riesling Trail	45
Chapter 9	The Barbed Wire Pub	49
Chapter 10	Golden North Ice Cream	55
Chapter 11	King Tree and Over the Edge	61
Chapter 12	Schnitzel or Fish	68
Chapter 13	Camels, a Wobbegong and the First Telegraph Pole	75
Chapter 14	A Visitor and a Phantom	81
Chapter 15	Morse Code, Mawson and Todd	87
Chapter 16	Insulators and Fossils	95
Chapter 17	Beltana Repeater Station and Telephone Communication	103
Chapter 18	Wind, a Dead Roo and Celebration	110
Chapter 19	The Twin Tub and the Railhead	116

Chapter 20	The Afghans and Hunting for Reg Dodd	119
Chapter 21	Precious Water	125
Chapter 22	Unlikely Cameleers and the William Creek Hotel	132
Chapter 23	The Peake	138
Chapter 24	Oodnadatta, the Angle Pole and Eringa	143
Chapter 25	Chambers Pillar	149
Chapter 26	Halfway and Nowhere to Stay	155
Chapter 27	Back to Alice Springs	160
Chapter 28	M.K. Turner	169
Chapter 29	Ngangkere Frank Ansell	176
Chapter 30	Gillen, the Ghan and *First Citizen*	182
Chapter 31	Calling Australia Home and Up the Stuart Highway	190
Chapter 32	Barrow Creek and a Boulder	194
Chapter 33	Nuggets of Gold	201
Chapter 34	The Joining of the Line and a Stuart Lookalike	208
Chapter 35	Floating and Flooding	217
Chapter 36	Pools and Poles	225
Chapter 37	The Undersea Cable and the Telegraph Station	230
Chapter 38	The Mills Family	239
Chapter 39	Connection	244
Selected Bibliography and Further Reading		248
Author's Note		250
Acknowledgements		251

Preface

In his book *Dreamgates*, author Robert Moss writes that according to Australia's First Nation Peoples, 'the stories worth telling and retelling, the ones in which you may find the meaning of your life – are forever stalking the right teller, sniffing and tracking like predators hunting their prey in the bush'.

A journey is never just about going from A to B: it's also about uncovering layers of stories along the way – of people and places, tensions and beauty. And now I realise that the idea for this journey was taking shape long before it became fully formed, quietly nudging me in its direction.

Was the seed planted when Burnum Burnum, the inspirational Aboriginal activist, came to my office for the last time and gave me a photograph of himself standing next to a spear tree? Or maybe it was when my husband, Steve, and I made an unsuccessful attempt to drive a Holden Commodore along a rough dirt track to Cameron Corner, where the borders of South Australia, Queensland and New South Wales meet. I sat clasping a bar of soap in my hot hand, having been told that soap was useful for repairing a ripped sump. We listened to the sound of stones hitting the undercarriage, as we inched along at barely 20 km/hr. But I knew for sure 10 years ago, when we were travelling through the Flinders Ranges, that the idea to follow the Overland Telegraph Line – the 3200-kilometre wire constructed in the 1870s to connect Adelaide to Darwin – had firmly attached itself to me, and I couldn't shake it off.

I tried not writing this story. I tried to find another, simpler story to write. A story that didn't involve a long journey and didn't need time and money. But perhaps we have no choice in our stories. Maybe stories find us and insist that we tell them.

CHAPTER 1

Planning and Preparing

I am Irish born. Fifteen years ago I asked a Wiradjuri woman how I could belong in Australia, the place I now call home. She told me to first go back to the country of my birth and understand how I belong there. So I did. I returned to Ireland and walked an ancient pilgrim path. While I was writing about my experience of following St Declan's Way, I realised I wanted to make a journey across Australia, in a way that connected me to the land and its people, and to experience the enveloping stillness and silence of the continent's vast interior.

When Steve and I visited the small town of Melrose in the Flinders Ranges and I picked up a leaflet about the Mawson Trail, a cycle route from Adelaide to the Northern Flinders Ranges, I was gripped by the impulse to cycle the first part of my journey from Adelaide, and follow the Mawson Trail wherever possible. Not keen on cycling, Steve said he would drive the off-road section of the Overland Telegraph Line route along the Oodnadatta Track and up to Alice Springs with me. From there I would either take a bus or hire a car and drive to Darwin.

So here I am, on a plane from Sydney to Adelaide with my bicycle. At my feet is my small red pannier that doubles as my handbag. In the overhead locker sits one of my large panniers that attaches to the bicycle's rear rack, which the woman at the Qantas check-in desk kindly suggested I take as hand luggage so I didn't have to pay an excess baggage fee. This was after I'd emptied the entire contents of my panniers several times onto the floor in front of the check-in counter, because I remembered I'd packed a lighter, several spare batteries and an aerosol can of WD-40 – all on the dangerous items list – while the queue of people waiting behind me lengthened.

Whispering Wire

A maxi taxi transports the bicycle box and me to North Adelaide, where I'm staying with Denise Miller. Now in her mid-80s, Denise is a schoolfriend of my mother. She directs the driver to the garage around the back of her terrace house.

'Are you taking all that with you?' she asks, when I extract my bulging panniers from the vehicle.

Denise insists we watch the six o'clock news, explaining that she was within metres of a shootout this morning. She had driven to the Central Market to buy king whiting for dinner, unaware the city was in lockdown as a man, surrounded by snipers, held four women hostage in a brothel. Policemen directed her through the deserted streets. We learn the man released the women unharmed, but shot himself. Denise is convinced the king whiting was worth running the gauntlet for, and I agree it's delicious.

A vase of fresh daffodils stands on the chest of drawers in the room where I'm sleeping, and a watercolour painted by my father of the Knockmealdown Mountains hangs on the wall. Seeing the picture, I feel a strong sense of belonging and connection; my mind floods with memories of Ireland – my father quietly humming as he mixed his paints and my mother's sweeping gesticulations as she chatted on the telephone.

I fall asleep almost as soon as my head touches the pillow, then wake several hours later as the grandfather clock in the hall strikes midnight and think about the trip ahead. I first learned about the Overland Telegraph Line eight years ago, when Steve and I drove along the Oodnadatta Track. A couple of telegraph poles with their porcelain insulators stood at the abandoned Curdimurka siding on the Old Ghan Railway. I was intrigued by the single strand of wire that once ran through the heart of Australia. This extraordinary feat of engineering, built between 1870 and 1872, connected at Darwin to an undersea cable to Java, enabling news to travel from Europe to Australia in hours, rather than the many months it took for mail by ship.

In Alice Springs we visited the telegraph repeater station, entering the small sandstone building where the telegraph operators tapped out the Morse code messages and transmitted them down the line. These labour-intensive telegrams were the precursors to today's instant communication.

When the Overland Telegraph Line was built, two-thirds of it was on

Planning and Preparing

country not settled by white people. With the line came the displacement of Australia's First People, who had lived on this land for tens of thousands of years. I became captivated by their stories. When the Alice Springs Telegraph Station ceased operations in the 1930s, it became a home for Aboriginal children – the Stolen Generations – children of white fathers who were taken from their Aboriginal mothers.

For several years I ruminated on my plan. Steve and I had just acquired a large mortgage and it seemed unjustifiable to take a couple of months off for this trip. The idea, though, had taken hold of me, and my obsession with carrying it out only grew.

I wanted a companion to cycle the first section, but who would be able to take the time, and also be happy to travel at my pace?

'I'll come with you,' said Fleur Dare, 'but I won't camp.' I was more than happy to agree, as it meant we didn't have to carry a tent, bedding and cooking equipment.

My mother, Marabella, became unwell, and I visited her in Ireland a couple of times. Between my filial duties and my work commitments, the trip was delayed, and it was another year before I rang Fleur to ask if she was still up for the expedition.

I've known Fleur since I first arrived in Sydney. Her aunt was also at St Hilda's School in Southport, with Denise and my mother. We've been friends for a long time – we'd been to each other's parties, she had been a guest at our wedding – but we'd never spent any length of time together. So we tentatively started to plan. I'd bought maps of the Adelaide Hills, South Australia's Mid North and the Flinders Ranges, and had ones of the Mawson Trail. Spreading them out on the dining table, we soon realised that much of the Mawson Trail was not a direct route northwards. We also needed to end up in a place with accommodation each day. A distance of about 50 kilometres a day would be doable, erring on less at the start because we wouldn't be fit, with slightly longer distances once we'd got into our stride. Counting a couple of days in Adelaide, we allowed ourselves three weeks to reach the outback town of Farina.

With a highlighter pen we marked the sections of the Mawson Trail we would follow, and the route we'd take where the trail deviated. We planned to leave Adelaide in the second week of June, when I could take time off from my part-time job.

'It's the worst time of year to cycle,' Steve pointed out. 'It's winter, and will be wet and cold.'

As I began a campaign to get fit, it became obvious to friends, who had only ever seen me pedalling slowly to the local produce markets, that I really was about to undertake this epic ride. They offered advice.

'You need a better bike,' said one. 'You can't cross Australia on that old bike.'

'I'm not crossing Australia,' I replied, 'I'm only going a quarter of the way.' And I was assured by Jordan Wilson – owner of the Ride In Workshop, who had cycled through India and the Himalayas – that my bicycle had a strong frame and was most suitable for this trek.

Fleur, her husband, Martin, and I signed up for a bicycle maintenance course run by the City of Sydney. We assembled one Sunday morning with a handful of people at Green Square Plaza, a hub of urban renewal in the city's inner-east. After instruction on chain maintenance, the instructor turned to tyres.

'Changing an inner tube is easy,' he told us, before proceeding to demonstrate. He instructed us to deflate our tyres and, using our tyre levers to remove the tyres from the wheels and take out the inner tubes, put the inner tubes back into the tyres and onto the wheels. Effortlessly he pressed the tyre back into the alloy rim with his thumbs. Cradling my wheel, I now tried to do the same, but no amount of thumb pressure would push my tyre back into the rim. Martin and Fleur and the rest of the group were already fitting their tyres back between the front forks, but I was still struggling.

Instantly I was overwhelmed by doubt, wondering why I had thought I could cycle through remote South Australia if I couldn't even change a tyre. The instructor came over and explained how to use my thumbs to ease the tyre back in, a small section at a time, and the recalcitrant piece of rubber eventually slipped in.

A friend who had cycled part of the Mawson Trail a couple of years earlier told me parts of it were rough and stony and that I would need mountain bike tyres. Fleur and I settled on thornproof inner tubes which, being five times thicker than a standard inner tube, would radically reduce the likelihood of a puncture. I was priding myself on my bicycle maintenance skills, having effortlessly removed the old inner tube and

Planning and Preparing

replaced it with the thornproof one. Now I just had to get 15 centimetres of tyre edge into the alloy rim, but no amount of thumb pressing, pushing or pummelling worked. Again, it wasn't boding well for the self-reliance required for this long, off-road cycling adventure. Defeated and with wheel in hand, I walked up the street to the Ride In Workshop.

'You just need to give the inner tube a bit of a shake,' Jordan said. I jiggled the wheel frantically, reapplied the thumb pressure and in it went. I couldn't wipe the grin off my face.

But now in the darkest hour of the night my mind churns over my fear and plays images of me beside the road, jiggling and shaking the tyre but unable to get it back in the wheel rim. The clock strikes one, the quarter hour, then the half hour and finally I fall back to sleep.

CHAPTER 2

Adelaide

The following morning Denise drives me into the city and I head down King William Street to the General Post and Telegraph Office. This impressive Victorian edifice, with its tall clock tower, was constructed in 1872, the year the Overland Telegraph Line from Port Augusta to Darwin was completed. It was the most expensive building in Adelaide at the time, a monument to the engineering marvel that the telegraph line represented. Established less than 40 years earlier in 1836, the small colony of South Australia had, through its telegraphic communications, linked Australia with England.

I walk up the steps and through the marble-floored main entrance into the grand Central Hall. The 20-metre-high walls curve up to a half-domed glass skylight, and from the large ceiling rose, suspended on a long thick chain, hangs a massive chandelier, each of its 12 branches holding a large round light ball. The floral mouldings, detailed cornices and ornate archways are painted in gold and shades of terracotta and vibrant green. It was here on the upper floor that the telegraph operating room was situated. At the far end of the long hall, beyond the post office's modern plastic display units holding an assortment of stationery, books and stuffed toys, is an imposing gilt-framed portrait of Charles Todd, presiding over today's comings and goings. This is the man who came from England to South Australia in 1855 to take up the position of Government Astronomer and Superintendent of Telegraphs – the man who dreamed of bringing Australia and England into telegraphic connection.

An elderly woman wearing a burgundy-coloured felt hat queues to buy stamps, a young mother waits to collect a parcel while her blonde, curly-haired daughter arranges the teddy bears on a shelf, and a middle-aged man is here to lodge a passport renewal application. The post office workers bustle back and forth behind the counter on this Friday morning, while I stand in the middle of the vast room. Only now, after so much planning, does it strike me that this is the start of my journey, because it was here that the first telegraph from England was received.

The General Post and Telegraph Office is on the corner of Tarntanyangga – Victoria Square. Before colonisation, the Kaurna people knew the Adelaide city and parklands area as Tarntanyangga, 'the Dreaming place of the red kangaroo'. On a stone pedestal across the square stands a marble statue of John McDouall Stuart, commemorating the Scottish explorer's 1861–62 expedition from Adelaide to the Indian Ocean, which paved the way for the Overland Telegraph Line 10 years later. Stuart had made several previous attempts to cross the continent. On his return from this last successful expedition he was plagued by ill health and near blindness, and was so weak that he had to be carried much of the way by stretcher. To Charles Todd, Stuart's success meant his own dream was becoming a reality. Todd quizzed Stuart about his journey, wanting to know about trees en route that would make suitable telegraph poles, and the location of permanent water. As I look up at the statue, I think of these two men, both small in stature, one a hard-working public servant, the other a surveyor and explorer prone to excess drinking. Between them, they changed the destiny of the fledgling state of South Australia.

My next port of call is the State Library on North Terrace. As soon as Charles Todd arrived in Adelaide and took up his position as Superintendent of Telegraphs, he began building telegraph lines. By 1870 South Australia's northernmost line was at Port Augusta, so the Overland Telegraph Line was constructed from there to Darwin, and I'm keen to see a map of the route.

Within 20 minutes, librarian Suzy Russell has not only found a map of the Overland Telegraph Line, but also sourced a typed booklet listing the opening dates of all the telegraph stations in the state. When I explain that I'm also interested in the explorations of John McDouall Stuart, she asks if I would like to see some of the original journals from his fifth expedition and second attempt to reach the north of the continent.

Whispering Wire

Half an hour later I'm told the archives have been retrieved from deep within the bowels of the building and I can view them in the Somerville Reading Room – an inner sanctum with precisely controlled air temperature and humidity. I'm not allowed to take my bag in – only a pencil, paper and my camera.

I lay the map on a brightly lit table and turn a couple of pages of the typed booklet. There is the list of the Overland Telegraph Line repeater stations north of Port Augusta that opened in 1872: Beltana, Strangway's Springs, Peake, Charlotte Waters, Alice Springs, Barrow Creek, Tennant Creek, Daly Waters, Katherine, Yam Creek and Port Darwin – and Powell's Creek, which opened on 1 January 1874.

When I return to the desk I'm given a box labelled 'Stuart, John McDouall Diaries & 2 MS Leaves 1860–61'. Inside are two small, worn, leather-bound notebooks. I open one. Some of the pencil script has faded, but other sections are readable.

Thursday 13th Dec, Chambers Creek

Sent some of the men back for the horses that we left behind yesterday. The rations only arrived here on Saturday night. The dried meat is not all prepared, we have still three bullocks to kill and dry which will take more than a week. It will be a fortnight before I am able to make a start ...

The writing fades and I can't make out the next words. I carefully turn the pages.

Tuesday 5th March, The Finke

Started at 5m 8 oc on a bearing of 345 00 00 for the Hugh with Thring and Lawrence. At the ck [creek] at 8 oc PM water nearly all gone, only a little in a well dug by the natives, cleared it out but it took us until 12 oc PM before we watered the four horses. The line of country passed through today was sand hills with spinifex, grassy small plains with mulga and other scrubs and occasional low table toped hills comprising of sand, lime and ironstone, also the hard-whitish flinty rock. Kangaroos plentiful but very wild ...

I can't make out the next couple of sentences.

Adelaide

The second book is a Letts diary. The opening page says 'Bills Due Book and Almanac 1861'. It's a week to view, but Stuart has ignored the dates, and in his tiny, neat handwriting he has recorded each day, sometimes in only a paragraph.

I sit at the table in the reading room, not quite believing that I'm allowed to hold John McDouall Stuart's diaries. Looking through these battered leather books, I can picture this determined Scottish surveyor every evening diligently recording his bearings, his whereabouts and descriptions of the country that the exploring party had passed through that day.

***

This evening Denise has invited to dinner her stepson and his wife, cycling enthusiasts in their 60s. Jill recounts their weekly morning rides and the cycling holidays they've been on, in both instances covering many more kilometres than I would ever attempt in a day. Denise explains that Fleur and I are setting off on our bicycles to Farina.

'That sounds wonderful,' Jill exclaims. 'Who's organising the tour?'

'We are,' I reply. Jill looks impressed.

'And how big is the group?'

'Just two,' I respond, realising that she has a vision of a 30-odd Lycra-clad pack whizzing across the country, followed by a support vehicle carrying a gourmet lunch. I explain we'll be cycling very slowly with heavy panniers and a picnic.

The following morning I decide to assemble my bicycle in Denise's garage, but it's jammed so tightly into the box that I can't lift it out. As I slowly hack, tear and cut away the cardboard, using alternately a Stanley knife and a pair of scissors, I wish I were a six-foot Amazon endowed with herculean strength, and not a scrawny, five-foot-three weakling. One strength I do have, however, is persistence, and eventually I've cut away enough of the cardboard to free the frame.

Now it's only a question of turning the handlebars and attaching the front wheel and the bicycle will be ready to go. But, hard as I try, I can't move the handlebars. I push, shove, strain and struggle, until my grunts become so loud that Denise appears.

'You're not filling me with confidence,' she remarks. She holds the rear rack so the frame stays put, but I still can't get the handlebars to move.

'It's fine,' I say, trying to sound confident. I promptly discover, with the front wheels clasped firmly between my knees, I have the leverage to turn the handlebars. Now, feeling competent, I pump up both tyres, before realising the back brake isn't working and I can't figure out why.

Given that we are about to embark on a 19-day ride, I've decided I need an expert to double-check the bicycle, so I wheel it around the corner to North Adelaide Cycles. Operating out of a small garage, the shop is run by Kim Hentschke. Not only does Kim check the bike and employ basic mechanics to fix the back brake but he also knows the Mawson Trail. He suggests I take a couple of spokes and a spoke key in case of a wheel buckle. He asks if I'll be carrying more than 20 kilos. 'Oh, no,' I say blithely. But as I cycle back to Denise's, I wonder why he wanted to know. I realise the pannier I checked in for the flight from Sydney weighed nine kilos, and the other one is probably equally heavy, so with my two water bottles and the contents of my handbag, it might amount to the ominous-sounding 20-kilo threshold, but I don't give the matter another thought.

CHAPTER 3

Old Photographs and Charles and Alice Todd

That evening Denise and I look through some of her old photographs. There's one of all the St Hilda's School prefects. Denise, Marabella and Fleur's aunt, Maudie, are lined up in their white school blouses, ties and pinafore dresses. Denise with her effervescent smile, Maudie standing casually at one end, and Marabella, with her beautiful features, in the centre. The camera doesn't pick up the large red birthmark covering the right-hand side of her face, which plagued her throughout her life. Then Denise shows me a photo of herself as Elizabeth Bennet, and Marabella, dressed in a morning jacket, playing Mr Darcy in the school production of *Pride and Prejudice*. Apparently, Dum, my grandmother, sent a message backstage to Marabella in the interval: 'A gentleman never sits on his tails. Flick them up.' So she spent the second half attempting to do just that.

Denise tells me that Marabella used to come home from school and cook the dinner every night, and she was the one who kept the ration books for the family.

'What did Dum do?' I asked.

'Painted her nails,' Denise replies, 'but your mother adored her. And we didn't like Mr Clifford.' Denise adds. He was Dum's boyfriend. My grandfather was with the British Consulate in Shanghai. As a result of the Sino-Japanese War, he was posted up the Yangtze River to the British Embassy in Chungking. My grandmother, with my 11-year-old mother and my nine-year-old uncle, were evacuated to Australia, arriving by ship in Sydney just before the bombing of Pearl Harbor. My grandmother met Mr Clifford on the ship. He was stationed in Brisbane with the air force, so she moved from Sydney to the Gold Coast to be nearby. Before

Whispering Wire

the war he had been involved in the theatre. In 1948 Vivien Leigh and Laurence Olivier were touring Australia and they came to tea with Dum and Mr Clifford. Marabella, who idolised the actors, wasn't told they were coming, and arrived home on her bicycle just in time to see the two stars driving away.

After she finished school, Marabella boarded a ship to England, but she kept in touch with her schoolfriends and, 45 years later when my father retired, she returned to Australia with him. They bought a 1980s two-tone Ford Falcon sedan, which they called the Limo, and drove through Queensland, NSW, Victoria and South Australia, visiting friends. Six months later they returned to Ireland but didn't sell the Limo, and when I got a job in Sydney, they told me it was in a shed on a friend's property, eight hours drive north of Sydney, where I was to go and collect it.

Marabella fell into a quagmire of anxiety and depression when my father died 10 years ago, from which she's never recovered, and now she's in a nursing home in County Tipperary. As her only child, part of me feels guilty that I've failed to make her happy, and as I embark on this adventure I feel torn, because if I'm not at work or with Steve, I feel I should be in Ireland with her, rather than gadding off on what she would call 'a hare-brained jolly'.

***

On Sunday afternoon Fleur pulls up at Denise's front door in a large taxi with her bicycle box in the back. After cups of tea and Denise's homemade Afghan biscuits, Fleur decides to assemble her bicycle. Despite being highly practical, she's stumped by the front wheel axle. She removed the quick-release spindle for the flight and now it won't go back in. Being a long weekend, no bicycle shops are open, but we decide to take it to Kim at North Adelaide Cycles first thing on Tuesday morning before we set off.

I mentioned to Denise a couple of days ago that I planned to visit Charles Todd's grave at North Road Cemetery, three kilometres northeast of here. On Monday morning Denise insists on driving us there, because she wants to check on the grave of her first husband, who died when their three children were still at school. Having visited Dick's grave, we trail up and down the rows of headstones searching for Todd's.

Old Photographs and Charles and Alice Todd

I ask two women who are putting flowers on an enormous white marble tomb. One suggests we look in the old part of the cemetery and points us in the right direction. Denise, who is starting to get cold, heads back to the car, while Fleur and I scour the rows.

Then I see it. At the base of a tall stone cross stand the marble headstones of Sir Charles Todd, and his wife, Alice. Beside them is a smaller cross and a stone grave marker that commemorate their son, Hedley Lawrence Todd, who died three years before his father. The other grave markers on the Todd plot include one in memory of Charles and Alice's eldest son, Charles Edward, and their youngest daughter, Lorna.

Here lies the woman after whom Alice Springs was named. And alongside her rests the small, bespectacled man who arrived in Adelaide in 1855 with the dream of constructing a telegraph line that would connect Australia with England. A dream which, against all odds, led to the completion of the Overland Telegraph Line in less than two years.

Born in London in 1826, Charles Todd was seven years old when the family moved to Greenwich. His father ran a shop selling English wines and, despite being a Dissenter, drank to forget his troubles, according to author Alice Thomson, who wrote about her Todd ancestors and the building of the Overland Telegraph Line in *The Singing Line*. Meanwhile, Charles's invalid mother spent her days lying in bed or reading religious texts.

Charles had a gift for mathematics and, aged 15, started working at the Royal Observatory in Greenwich, analysing observations of the moon and the planets accumulated over the previous 90 years. He worked 15-hour days with one meal break. Six years later he was appointed Assistant Astronomer at Cambridge Observatory.

While in Cambridge he visited his distant cousins, the Bell family. This shy, awkward 22-year-old sat in the drawing room, drinking sherry and eating Madeira cake, as he talked to Mrs Bell about his new position.

'You should get married, Mr Todd,' Mrs Bell told him.

'I fear no one would want to marry such a dull fellow as I,' he replied. At that moment Mrs Bell's 12-year-old daughter, Alice, jumped up from behind the sofa.

'I will marry you, Mr Todd,' she said. There was a long silence.

'You are far too young,' he said.

'You can wait for me,' said Alice.

The following day Charles Todd sent Alice a copy of *The Pilgrim's Progress*, and every birthday she received a religious tract from him, in which he initially inscribed 'Alice Gillam Bell, from her friend, Charles Todd', then in later years, 'her admirer' and eventually, 'her devoted admirer'.

Todd remained in Cambridge studying the stars for seven years before returning to the Royal Observatory at Greenwich to head the Galvanic Department. He used the telegraph to ensure that the time balls at Greenwich and in London's Strand were dropped at exactly 1 pm each day. Those in the business world set their watches to Greenwich Mean Time, but this precision was of greatest importance to ship captains, who set their chronometers so they could accurately calculate longitude wherever they were in the world.

In 1855 this 28-year-old slightly built man with his black beard and black-rimmed spectacles paid another visit to the Bells in Cambridge. He explained to Mrs Bell that he had been offered the position of Government Astronomer and Superintendent of Telegraphs in the newly founded colony of South Australia.

'And would you be taking anyone with you, Mr Todd?' asked Mrs Bell.

'I would hardly ask anyone to share what would be a very rough and lonely life,' he replied.

There was another long silence.

'I'll go with you, Mr Todd,' said Alice, who was now an attractive 18-year-old woman and three inches taller than him.

Alice was one of 11 children, but five of her siblings had died by the time she was 12 years old, and now only one sister and two brothers were still alive. This was an opportunity to put behind her a childhood peppered with tragedy and start a new life. In his wedding speech, Charles declared he would like to see a telegraphic string stretching around the world, like the necklace of pearls around Alice's throat, and at his leaving party at the Royal Observatory, he announced that he wanted to be 'instrumental in bringing England and Australia into telegraphic communication'.

The newlyweds sailed on a ship called *Irene* with Edward Charles Cracknell, the one assistant Charles Todd had chosen, and his wife. With no foresight into the devastation these species would wreak, Captain

Bruce had encouraged the passengers to bring foxes for hunting and pet rabbits. Alice brought her cat. During the four-and-a-half-month voyage the Cracknells' baby died and was buried at sea. The ship arrived at the Adelaide port of Glenelg on 4 November 1855, the same day that a private electric telegraph had been opened from Adelaide city to Port Adelaide.

Within a month, Todd had started building a government line, which soon put the private line out of business. Five months later Todd began the construction of a line from Adelaide to Melbourne, extending it as far as the South Australian border where it was connected to a Victorian government line. This first intercolonial telegraph line in Australia transmitted its first messages in July 1858.

But the mail service between Britain and Australia was still by ship. It took three months or more, and there was only one mail service each way a month, so a response to a letter to a friend or relative could take nine months, or sometimes more, to arrive. Politicians waited as long for correspondence on government matters, as did exporters of Australian wool, wheat and gold to hear of the price their produce had fetched.

***

In the afternoon Fleur and I visit the Art Gallery of South Australia on North Terrace. I am captivated by the two gnarly red gums dappled by evening light in Hans Heysen's painting *Red Gold*. It's a scene near where the artist lived in the Adelaide Hills. When I spoke to Helen Vonow, collection manager at the Botanic Gardens of South Australia, she said we would see plenty of 'these iconic red gums' as we cycled through the region.

But the painting that intrigues me is by Nicholas Chevalier, depicting the start from Melbourne of the 1860 Victoria Exploring Expedition to cross Australia. Robert O'Hara Burke, on horseback, heads the party, and behind him are half-a-dozen men mounted on camels, while others lead horses. They are surrounded by the huge crowd that has gathered to see them off. Men in black frock coats and grey-striped trousers wave their silk top hats in farewell. South Australia was not the only colony wanting to find a route across the continent for a telegraph line. While John McDouall Stuart travelled light with a small band of men from Adelaide, the gold-rich colony of Victoria spared no expense for its expedition.

We walk from the city back to North Adelaide, stopping at the Adelaide Bridge to look down at the paths running along either side of the River Torrens. Denise told us that both paths go all the way to the weir 15 kilometres upstream where the Mawson Trail starts, so we'll be following one of these paths when we set off tomorrow. I feel my stomach tighten. Now we're actually here in Adelaide, the journey ahead feels monumental and I just pray I'm up to it. I can tell Fleur is anxious too. We walk quickly up the hill.

CHAPTER 4
On Our Way

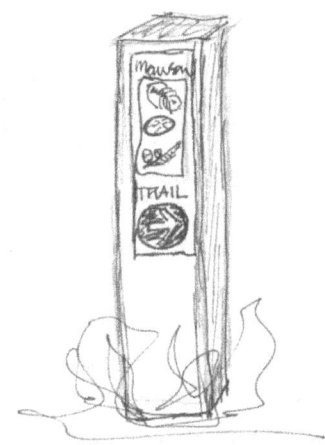

I wake up when my alarm goes off at half past six feeling excited but apprehensive. Fleur's bedroom door is open, and I stick my head in to find her already dressed.

'How did you sleep?' I ask.

'Not well. I'm too nervous,' she replies. I put on my Bonds vest, a long-sleeved thin woollen top, a thin cotton shirt and scarf, a zip-up sleeveless top, woollen long johns under my shorts and thick socks. Next is the pair of Australian green jade earrings I bought when Steve and I travelled to Port Lincoln a couple of years ago. I feel they are not only pretty but also lucky.

Denise was adamant last night that she would cook us breakfast before we set off, so at half past seven we sit down to fresh fruit, bacon and eggs, followed by toast and marmalade, and mugs of tea.

At eight o'clock Fleur and I walk around the corner with her front wheel to North Adelaide Cycles. Kim clears the axle shaft in an instant but suggests that we wheel past when we're on our way, so he can give Fleur's bike a quick check before we head off. Fleur returns to Denise's to assemble her bicycle, and I head to the bakery to buy bread rolls for lunch.

In Denise's garage Fleur attaches her compact panniers to her rear rack, while I wrestle to secure my two large heavy ones to my bike. Denise waves us off with a final gift of a bag of hard-boiled eggs, and we cycle around the corner to the bicycle shop.

'You've got a lot of gear if you're not camping,' Kim says when we pull up. Taking a closer look at my two bulging panniers, he adds, 'If it's more than 20 kilos, I'm worried your rack may break under the strain.' After weeks of culling to reduce my clothes, books, and equipment down to the bare minimum, the thought the rack might give way on a bumpy track in the outback hadn't occurred to me. But when Kim starts talking about attaching a trailer to the back of my bike, I decide I'll take my chances with the rack.

He catches sight of the odometer I've borrowed from a friend. Laying a tape measure out on the pavement, he measures a rotation of my wheel. He says the odometer needs to be recalibrated, because it's slightly overestimating distance. But then he discovers it can't be adjusted.

Kim is used to preparing cyclists for long rides, but two women in their 50s planning to ride 800 kilometres impresses him so much that he prises his wife, Melissa, out of her hairdressing salon next door, along with her client – who has half her hair pinned up and the other half down mid-dying – to wave us off. Kim hugs us both and says to ring if we have problems.

As we freewheel down the hill from North Adelaide to the river, I'm elated to be starting this journey. Seeing the city skyline with its skyscrapers and multiple high-rise buildings, I try to imagine how Adelaide would have looked when John McDouall Stuart arrived here from Scotland in 1839 a few years after the colony of South Australia was founded. Colonel William Light had drawn up his plans for the city, Holy Trinity Church has been built, and there was a scattering of single-storey buildings. There were no trains, no bicycles – let alone cars – and people travelled by foot, on horseback, in horse-drawn carriages or in wagons pulled by bullocks.

Both of John McDouall Stuart's parents died when he was only 11 years old. At the time he attended with his older brother the Scottish Naval and Military Academy in Edinburgh. John's two younger sisters were sent to boarding school, and a family servant kept house for the two boys and their eldest brother, who was studying medicine.

Short, shy and not good with words, John McDouall Stuart was considered unsuitable for military service, the civil service or the church. He trained as a civil engineer, and a career in the colonies was considered the best option. There is a story that Stuart was engaged to a woman named Mary Russell, but before asking her to accompany him to Australia he saw her kissing another man. Unknown to Stuart, the man was Mary's cousin, who was also emigrating to the colonies. Consumed by jealousy, Stuart sailed to Australia and never saw his fiancée again. He was 23 years old and showed little interest in women for the rest of his life.

In 1844, employed as a draftsman, he joined Charles Sturt's expedition to find the geological centre of the continent and to determine whether there was an inland sea. After setting out from Adelaide they spent months stranded in desert country in western NSW at a lagoon they named Depot Glen. The party suffered scurvy, which killed the surveyor, James Poole, and Stuart was promoted to expedition surveyor. After 18 months the party limped back to Adelaide, reporting that it looked as if the new colony of South Australia was hemmed in by scrubland and dry salt lakes with limited pastoral land.

In 1858 the South Australian government offered rewards for the discovery of new grazing country, and pastoralist William Finke commissioned Stuart to explore country west of Lake Torrens. He set out with an assistant bushman, an Aboriginal tracker and a month's food. The pace of travel on Charles Sturt's earlier expedition had been dictated by the 200 sheep they took for food, but Stuart was determined to travel much faster. He rode Polly, a small bay mare he had recently bought. North-west of Lake Torrens, Stuart discovered a running river, which he named Chambers Creek, after James Chambers, Finke's business partner, who would finance his future expeditions and become a close friend. They continued to what is now Coober Pedy and southwards. They ran out of supplies, the tracker left Stuart and the bushman, and three weeks later the two emaciated white men, having survived on mice, pigface plant and the odd crow, finally reached a remote outstation hut.

But Stuart returned to Adelaide a hero. At almost no cost to the colony he had found grazing lands larger in size than the whole of Norway. As his reward, the South Australian government granted him a lease on a thousand square miles at Chambers Creek. That he had mapped such a vast area so impressed the Royal Geographical Society in London that he was awarded a gold watch.

Financed by William Finke and James Chambers, Stuart set off again almost immediately to survey his land claim, and to search for gold in South Australia's quartz-rich Davenport Range, before pushing northwards through the continent. His companions were David Herrgott, a Bavarian artist and naturalist, and Louis Müller, a stockman and amateur botanist, who both had experience in gold mining. One of James Chambers's stockmen also rode part of the way with them.

The group travelled between Lake Torrens and Kati Thanda-Lake Eyre. Desperate for water in the desert country, Herrgott discovered a group of freshwater springs bubbling out of the top of mounds. Stuart named them Herrgott Springs (later the town here was also known as Hergott Springs, until renamed Marree in World War I due to anti-German sentiment). Travelling north-west, the men found more mound springs. Stuart realised this chain of springs provided a permanent water source for a route across this section of the continent. The party ventured 150 kilometres further north than any previous explorers. But they ran out of shoes for the horses and, unable to find water, they were forced to turn back.

***

'We'll get there,' Fleur says as I photograph her on the bridge. Her strong affirmative statement reassures me. My entire focus has been on setting off, and although we've planned our route day by day, I've given little thought to any obstacles we might encounter.

At half past ten we eventually start cycling. The first 15 kilometres to the start of the Mawson Trail follow the River Torrens through city suburbs, and as the cycle path is flat we estimate it will take us about an hour. Already I'm hungry.

Denise told us a cycle path runs along both sides of the river; we decide to follow the one on the north bank. But it deviates onto a street, so we backtrack until we find a bridge to the opposite bank. Kim's parting words were 'When you're cycling along the Torrens, always make sure you can see the river'. I thought he was joking. But heeding his words from then on, we zigzag from one bank to the other following the most prominent path.

We cycle through a park, where three children chase each other around a river red gum while their mother watches from her picnic rug. Then, barely out of Adelaide's CBD, we lose the river completely. Fleur tries to bring up Google Maps on the iPhone she has borrowed from a friend, while I wave the map in the face of a young Asian mother standing in a driveway and demand directions. Returning, I explain we need to go to the right.

'No, we head this way,' Fleur replies, indicating to the left.

'We're here,' I say, jabbing the map.

'No, we're there,' she responds, peering at a dot on the phone.

Each of us is adamant we should head in opposite directions. Fleur is about to pedal one way and I'm taking off in the other direction when it dawns on me that although we know each other well in many ways, in others we don't know each other at all. I have no idea if Fleur has any sense of direction, but even if she doesn't, I realise it isn't a good idea to lose my companion so early in the piece, particularly as most of the food is in her panniers. So I turn tail and follow her. Several U-turns and river crossings later, we're back on the north bank. The path doesn't deviate from the river again, and we continue until we reach the weir. It has taken us two and a quarter hours to get here, and now I'm very hungry. I lean my bicycle against a huge stone pier of an old aqueduct.

'This is the perfect place for lunch,' I say.

'Rossie, we're not yet halfway,' Fleur points out, as she studies the map. 'We should get a few more kilometres behind us before we stop.' I agree reluctantly. 'But we need to have lunch soon.'

We cycle along Gorge Road, a winding route that follows the river. Lined with red rocks dripping with orange-tipped she-oaks, this road brings us to a sign for Mawson Trail, which indicates a dirt track heading up into the hills. Ten minutes later we're wheeling our bikes, as the track is too steep to ride. Even pushing my bicycle is hard. I have to stop every 50 metres to catch my breath, and all I can think of is how long it's been since Denise's delectable breakfast. When I suggest that now would be a good time for lunch, Fleur insists we press on. I lag further and further behind her, seriously questioning if I have the stamina to make it to Woodside today, let alone cycle to Farina. No amount of water quenches my thirst and I'm sweating profusely.

At two o'clock I see Fleur stop at the top of a hill. By the time I push my bike up to her she has taken out her homemade Anzac biscuits and a tin of salmon. From my pannier I dig out the bread rolls and a tomato. It's such a relief to rest and finally eat. We sit looking back down the red-earth track lined with red gums and grass trees towards Adelaide and the ocean in the far distance. There is no breeze, and not even the sound of a bird breaks the silence.

Minutes after we set off again we find ourselves on a slope so steep that even pushing our bikes is nearly impossible.

'What about both of us pushing one bike at a time up the hill?' I suggest, as once again my boots slip back over the stones.

'No!' Fleur replies, ever practical, but with no explanation as to why she thinks my logic is flawed. She has set the pace all day and coaxed me on when all I've wanted to do is stop, so I don't argue. I feel physically drained. Fleur is ahead, as usual, doggedly pushing on. The space between us widens, but I'm powerless to go faster. My arms ache from holding the handlebars in one hand and the saddle in the other, and it's only with immense effort that I can push my bicycle, with its bulging panniers, as my soles have no grip on the steep incline. I inch up this remote forest track in the Adelaide Hills, stopping every few steps to catch my breath. It's three o'clock and already there's a coolness in the air.

The day is slipping away and it will be dark in a couple of hours. We haven't seen either a vehicle or another person on this track. I am exhausted and unsure if I can go much further. As I lose my footing on this stony incline yet again, I'm gripped by a fear that we won't make it. Despair is creeping over me until two elderly men appear at the top of the hill and stroll down the track towards us.

They walked out this way this morning and are now on the return. 'After this hill,' one assures us, 'the track is not so steep.'

'There are hills,' says the other, 'but on a bicycle, it shouldn't be too bad, as there are parts where you'll be able to cycle.'

Filled with renewed hope, we press on. Fleur has raced ahead – again – and I follow as fast as I can, wishing I was fitter. I feel jealous, seeing how the hours Fleur spent at the gym over the last few months are now paying off. Already, on this winter afternoon, the daylight is starting to fade.

We cross the Heysen Trail, the 1200-kilometre walking track from the Fleurieu Peninsula to the Flinders Ranges, named after the artist Hans Heysen, whose paintings we saw at the art gallery. The Mawson Trail veers to the left round a hill. We follow it, but then think that we missed a signpost as it feels as if we have completed a large circle and are now going back on ourselves. We reach a gate and lift our bikes over the low wooden pole beside it. It's four o'clock. The sun is sinking. It's getting cold and we're lost. We pore over the map, wondering where we are and, more to the point, where we should be going. There is no mobile phone reception up here and no houses visible.

I have a vision of us spending our first night huddled together on a hillside in sub-zero temperatures. It's reassuring to know that inside my pannier is Steve's EPIRB – emergency position-indicating radio beacon – which he takes on offshore yacht races. If we really find ourselves in dire straits, this device can send a distress message to the nearest rescue services.

We are walking our bikes into an open area when a ute pulls off the track and stops. We explain to the driver that we're trying to get to Woodside.

'It's a long way,' he replies after a pause. He suggests we take the track from here to a village called Lenswood and go to Woodside from there.

'That's the quickest route,' he says.

Luckily it's mostly downhill to Lenswood. Our mobile reception returns when we get there, so I ring Steve to let him know that we're nearly at the hotel. 'Why aren't you there already?' he responds, as someone who is always early.

The final stretch to Woodside is along Tiers Road, which runs through rolling hills bathed in soft evening light. These last kilometres seem endless and by the outskirts of the small rural township I know I'm unable to make it up another hill. But to my relief, the hotel is at the bottom of the main street immediately ahead of us.

I look down at the odometer and see this was not the modest 35 kilometres that we planned for our first day but 46 kilometres. Maybe it was our numerous deviations along the River Torrens, or getting lost in the hills that added the extra kilometres or, as Kim had said, the odometer could need recalibration. Perhaps the extra kilometres are just a gross exaggeration.

Fleur goes into the hotel and reappears with a young woman, who shows us a shelter at the back of the Victorian brick building, near the kitchen, where we can leave our bicycles for the night. She gives us a key to our room on the first floor.

Fleur takes the single bed and gives me the double. A flat-screen television hangs on the wall, but there are no bedside tables or lights. The carpet has a faint stale beer smell and is slightly sticky, but the sheets and towels are crisp and clean.

Immediately I empty the contents of my panniers onto the bed, knowing it's imperative to lighten my load. The tome on inland plants of Australia has to go, as does my copy of *What Bird Is That?* The checked shirt and my deck shoes, which I put in as evening wear, aren't essential. I also jettison a T-shirt and cotton knapsack.

Next door to our room is a small kitchen. It has a door onto the wide wooden verandah, where there are several old armchairs and ashtrays brimming with cigarette butts. The only table in the kitchen is piled with dirty plates. It's not a place to linger, so we make ourselves two mugs of tea and retreat to our room.

'I usually stay in five-star hotels when I'm with Martin,' Fleur remarks, sitting cross-legged on the bed. After a day of goading me along and now these gloomy surroundings, I fear she might want to give up on our expedition. But an hour later in the recently renovated dining room, as we sip red wine and tuck into delicious lamb shanks, she turns to me with a satisfied smile.

'I like a challenge,' she says.

CHAPTER 5

Tea and Todd

The pile of dirty dishes in the kitchen is higher this morning and is surrounded by empty Heineken bottles, but Fleur finds a couple of clean plates, and some bread, butter and Vegemite sachets. I make two mugs of tea and we retreat to our room. Rummaging through my belongings, I unearth Denise's hard-boiled eggs, and we picnic on our beds.

Before I change my mind about last night's jettisoned items, I head up the street to the post office and mail all 2.7 kilos of them home. With fresh bread rolls from the bakery for lunch, I return to the hotel to find Fleur has already brought the bicycles around to the side door and is assembling her gear. I collect my panniers from the room, and staggering downstairs I realise they are still large and cumbersome. A spotty teenager stands at the pub door watching me struggling to attach them to the rear rack.

'You've got a lot of luggage,' he comments.

We had planned to get back on the Mawson Trail this morning, but we decide to take the shortest and easiest route to Mount Pleasant, where we are staying this evening. We follow the Amy Gillett Bikeway built to commemorate the South Australian cyclist killed in a road accident while training in Germany. Formerly a railway line, this section from Woodside to Mount Torrens runs alongside the road for 12 kilometres.

Musk lorikeets dive into the huge red gums either side of the trail, and a cuckoo-shrike, with its white fanned tail, flies above the winter wattle that is just coming into flower. As we cycle side by side along the flat bitumen, Fleur tells me about the pet goat she had as a child, after which she named her bicycle. Fleur grew up with her three brothers at Dunmore Park, their family property near Dalby in South East Queensland.

'Sulemon was black and white, like my bike, and used to run around the paddock with me every afternoon after school.'

My sturdy black bike is called Juniper.

I questioned the bicycle as an optimum mode of transport yesterday, but today I have no doubt it was the right decision for this first section of the journey. In a vehicle, it's easy to cover hundreds of kilometres in a day, but on bicycles we must rely on leg power. Our daily distances are far less, but I feel we are in the country, not just passing through it.

As we planned the journey, Fleur admitted that she hadn't had a holiday without Martin in the 10 years they had been together. The last time she had been on an adventure with a girlfriend was in Europe when she was in her 20s. Pedalling along the path I feel utterly liberated from my usual commitments and hectic routine. What a joy to have the freedom to cycle every day. I can't help smiling at our illicit escape.

By midday we've cycled 19 kilometres and reached the town of Birdwood. I have learnt that Fleur likes to have done over half the day's kilometres before stopping for lunch, so having reached that milestone we are sitting on the grassy top of a stock loading ramp in the deserted showground, devouring tinned salmon rolls and more homemade Anzac biscuits. Life could not be better.

Fleur's love of tea extends beyond a tea bag. In Adelaide she presented me with a bright green, perforated rubber pouch and showed me a similar pink one she had bought for herself. Now she fills the pouches with leaf tea and places them in our mugs, which she fills with hot water from the thermos.

Charles Todd, Superintendent of Telegraphs, also had a great liking for tea and used to tell the men working on the Overland Telegraph Line, 'Without my T I'd be odd.'

As early as 1857 Charles Todd had suggested to the South Australian governor, Sir Richard MacDonnell, the idea of building a telegraph line from Adelaide to northern Australia, which would connect from there with an undersea cable to Asia and eventually to England.

By 1858 plans were being made for a telegraph line to stretch as far as the Indonesian island of Java, but where would it come ashore in Australia? The Western Australians wanted it to come to Albany on King George Sound. The Queenslanders were arguing for a cable that ran through the Torres Strait, or which came ashore on Queensland's north coast and connected to a landline built to Brisbane.

Charles Todd stressed to Governor MacDonnell that a telegraph line brought ashore in Australia's north and then stretching overland to Adelaide would ensure that Adelaide continued to be the hub in the eastern colonies for international news.

Mail ships from England stopped at Albany in Western Australia – where they took on coal and stores – before sailing on to Melbourne. The mail for Adelaide was offloaded at Albany and loaded onto a fast mail ship, usually arriving 36 hours earlier than the ship sailing to Melbourne. Newspaper reporters would therefore flock to Adelaide to transmit, via the telegraph lines, the overseas news to their respective publications. One reporter was so determined to be the first to transmit the news that he hogged the line sending chapters of the Bible while he wrote his copy.

Cable entrepreneur Lionel Gisborne and American financier Cyrus Field had raised nearly £1 million in share capital, an enormous sum of money at that time, to lay a cable across the Atlantic. It was laid from the west coast of Ireland, but it broke after 1600 kilometres. Gisborne and Field found finance for a stronger cable, which was successfully brought ashore in Newfoundland in August 1858.

With this success behind him, Gisborne now had a plan to connect Australia with an international line via Batavia – present-day Jakarta – to Brisbane's Moreton Bay. In July 1859 his brother, Francis Gisborne, arrived in Australia to talk to the colonies, proposing each one pay a proportion of the cost. With the exception of Victoria, none of them agreed with the proposed contributions. South Australia's Governor MacDonnell, on the advice of Charles Todd, argued that rather than pay £58,000 towards the venture, it would be more cost effective to construct a line overland from the north of the continent to South Australia. The other problem the Gisborne brothers faced was that the transatlantic cable had failed less than a month after the start of telegraphic transmissions.

***

We stay our second night at the Mount Pleasant Hotel, and before setting off the following morning, as neither of us are particularly tech savvy,

Fleur rings Martin to get instructions on how to operate the Telstra iPhone. While's she's talking to him I call Steve.

'I rang Mount Pleasant Police Station last night,' he tells me.

'What?' I respond. 'Why?'

Before I left Sydney, in case of an emergency, Steve insisted that I give him a list of the places we're staying, and the contact details for the police stations in each area.

'The policeman on duty told me the road from Quorn to Hawker is very busy,' he continues.

'But Mount Pleasant is nowhere near Quorn or Hawker, and neither are we,' I reply. 'It'll be days before we get there.' I pray Steve isn't going to ring every police station between here and Farina.

'We're back on the Mawson Trail today, and it won't be busy at all.'

'Good. Be careful,' he replies. 'Got to go. Bye.' The line goes dead. I hope he is reassured and stops worrying.

It's nearly 9 am when we cycle through the town and turn onto a gravel road. Beneath a river red gum flowers yellow wood sorrel, and the silence is broken by the caw of crows. After five kilometres we rejoin the Mawson Trail, which also follows this road.

Young stags on a deer farm turn their antlered heads to look at us and the roes' tails quiver. Fleur cycles and I push my bike up the hill to High Eden, where grass trees and granite boulders pepper the rolling hills. Several sheep scarper across the road and half a dozen blue fairy wrens whirl up from the ground and into a bush. We pass the entrance to Leo Buring's vineyard.

'Their Rieslings are superb,' remarks Fleur, who I'm starting to realise is rather a wine connoisseur.

A Mawson Trail sign directs us to the right through a large wooden gate. The track is on a ridge, the green hill rolling down to the flat plains stretching into the distance. We sit eating our lunch in nature's amphitheatre, watching two falcons circle above a flock of sheep grazing below us.

It starts to rain as we are packing up, so I clamber into my waterproof trousers and jacket, and Fleur puts on her raincoat. We cycle past the rows of bare vines in the Jacob's Creek Steingarten Vineyard. With dusky wood swallows sweeping in broad circles beside us, we coast down the hill to Rowland Flat.

Tea and Todd

The rain has eased by the time we reach the main street of Tanunda and see a two-storey sandstone building bearing the words 'Telegraph Station' across the arched doorway. No longer a hub for Morse code messages, the building is now a museum and a bicycle shop. Fleur buys a can of oil and the proprietor, Evan Schulz, tells us that his German Lutheran ancestors, having been persecuted for their religion, came and settled here in the 1840s with Pastor Kavel, one of the founders of Lutheranism in Australia.

The Lutherans were mainly farmers. Some settlers had experience in viticulture and planted vines, giving birth to the Barossa Valley vineyards. The community kept its language: lessons at the Lutheran school were in German, as were services in the Lutheran churches, and German-language newspapers were widely read.

Fleur and I walk around the museum looking at the memorabilia – china, clothes and photographs – from these self-sufficient early Lutheran families. There is a small jaunty white butcher's cart with large red wooden wheels, but no white frills for a bride, instead an austere high-necked black wedding dress.

In World War I, Evan tells us, an intern camp was set up near here. Despite many internees being Australian citizens, they were treated as prisoners of war, and instantly became targets of a hate campaign. The descendants of the Lutherans, who had come to South Australia to escape religious persecution, were verbally abused, sometimes physically assaulted, and their churches were attacked. In truth, a considerable number of German-Australians believed very strongly in the war against Germany and fought with the Australian forces at Gallipoli and on the Western Front.

At the supermarket we buy food for tonight's dinner and tomorrow's breakfast and lunch. We pick up a bottle of Barossa Valley Shiraz and head to our cabin in the caravan park. Fleur has the double bed and I'm in a bunk and despite temperatures dropping to four degrees or lower at night, it has no bedding. At the office, I'm told that bedding for the bunk bed isn't included in the price of the cabin, so I must pay $15 for two blankets.

Fleur fires up the oven and bakes two chicken breasts slathered with honey and lemon juice. We sit at the kitchen table eating biscuits and a locally made goat camembert, and I think about the struggles and the persecution endured by Evan Schulz's ancestors, despite the idealism behind South Australia's foundation.

The colony of South Australia was established in 1836 with the idea of creating a middle-class utopia with political and religious freedom. There was to be no convict transportation to the new colony. Unlike the other Australian colonies, it was not formed under the concept of *terra nullius*, and Aboriginal use of the land was acknowledged. The *South Australia Act*, passed by the British parliament two years earlier, had decreed that no actions could be undertaken that would 'affect the right of any Aboriginal natives of the said province to the actual occupation and enjoyment in their own persons or in the persons of their descendants of any land therein now actually occupied or enjoyed by such natives'.

The founders of South Australia wanted their province to be 'unstained by native blood', and the Colonisation Commissioners assured the Colonial Office that the Aboriginal people would be compensated for any loss of land.

When the first settlers arrived, the Kaurna of the Adelaide Plains thought they were just visiting, because whalers and sealers who lived on Kangaroo Island had come on forays to the mainland before. But the newcomers stayed.

They claimed land by building fences. They introduced crops and farm animals and destroyed traditional sources of food and water. By 1850 the first mission had been set up and Aboriginal people were receiving government rations to compensate for the loss of their traditional hunting grounds. In the settlers' rush for land, the original noble colonial ideals were forgotten. After 10 years, South Australia had over 22,000 immigrants and the local Kaurna population was reduced to less than 300.

While in Adelaide I had visited Rosemary Wanganeen at her home in Ethelton. Paternally, she proudly identifies as Kaurna; her maternal side is Wirangu, whose people's lands are the Western coastal region of South Australia. She is equally proud of her English heritage.

'*Niina marni.*' She welcomed me in Kaurna, opening the flyscreen door.

Rosemary Wanganeen is a counsellor and the founder of the Healing Centre for Griefology. We met a year earlier, when she came to Sydney to speak to the Australian Medical Association. In her 60s she has a streak

Tea and Todd

of pure white in her black hair and a youthful face; when she laughs it lights up with joy. She exudes warmth and I feel a great sense of ease in her presence.

She made me a mug of tea and coffee for herself, and we sat at her kitchen table. She told me that she lived on an Aboriginal mission until the age of five, when her parents gained an exemption under the *Aborigines Protection Act.* They were hoping to make a better life for themselves and their family by living outside the mission. It required cutting all ties with their Aboriginal culture, including not speaking their traditional languages. The family moved to the town of Clare, where they were the only Aboriginal family.

Her mother died when Rosemary was 10 years old. She and five of her eight siblings were removed from their father, separated from one another and put into foster homes. Rosemary experienced many forms of abuse in those homes. By the age of 17 she was married and a mother. She experienced family violence in both her marriages, to white men who were drinkers.

She was living in Sydney when her second husband badly assaulted her and she was taken to a women's shelter. As she stood looking at her battered face in the mirror, it transformed into an old, traditional Aboriginal woman's face. This woman, who Rosemary believes was an ancestral grandmother, told her she was about to find faith and trust in her own abilities. This was the start of her five-year healing process.

Taking her children, she left her husband, returned to Adelaide and began her journey of inner healing. She looked at how she had been victimised at school, how she was taken away from her family and had become part of what we know now as the Stolen Generations. Asking why anyone had the right to do that to her led her to investigate Australian and English history, and even the history of ancient Greece. She discovered that Plato, after the loss of his beloved teacher, Socrates, coined the idea that to express grief was a sign of weakness. It was then, she believes, that Europeans started to shut down and suppress their grief because they didn't want to be seen as weak.

'But,' Rosemary emphasised, 'if you suppress your grief it becomes externalised, and the grief anger, which is a normal part of the grieving process, can turn to rage, which can become violence.' It was very important in Aboriginal culture that relationships both within and between tribes were maintained, as well as maintaining relationships with animals and the land. Rosemary believes that when people across Europe stopped grieving freely, many of them started to lose connection with nature and the earth, as well as with the animal kingdom.

As Rosemary gained understanding of her own trauma and that of her ancestors, she believes she released the suppressed contemporary and unresolved intergenerational grief inside her.

Growing up, she was ashamed of her Aboriginality. 'I knew I was Aboriginal, but I didn't feel Aboriginal, because my pride was missing.' Today she has a strong Aboriginal identity.

'Loss and grief aren't in our everyday language,' Rosemary told me, 'but our ancestors used to have very strong, structured grieving ceremonies.' She believes that the body is like a container, and with every loss we experience from birth onwards, our body fills with this invisible grief energy, so we need to have a grieving process from the cradle to the grave to empty it out. So much of the dysfunction in both Aboriginal and non-Aboriginal communities – alcohol and drug addiction, anger, violence and abuse – she believes stems from suppressed grief.

As she talks, I can't help thinking of Marabella – how miserable she is, and how much of my life has been spent trying to fill that empty chasm inside her. She is loving, and a loyal friend, helping people in ways that have proved life changing. But because she is highly sensitive and insecure, she is critical of both herself and others in a way that cuts like a knife. As a teenager, I noticed how her mood would spiral downwards, like a bird falling from the sky. My father's eyes would cloud with sadness, and with his stiff upper lip he'd announce it was because of her French blood. I think of my grandmother, married off at 18 by her French father to my much older Welsh grandfather, who was estranged from her mother for most of her life. Then how throughout her adult life my mother was estranged from her father.

'If you look at Aboriginal history, it could be said that we were in the wrong place at the wrong time,' Rosemary continues. 'And those white Australians who came out here in many cases were forced from their Country, culture, language and families, and today I believe there is what I call "grief guilt" for what their ancestors did to another people who didn't know how to fight back.'

We walked outside. Rosemary stood on the street in front of her house and with a broad smile, she threw her arms out wide. Behind her a bottlebrush and a white-barked pink flowering gum, like emblems of her Aboriginality, sprawl over her fence onto the pavement. Beside them grows an olive tree – the European part of her heritage and the branch of peace she extends to white Australians. I deeply admire the way she has not only transformed her own life, but also supported Aboriginal and non-Aboriginal Australians in their healing.

I dwell on Marabella's emotional pain. I see patterns in my mother's life – the choices she has made that do not value her dreams and desires, and the prison this intelligent vivacious woman has made for herself. As her daughter I feel its effect, this DNA pulsing through my veins, this learnt behaviour in me, which manifests as doubt and insecurity, and I know I need to let that go and choose differently. I am exhausted after another day's cycling, but tingling with joy that I am fulfilling my dream of following the Overland Telegraph Line.

Fleur takes the chicken out of the oven. We are both ravenous and devour her delicious dish with quantities of salad. It's growing cold, so Fleur turns on the reverse-cycle air conditioning, but despite the remote reading 31 degrees, it whooshes out cold air. The office is now closed, so we can't ask for assistance. I put on all my layers, including my woolly beanie and scarf. Fleur, determined to manifest warm air, spends the evening standing on a chair, a glass of Shiraz in hand, pointing the remote at the air conditioning unit mounted above the door and pressing various buttons. Despite her tenacity, only cold air billows out.

CHAPTER 6

Rain, Maggie Beer and Sir Sidney Kidman

The clouds are grey and ominously low this morning, and it's already raining lightly. It's time to find Fleur a pair of wet-weather pants. First we stop at the Apex Bakery to buy its famous sourdough bread. The shelves behind the counter are stacked with loaves of different sizes and shapes, all baked in the original 90-year-old woodfired Scotch oven. We select a small round loaf for our lunch, and add the peanut biscuits and an apple scroll.

Diane, who serves us, recommends the Mitre 10 hardware store in Nuriootpa for waterproof trousers. We cycle three-and-a-half kilometres there to discover it doesn't sell them, but Fleur is told to try Spot On Fishing about a kilometre across town. A sign on the window advertises snakes and lizards, and although the shop also stocks every conceivable fishing accessory there are no waterproof pants for sale. Just up the road, though, is Farmer Johns, which sells agricultural equipment and supplies. Here Fleur finds a pair of fluorescent green plastic trousers and a jacket to match. She dons her new outfit as the heavens open.

Fleur wants to visit the farm shop of Maggie Beer, the Australian doyenne of seasonal home-cooked food. So we cycle the few kilometres across Nuriootpa in the heavy rain. Having a great appreciation of fine food as well as being an excellent cook, Fleur is delighted that we can sample the full range of Maggie Beer's products. It's now 11.30 and I'm very hungry. We taste all the gourmet pâtés, pastes and pickles and I tuck into chunks of bread dunked in extra virgin olive oil.

Still ravenous, I'm looking for a spot to eat our picnic lunch when through a window I spot Maria Horgan, a friend from Sydney, sporting a black-and-white striped apron. She and several girlfriends are spending a few days in the Barossa Valley, and in the middle of a private cooking demonstration of recipes using Maggie Beer's verjuice, an unfermented grape juice.

Maria and her friend Samantha join us, glasses of sparkling Ruby Cabernet and large plates of verjuice chicken and salad in hand. They are curious to know why Fleur and I are wandering around Maggie Beer's Farm Shop in plastic trousers, and I explain about following the Overland Telegraph Line. Samantha, originally from Adelaide, believes her ancestors had a connection with John McDouall Stuart, who crossed the continent in 1862 and paved the way for the telegraph line but, much to my disappointment, she can't recall the family history.

Maria and Samantha eat the occasional mouthful of salad as they talk. I am so hungry now that I don't trust myself not to head straight to the leftover chicken salad on the counter and pile up a large plate. To make matters worse, they both toy with their food in a foody weekend way that suggests they had a large dinner yesterday and a substantial breakfast this morning.

At that moment Maggie Beer herself appears, extolling the versatility of verjuice – for cooking and as a refreshing non-alcoholic beverage. She eyes Fleur and me, dripping and bedraggled in our wet-weather pants unlike the other dry well-dressed attendees. I explain we're cycling to Farina, and she gives her best grande-dame smile as Maria takes a photograph of the three of us.

Maria, Samantha and friends leave. Fleur and I, having discovered we are not allowed to eat our picnic on the premises because it hasn't been bought from here, adjourn to the café and order two delectably rich chocolate brownies. Fortified and spurred on by our sugar high, we ride off.

We abandon our original plan to follow the scenic Mawson Trail, as the rain shows no sign of easing and it's cold and windy. I wear my fluorescent belt and turn on my rear light, hoping motorists will notice us in the gloom as we edge along the main road. Initially we're blown along – until the road changes direction and we are blasted from the side by the south-east wind. As I watch the numbers slowly clicking over on the exaggerometer, the 14 kilometres to Kapunda feels endless. With our hoods up and the rain pelting down, it's hard to hear vehicles approaching from behind, and the force of the air blast from a fast double road train sends us both wobbling onto the verge. Our wheels skid over the loose gravel, but neither of us fall off.

'Are you all right?' I ask, shivering in shock and feeling vulnerable. Fleur grits her teeth and nods.

'We have to listen for road trains,' she says.

'And get off the road,' I add. But we have no option except to keep riding the seven kilometres to Kapunda in the driving rain.

Approaching the town, we see an information board under a shelter and stop. Fleur is wearing two pairs of gloves, so she asks me to get the details for the caravan park out of her front pannier. As I pull them out, her Qantas flight information takes to the air, dances in the wind, lands on the wet gravel and is swooshed into the air again as I chase after it.

'I've got it,' I shout, when it finally falls in a sodden heap in the mud. Fleur doesn't reply as I hand back the soggy brown lump of paper – her ticket back to Sydney, away from this wind and the rain. She looks miserable; having grown up in sunny Queensland, she hates the cold.

Kapunda was the home of the cattle king Sir Sidney Kidman. I had thought we would explore the various Kidman haunts in town, but we're both wet through. Neither Fleur's new fluorescent plastic fantastics nor my waterproof trousers purchased at an Irish horse fair have stood the test of this torrential downpour. Our only thoughts now are about getting out of the rain. So my sightseeing of Kapunda is confined to the IGA supermarket aisles, and Sip*n*Save, the drive-through bottle shop attached to the Prince of Wales Hotel. It was here that Sidney Kidman stayed the first night after he left home, aged 13, on a one-eyed horse with five shillings in his pocket.

Brad and Emma Valentine greet us at the caravan park reception. Emma checks us into the cabin with the best heating, and she lends us her large umbrella so we can get to the industrial dryer in the communal laundry without undergoing a second drenching.

Standing under a hot shower, my toes tingling with the heat, is blissful. The clothes in our panniers packed in plastic bags are dry but we face the task of drying out all our other belongings and our panniers. We use the tea towel and a hand towel to get the worse of the moisture out of our panniers and throw all our dripping clothes into the washing machine, then, under the giant umbrella, Fleur takes them to the dryer. Having sent my docksiders back to Sydney two days ago I have no dry shoes, so I borrow Fleur's pair and go back to reception to ask for newspaper to stuff in our shoes in the hope of speeding up the drying process. Brad says he is going to town and can get some for us. We eat copious amounts of cheese and biscuits while we await his return, and I ponder the life of Sidney Kidman.

Born in 1857 on a farm in Payneham, now a suburb of Adelaide, Sidney was not even a year old when his father died. His mother, who had five boys aged under 10, was pregnant at the time with their sixth son. When Sidney left home at 13 he worked his way north to the Barrier Ranges, near Broken Hill, to join several of his elder brothers. His brother George found him work shepherding stock. A year later Sidney got a job as a rouseabout at Mount Gipps Station, where three of his brothers were working. Exposed to every facet of station life and constantly questioning the older men, he gleaned both knowledge and skills.

Sidney sat around campfires at night listening to numerous tellings of the story of the great cattle-thieving feat of Harry Redford, who stole 1000 head of cattle from Bowen Downs, an enormous Queensland property, and headed with them to Adelaide through the country that 10 years earlier had claimed the lives of explorers Burke and Wills. Among the herd was a white bull, which Redford sold as soon as he could, and he drove the rest of the mob through the arid, semi-desert country as far as Lake Blanche, east of Marree, where he sold the herd.

Redford and his two accomplices headed for Adelaide with the money before the theft was discovered at Bowen Downs. The police found the white bull, used in evidence against Redford when he was arrested and brought to trial in Roma three years later. One of his accomplices confessed, but because the jury was composed of stockmen, who were riveted by this droving feat, Redford was acquitted and, to the judge's dismay, regarded as a hero.

While the others around the campfire hooted with laughter at how Redford had walked free, young Sidney Kidman was earnestly considering this new 'back corridor' to the Adelaide markets.

In the late 1870s Sidney met Miss Isabel Wright in Kapunda. Training to become a schoolteacher, Isabel fascinated Sidney with her explanations of the inland river systems of Australia, including Queensland's Cooper Creek and Diamantina and Georgina rivers. He realised the floodplains of these rivers could make his back corridor possible. The pair married and had six children, two of whom died before they were 18 months old.

Sidney and his older brother Sackville ran a stock-dealing business, went into partnership in a coach business and started buying large pastoral properties, including several stations in the Channel Country. The telegraph line was essential to their business, as the Kidman brothers and their drovers and managers used it to report vital information, such as the location of feed and water, the identity of other drovers who were on the road and the size of their mobs, and the markets to which they were heading.

Sackville Kidman died in 1899, leaving Sidney to operate alone. The first large property he bought on his own was Eringa Station in South Australia, near the Northern Territory border. Several years later he bought the largest and grandest home in Kapunda and called the house Eringa after this property.

***

Brad arrives at the door with an old copy of the *Leader* from his mother-in-law. We stuff our shoes with the newspaper, turn the air conditioning on full blast, position every chair in the cabin in front of it, and hang the panniers, wet-weather jackets, trousers, hats and shoes on them to dry. Armed with the hair dryer, I set to work on Fleur's plane ticket and the equally wet map.

It's still pouring outside. Unanimously we decide we do not want to experience another day like this. So while Fleur creates another gourmet meal – this time a delicious pesto pasta – I get onto the internet and search for train services between Kapunda and Auburn. But tomorrow, being a Saturday, there isn't even a bus. All we can do is plot a route that avoids dirt roads.

CHAPTER 7

Telegraph Developments and the Hen Party

Fleur and I are equally reluctant to get on our bicycles. We slowly eat breakfast, drink numerous cups of tea and decide, after all of yesterday's rain, that we should oil the chains with the wet chain lube that Fleur bought from Evan at the Telegraph Station in Tanunda.

Hugh Richardson, who lent me the exaggerometer and cycled parts of the Mawson Trail a few years ago, is a man who knows bicycles. While attaching the odometer he told me I should clean my bicycle at the end of each day and check that nothing has come loose.

'That sounds like a good idea,' I responded. Immediately Hugh sensed my lack of expertise and reeled off a long list of spare parts he considered imperative for this expedition.

'I'm carrying two spare thornproof inner tubes,' I said, to demonstrate I was not entirely unprepared.

'Can you change a tyre?' he asked, looking me straight in the eye.

'Of course,' I replied.

Fleur and I clean the mud off our bikes and oil our chains and it's 10.20 by the time we clamber back into our wet-weather gear and set off. Our possessions are dry, with the exception of our damp hats and shoes. The heavy rain has reduced to light drizzle but, aware that we have to cover 50 kilometres today, I ignore the temptation to deviate to look at Eringa. In 1921 Sidney and Bel moved to Adelaide, and he donated their huge grand house on its magnificent grounds to the people of Kapunda to be used as a high school. It opened as a school in October 1922, and just short of 100 years later, in March 2022, it was sadly destroyed by a fire.

We take the road to Marrabel and from there to Saddleworth. Olive bushes, dripping with their small green fruit, grow wild beside the road. It rains on and off throughout the day, but we arrive at the Rising Sun Hotel in Auburn just before a dark-grey cloud breaks.

Ken and Paula Noack bought the hotel three years earlier and run it with their daughter, Sarah, and her fiancé, James Kolencik, who is the chef. Paula takes us into an alarmed shed, where all the hotel's alcohol is stored, and our bikes are locked in this stronghold for the night.

The Rising Sun Hotel was built in the mid-19th century, when up to 100 bullock drays a day, transporting copper from Burra to Port Wakefield, would pass through Auburn. The stables at the rear were part of the original premises, and the barn was used as a dance hall, a courthouse and the post office. It was from here that Charles Todd sent Auburn's first telegram.

Paula leads us into the barn with its high roof spanned by heavy, dark wooden beams.

'There's a hen's night in here this evening,' she explains, as we walk past a large 'Pin the Cock on the Jock' poster.

'The loft in here was used as a temporary office for the first Auburn telegraph,' she says.

Standing beside a long table festooned with phallic-shaped swizzle sticks, I try to imagine Charles Todd sending Auburn's first telegram from here in 1862, the same year that explorer John McDouall Stuart finally succeeded in crossing the continent and reaching the north coast of Australia.

In July 1859 Stuart had returned from his second expedition with David Herrgott and Louis Muller. They had discovered the chain of mound springs and this reliable water provided a permanent route north.

With talk about an overseas telegraph cable to connect England and Australia, the South Australian government urgently wanted to find a route from Adelaide to the north coast, and now offered a reward of £2000 for the first explorer to cross the continent. In just over a month after returning from his second expedition Stuart set out on his third. The colony of Victoria was also planning a transcontinental crossing, so a race had begun between the two colonies, and there was no time to waste.

Stuart took four men on his third expedition. One of them, William Kekwick, was a large, quiet man who had worked as a drover and a

Telegraph Developments and the Hen Party

goldminer. A Quaker and amateur botanist, Kekwick would accompany Stuart on all his futures explorations. Because the government disputed Stuart's land claim at Chambers Creek they resurveyed it, and under the instructions of his patrons, Chambers and Finke, prospected for gold west of Kati Thanda-Lake Eyre, but without success. Running low in food, Stuart decided to return to Chambers Creek before heading north. While they had been away Chambers' brother-in-law had stocked the land with 1700 head of cattle, and he and his men had built a stone hut and stockyards. Chambers had sent supplies – flour, tea, sugar and horseshoes – so Stuart and his party could kill some cattle and dry the meat and head north immediately. But, except for Kekwick, the men refused to set off again.

Determined to press northwards as soon as possible, Stuart gave Kekwick a letter to the manager of Moolooloo Station, a property 250 kilometres away in the Flinders Ranges that Chambers owned. The letter asked for fresh horses and six men. While Kekwick rode off on this mission, Stuart lay in the dark stone hut, avoiding the sun in an attempt to cure an eye infection.

A month later Kekwick returned with a string of horses and an overweight 18-year-old, Ben Head, the only person he had been able to recruit for the expedition. Three days later, on 2 March 1860, the three of them set off on Stuart's fourth expedition. A month later they crossed the border – a line drawn on a map by the Colonial Office in London – into the Northern Territory.

They reached a ridge of mountains that Stuart named the MacDonnell Ranges, after South Australia's Governor-in-Chief. Running low on food, Stuart cut their daily rations, much to the dismay of Ben Head, who was already half his original weight. They pressed on beyond present-day Alice Springs. Stuart was aiming to reach the Victoria River in the north-west, thought by the South Australian government to be a good route for the telegraph line. It was also known that the Victorian expedition was heading to the Gulf of Carpentaria. But unable to find a way north-west to the Victoria River, Stuart's only option was to push north. Despite scurvy and severe hunger, the three men travelled beyond Tennant Creek.

Stuart, Kekwick and young Ben Head were camped on a lagoon when two Aboriginal men visited them. In his journal, Stuart described the men presenting them 'with four opossums and a number of small birds and parrots'. He said the men were initially frightened, but they became bolder and came into the camp. Having no notion of their culture of exchange and sharing, Stuart wrote that they

> *wanted to steal everything they could lay their fingers on. I caught one concealing the rasp that is used in shoeing the horses under the netting he had around his waist, and was obliged to take it from him by force. The canteens they seemed determined to have, and it was with difficulty we could get them from them. They wished to pry into everything, until I lost all patience and ordered them off.*

Later that day two boys approached the camp. Aware that his party were set up at the only water in the area, Stuart told Ben Head to take them a dish of water. In the evening, one of the original men returned with two young men and an old man. Stuart and the old man tried to communicate using sign language, but failed. Then the old man made a hand gesture which Stuart recognised as a Masonic sign. He wrote:

> *I looked at him steadily; he repeated it, and so did his two sons. I then returned it, which seemed to please them very much, the old man patting me on the shoulder and stroking down my beard.*

The men left, and thanks to the gifts of possums and birds, Stuart, Kekwick and Head ate their first decent meal for a long time.

Three days later, as they continued northwards, the explorers found a creek with water, but the same people were camped there. Stuart led the party around the camp, hoping to find water farther down the creek. But it was dry, so Stuart decided to camp above where they had seen the Aboriginal people. Retracing their steps, the explorers saw footprints and realised they were being followed and soon after three tall men with boomerangs, waddies and spears blocked their path. Stuart rode forward with his palms upturned in a sign of peace, and 30 men came screaming out of the bush.

Obeying signs to clear off, Stuart started to turn his mare, Polly, but was bombarded with a shower of boomerangs. The men came closer, so Stuart gave orders to Kekwick and Head to fire. The packhorses bolted to the creek at the sound of the gunfire, so Kekwick and Stuart continued to shoot while young Head raced after them. Dragging the packhorses, the three men rode into the night, travelling beyond their previous camp.

The warriors would have had no difficulty killing the travellers if they wanted to, so it is likely that this was just a show of strength, to indicate in no uncertain terms that they wanted these foreigners and their thirsty animals to leave their land and precious water sources. What Stuart interpreted as Masonic signs were probably gestures indicating they should leave. Realising their vulnerability after this incident, Stuart decided the three of them could go no further, so they turned south for Adelaide.

From Moolooloo Station, Stuart wrote to James Chambers: 'The Telegraph could be laid down, there is no obstacle but what can be overcome as far as I have gone.'

When the trio arrived back in Adelaide in October 1860, the Royal Society of Victoria's grandiose transcontinental expedition with its 27 camels had already been travelling for a month and a half. But the South Australians were certain that their man – who was able to travel both light and fast – could still win the race to cross the continent. Two days after Stuart arrived back in Adelaide the South Australian government was already planning his next journey. The prospects for the small South Australian colony and its plans for a telegraph line lay in his hands.

***

It feels like we're on holiday this evening. It's Saturday night, tomorrow is a mere 30 kilometres to Clare, and we're staying in this grand old hotel with its high ceilings and stained-glass windows. Having showered, we head to the bar. The hotel is renowned for its food, and dotted throughout the hallway, dining room and bar are tables, covered in crisp white linen tablecloths, set for dinner. We sit at a table near the fire. Fleur is in the mood for a good meal and orders lamb rack with harissa and chickpeas. I decide on a chicken schnitzel which, although not as gourmet, looks deliciously large and like perfect cycling fodder. We order a bottle of Rising Sun Shiraz, made from grapes grown on Ken and Paula's vineyard a couple of kilometres away.

'We haven't had time to make a label,' Paula says, placing the bottle on the table.

Whispering Wire

Fleur reminisces about her three brothers and their four cousins catching the bus to school in Dalby every morning.

'Mum and Dad wanted to send me to St Hilda's. But I said, "If you send me to boarding school, I'll run away."'

When I first arrived in Sydney I met Fleur because of my mother's network of old schoolfriends. She took me to Randwick Races. I lost on every horse I backed, but Fleur had an uncanny ability to pick a winner. I knew Fleur had always had an eye for horses, but only now does she tells me that her ancestor, James Winten, was a 20-year-old stableboy in Tunbridge Wells in Kent when he was transported to NSW in 1817.

Two generations later the family moved to Queensland. Between the five sons, the Wintens owned four pastoral properties, and in the 1890s they went from breeding only workhorses to filling their stables with thoroughbreds. The Winten passion for racing was ignited. Three of the brothers' horses won the Queensland Guineas, including one owned by Fleur's grandfather, Rowland Joshua Winten. Fleur's great-uncle, Harry Winten, bred the Australian 1940s champion Bernborough. So now I understand where Fleur gets her love of racing.

CHAPTER 8

Rattling Along the Riesling Trail

I woke briefly in the night to the sound of a possum pounding around in the roof. But sitting up in bed and drinking tea this morning, Fleur recounts that she was kept awake by the long, loud lovemaking of the couple in the room next door.

It's drizzling as we walk around the town, looking at the old buildings made from locally quarried Auburn bluestone. One of these buildings is the two-storey post office, its blue-grey stone walls glimmering in the wet. It was built in 1862, so the telegraph office was not based for long in the barn at the Rising Sun.

As we return to our room we see two women cleaning a bedroom, one of whom was working in the bar last night. There was considerable speculation about the cake for the hen's party yesterday, and she now gives us the lowdown.

'It was the shape of a penis, and enormous – 50 centimetres long – with perfectly round balls, and pubic hair made of coffee icing. And in icing beside it were the words *The Best is Yet to Come*,' she recounts. 'The bride-to-be cut the balls and out squirted a creamy white substance.' As we roar with laughter, the other woman, who is probably in her early 30s, says that before she got married she had a morning tea with her mother, grandmother and their friends, and was given rice and pasta for her store cupboard. The stark contrast in the rites of passage sends us all into more peals of laughter.

I think of my hen's night at a Lebanese restaurant in Surry Hills with three girlfriends. We drank sparkling wine and lounged on brightly coloured cushions eating hommous and baba ganoush before I was

Whispering Wire

coerced into attempting to belly dance by a voluptuous Lebanese expert with scarlet lipstick and eyes heavy with mascara.

I start the day thinking I don't have the energy to cycle another kilometre, but that feeling melts away once we're rattling along the Riesling Trail. Even though it's raining, it's delightful following the route of the old railway line to Clare, which is also part of the Mawson Trail.

Rosehips grow beside the track and spider webs glisten with the tiny droplets, hanging like glass baubles on the fine threads. Chickens slowly strut and peck the dirt at a homestead. A pepperina grows beside the tin-roofed house, two sheep graze in the home paddock, and a willie wagtail quivers on a fence post.

The sun emerges from behind a cloud and, for the first time in three days, we peel off our plastic tops and trousers. At an old railway cutting we pick up the grey and black slate-like pieces of siltstone; a sign tells us these stones were deposited 750 million years ago as sediment in a shallow sea that extended from Antarctica to Central Australia. I'm pondering the great hand of time when a grey cloud bursts and we scrabble back into our waterproofs. Adelaide rosellas, with their long, dark-blue tails and red brows flit through the bare vines and a huge red kangaroo bounds along the top of the siding beside us. It stops and turns to look back in our direction before bouncing across the trail ahead.

Being in the heart of Australia's prime Riesling region, we stop at a small winery. Shut the Gate's owner, Richard Wood, explains how the precious *terra rossa* soil differs between one hill and the next and how that affects the Riesling grapes. As Fleur makes discerning remarks about the fragrances, acidity and the citrus aromas of the three wines we taste I focus on the labels. There is a striking line drawing of goat on The Forager Shiraz; another bottle displays an elephant.

It's still raining when we reach Penwortham and deviate from the trail to look at the cottage of the pastoralist and explorer, John Ainsworth Horrocks. This old stone building opens only on the first Sunday of the month, so we can't see inside. But looking at the grounds, it's intriguing to think that here was the home of Australia's first camel. The big bull, named Harry, was the only survivor of a shipment of six camels from the Canary Islands to Port Adelaide in 1840, the other five having died when the ship hit a gale.

Harry, acquired in exchange for six cows, lived for several years at Penwortham before Horrocks took him on an expedition around Lake Torrens and the head of the Spencer Gulf to search for pastoral land. Harry was apparently a bad-tempered beast and became known as Harry the Horrible, often chewing holes in the flour bags and biting not only the goats but also the men.

North of Port Augusta, Horrocks and two other men – with Harry carrying the baggage – set out on foot to explore the plains. Horrocks stopped Harry to get his shot belt. He was preparing to shoot a bird when the camel lurched, his pack caught in the cock of the gun and discharged a barrel. It took off two of Horrocks's fingers and a row of his teeth, and he died three weeks later from infection. Lying on his deathbed at only 28 years of age, he asked that Harry the Horrible be shot. But before the dying man's wish was carried out, the bull took a bite out of an Aboriginal stockman's head. Harry was buried here under a large gum tree.

'I love camels,' Fleur announces an hour later when we're eating our picnic in the grounds of the Jesuits' Sevenhill Cellars. 'Beth McWilliams, my cousin, was married to a cameleer called Gool Mohamed. I met Beth and Gool when they visited my grandmother at her nursing home in Toowoomba. I was 18, and all I remember was this Afghan man who had huge feet and looked after camels. I thought that was really something.'

The buildings made from stone quarried on the property and the statue of the Virgin Mary overlooking the rows of vines give Sevenhill Cellars an air of serenity. It's the oldest winery in the region. The Jesuits first planted grape acres here in 1851, initially making only sacramental wine. We walk through the hand-dug cellar before making our way upstairs, past a stained-glass window and a large wooden cask labelled 'Altar wine', to the tasting room. After sampling an extensive range of reds and then, unsure which I prefer, trying half of them a couple more times, I feel decidedly lightheaded. We emerge to find it is raining again, but it's soft rain, a cool sobering spray on the face, as we cycle the six kilometres along the flat to Clare.

This evening we're in a Victorian edifice on the main street, the Clare Hotel, known as the Middle Pub. The woman behind the bar tells us to leave our bicycles in the laundry, so we wheel them round to the back of the building. We have been given an enormous corner room at the front of the hotel, with two three-quarter-size beds and a double bed. The bonus is the electric heater. Within half an hour this room resembles a laundry as several pairs of washed knickers and socks and a couple of shirts are arranged around the heater to dry.

Last night Paula Noack recommended Clare's Indian restaurant for dinner. Under the gaze of a large statue of Buddha, we spread out the map on a table and study it over roti and lentil dal. The Riesling Trail continues for several kilometres beyond Clare, and then we had planned to cycle along a dirt road, but after all the rain we don't know if that will be possible. The charming Indian waiters also have no idea.

Back at the Middle Pub, the woman behind the bar looks tired and disgruntled. She is pouring shots for a group in their late teens, and the music is full blast. Neither Fleur nor I feel inclined to sit and have a drink, so we mutter goodnight as we walk up to our room, directly above the bar. The thud of the bass reverberates round the room, as a clutch of Abba songs are transmitted loud and clear.

'I'm sure it'll be turned down shortly,' I say, sensing Fleur's irritation, while remembering that she was awake much of last night because of the enthusiastic lovemaking of our neighbours.

When Van Morrison belting out 'Brown-Eyed Girl' rises through the carpet, Fleur turns noticeably sullen, so I offer to go downstairs and ask for the music to be turned down. The bar woman places six shot glasses on the counter and pours a schooner of beer. The drinkers sway to the music and, standing at the corner of the bar, I'm ignored. I retreat to the room, admitting my failure, as Jimmy Barnes booms through the floorboards.

CHAPTER 9

The Barbed Wire Pub

Having followed the Riesling Trail for another nine kilometres, we are at a T-junction, hotly debating if we should take the dirt road, which I favour, or the main road, that Fleur advocates, preferring to make speedy progress. The decision is made when a man pulls up in his ute and tells us the dirt road is likely to be slippery; he recommends the bitumen route.

After several kilometres, we turn onto the RM Williams Way. Despite my initial reluctance to take to the tarmac, I like this road. It rolls up and down gentle hills and there is very little traffic. I cycle along thinking about the race between Victoria and South Australia to cross the continent.

For the Royal Society of Victoria's expedition to the Gulf of Carpentaria, 24 camels and their handlers were brought from Karachi, and several more camels, imported to Australia earlier for a vaudeville show, were also commissioned. There were 23 horses and six wagons, one of which could be converted into a punt. The equipment weighed over 20 tonnes and included a library of books, a dining table and a Chinese gong. The party consisted of 19 men, including four camel handlers.

Heading the party was Robert O'Hara Burke, a 39-year-old Irishman. He hadn't led an expedition before, but he was an adventurous and dashing man. Second-in-command was the camel expert, George James Landells. Neither Burke nor Landells had surveying skills, so 26-year-old William John Wills went as the surveyor.

On 20 August 1860, about 15,000 people gathered at Melbourne's Royal Park to farewell the expedition. Steve's aunt told me that among the crowd was Steve's great-grandfather, George William Reynolds, who had been on the staff of *The Times* in London and had arrived in Melbourne several days earlier with 40 other compositors to work on the *Argus*. It was a spectacle. The explorers all wore scarlet jackets, except Landells who, mounted on a camel, was dressed as a maharaja. On the first day, the expedition travelled 11 kilometres to Essendon on the outskirts of the city, and that evening Burke galloped back to Melbourne to propose to an 18-year-old actress, Julia Matthews.

It took two months to travel 750 kilometres to Menindee Lakes in NSW. Burke complained that the camels were too slow and took too long to load each day. Landells had brought along 270 litres of rum, claiming it was to ward off camel diseases and to rub into the camels' pads to maintain flexibility. When Burke insisted the rum be left behind, they had a roaring row and Landells resigned. But Burke forgave him and enticed him back before sacking him, making Wills his second-in-command.

While still in Menindee, the party received news that Stuart had reached the centre of Australia and was planning his next expedition. Wanting to be the first to cross the continent and knowing how fast Stuart travelled, Burke split the group. Half the original party had either resigned or been sacked by their hot-headed leader, and he now recruited William Wright, the manager of a sheep station he had met at the Menindee Hotel, and Charlie Gray, a sailor he encountered in another pub.

Leaving most of the equipment behind, Burke put Wright in charge of the Menindee party, with instructions to follow as soon as possible. Burke, meanwhile, set out for Coopers Creek with seven men. By mid-December Wright still hadn't arrived, so Burke decided to press north to the coast with William Wills, Charles Gray and John King, plus three months' provisions, six camels and a horse. He left William Brahe in charge of the remaining men, with instructions to build a stockade and wait for Wright to deliver more stores. Burke told them to return to Menindee if he and his party weren't back in three months.

Two months later the four men, having been plagued by heavy rain, mosquitoes and sandflies, reached a muddy estuary and the tidal salt water of the Gulf of Carpentaria. Wanting to reach the ocean, Burke left Gray and King with the camels, which were struggling on the slippery ground. Leading the packhorse, Burke and Wills pushed north through the mangroves. The following day they hobbled the horse and continued alone. After walking most of the day, they faced a wall of mangroves. The water was salty, but they couldn't hear the ocean. Exhausted and bitterly disappointed at not having made it to the open sea, they turned back.

***

Mid-morning we stop for a break and I eat a banana, now part of my daily routine. Fleur can keep pedalling all morning, but despite always having a substantial breakfast, I need an energy boost after an hour or so of cycling.

Back on the saddle, I feel my jaw tightening as I pedal up a hill. Inspired by the statue of Buddha in the Indian restaurant last night, I decide, rather than maintaining my grimace I need to find peace of mind and smile at the people in the approaching vehicles.

Large open paddocks span the rolling country. As the road curls around a cluster of granite boulders on a hill, a pair of kites ride the breeze above us before disappearing into the clouds. The only sounds are the call of the little black-and-white peewee and the clunking of the windmill as its halo of steel sails turns with the wind. A man in a car gives a friendly wave as he passes us. Another man waves from his ute, and I wonder if my beaming, Buddhist bicycling practice is making an impression.

Sitting in the centre of a network of rivers and creeks is the quiet rural town of Spalding. We stop at the general store, where a large, ruddy-faced man stands behind the counter. We enquire about the nearby aqueduct. He says he doesn't know it, he's new in town.

'Where are you from?' I ask

'William Creek,' he replies.

At last count, this remote outback town along the route of the Overland Telegraph Line on the Oodnadatta Track had a population of four. This man, Bruce Ross, and his wife, Mim Ward, bought the lease for the William Creek Hotel in November 2009.

'We sold it three years later to a couple whose dream it was to own an outback pub,' he says. 'The couple lasted three months before they put it back on the market, and it was bought by Trevor Wright.' Steve and I first met Trevor Wright in 2006. This pilot and owner of Wrightsair is one of William Creek's few residents.

Whispering Wire

Bruce and Mim bought this store only a few months ago, and it looks as if they are already providing a much-needed hub for the people of Spalding. In addition to the shelves of packaged goods there is fresh coriander and bok choy for sale, a large coffee machine sits on the front counter, and adjoining the store is a café.

Just up the street we see the Barbed Wire Pub. The door is open and publican Geoff Tiller is behind the bar. Our room isn't ready yet, he tells us, because three women walking a section of the Heysen Trail stayed in it last night, and their belongings are still there.

While we wait, Geoff suggests we look at his collection of barbed wire.

'There are over 500 varieties. And I've just found some strands on a nearby property which I believe date back to 1890,' he says.

On the wall in the hallway at the back of the hotel are numerous neatly labelled strands of barbed wire. This isn't ordinary barbed wire, but rather twisted sawtooth ribbon wire. Another label says 'A Barbed Net Fence for Hog Pastures' patented by Dodge and Warburton in 1882. There is thick, wiggly 'Snake Wire', vicious-looking 'Bull Wire' and the *pièce de résistance*, 'Flemish Four Braid', resembling a piece of crochet.

I catch sight of antique telegraph lines, including a single piece of iron wire. The caption says, 'Original Adelaide–Darwin Telegraph Line, 1872–80'. I'm ridiculously excited to see the wire that transmitted the first messages between England and Australia. I feel I'm slowly piecing together the history of the telegraph line, as we cycle across the country, but sometimes I doubt myself and what I've set out to do. This wire, though, is like a sign – a strand of encouragement.

Almost immediately a wave of confusion envelops me, because above this single strand is a two-stranded twisted wire; the caption reads: 'A Portion of Original Overland Telegraph Line, Adelaide–Darwin in 1872'. The Overland Telegraph Line was a single strand of No. 8 standard wire gauge galvanised iron, except on the first section south of Darwin where No. 6 gauge wire was used. I haven't read of a two-stranded twisted wire being used. What was it for?

We go outside and sit, basking in the afternoon sunshine at the front of the pub. The group that's walking the Heysen Trail dribble back in twos and threes. When our room is ready we shower and change and return to

The Barbed Wire Pub

the bar and order for dinner, at Geoff's suggestion, homemade soup and a beef schnitzel that we share.

Geoff – a large man with a big protruding belly, a long grey beard and a shiny bald head – bought the pub in 2010.

'Before that I worked for the Australian Leisure and Hospitality Group, a division of Carlton & United Breweries,' he tells me. 'I was there when it was taken over by Bruce Mathieson and the Woolworths Group. In addition to being the largest food retailer and takeaway liquor retailer in Australia, Woolworths's 75% share in the Australian Leisure and Hospitality Group makes it the largest hotel and poker machine operator in the country.' Geoff explains that he couldn't reconcile the company's drive to increase shareholders' profits at the expense of people with gambling addictions. 'So I bought the pub. I don't make as much money,' he says, 'but I'm my own boss and much happier.'

I greatly admire this man, who had the guts to walk away from his corporate job and all its perks because he didn't believe in the company's moral stance.

When Geoff hears we are following the Overland Telegraph Line, he brings out another coil of double-stranded twisted wire, attached to which is a cardboard tag with the following words:

> <u>1–7–03</u> CONFIRMATION WAS RECEIVED TODAY FROM MR ALAN NORTH THAT THIS TWISTED STRAND WIRE WAS DEFINITELY USED IN DARWIN AREA ON A PART OF THE ORIGINAL OVERLAND TELEGRAPH LINE, ADELAIDE TO DARWIN, 1870–1872. DONOR ROB GARDNER.

It's only months later when I'm back in Sydney that I discover that in some areas stranded wire was used as guy wire to secure the pole to an anchor post, although Todd had specified 17-foot poles to support angle poles. Also, every second pole had a lightning wire stapled to the pole, projecting seven centimetres above the insulator, with about 10 metres coiled and buried a metre underground at the foot of the pole. It's possible this twisted wire was used for that purpose.

In the bar we meet Bruce and Dee Lawson. She is from South Australia and he is from South Africa, where he trains guides at the Kruger National

Park. Dee tells us they live in the park in an enormous tent. They have taken three months away from Kruger so Bruce can walk the entire 1200-kilometre length of the Heysen Trail. Dee is walking much of the way with him, but she is also spending time with the rest of her family. They are halfway and Dee has just rejoined him. Their stay at the Barbed Wire Hotel for several nights is a luxurious interlude. Geoff will drive them to the next section of the walk and collect them at the end of the day.

Usually they carry food, water and camping equipment. I imagine them sitting in front of an open fire every evening, gazing at the stars, but Dee corrects this romantic vision. After walking all day, she says, they quickly cook a rice-based meal before hopping into their tent and falling sleep.

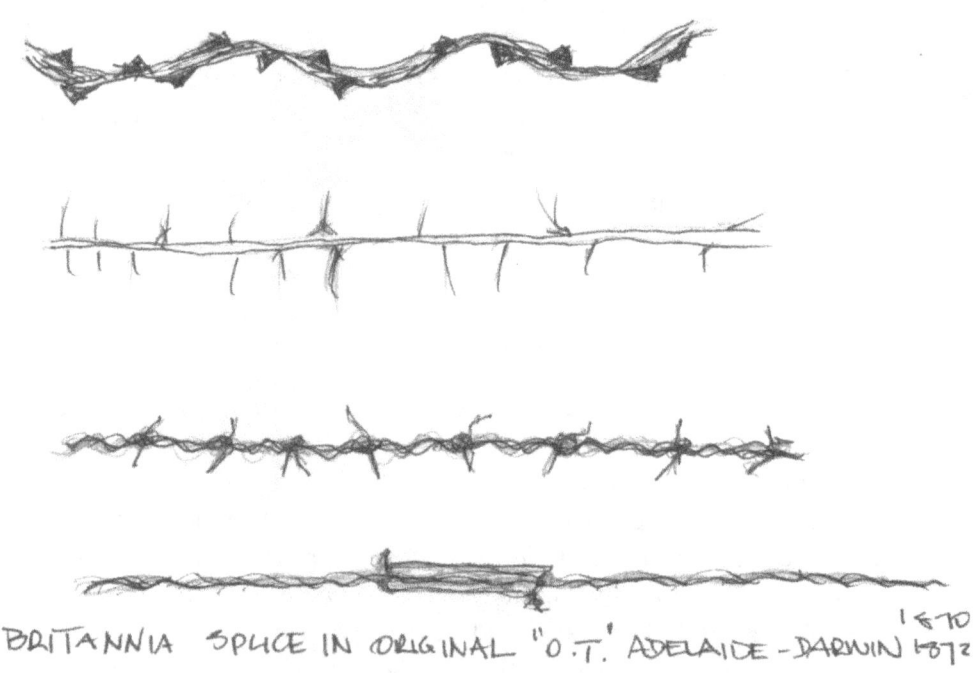

BRITANNIA SPLICE IN ORIGINAL "O.T." ADELAIDE - DARWIN 1872
1870

CHAPTER 10

Golden North Ice Cream

The task of making morning tea falls to the person with the most energy when the alarm goes off, which this morning is me. We sit propped up against our pillows under floral doonas contemplating the day ahead. It's 56 kilometres to Laura, our longest cycle stretch so far, and as usual I'm nervously wondering if I'll stay the course.

Bruce and Dee are outside the hotel waiting for Geoff, who pulls up in his minivan with Cooper, his kelpie. Today they are only walking for four hours and returning here for the night. I give Bruce and Dee a big hug. We'll be thinking of them tramping the Heysen.

A roaring spitfire heater bellows heat into the huge general store, and Bruce Ross is behind the counter. A schoolboy comes in to buy the local paper, and a council worker purchases a carton of coffee milk. Bruce greets them both by name.

Fleur and I decide to treat ourselves to breakfast at the café. Several wicker chairs have been positioned around a packing case, which serves as a coffee table, but we decide to sit at the red Formica-topped table by the window while Mim makes us egg and bacon rolls. As I drink my large cappuccino and Fleur her tea, our eyes are drawn to an arrangement of old wooden boxes and pale green-and-white enamel saucepans and kitchen utensils, and a large glass display case filled with old tins and bottles. The place is sparsely furnished, but Mim obviously has a creative eye.

Originally from Adelaide, Mim Ward has 11 brothers and sisters. She knows one of Denise Miller's sons and, it turns out, is a cousin of a friend of Fleur. No one else is in the café, so Mim, down-to-earth and vivacious, chats to us while we eat. Fleur and I are astonished by the connections, but Mim appears unfazed. With so many siblings and an extensive social network it might not be unusual to find a connection with total strangers.

Before we set off, I buy a large envelope at the post office and mail to Sydney the numerous pamphlets and papers I've collected since my possession purge at Woodside.

It's 9.30 by the time we leave. Fleur is out in front, and at the first hill I lag further behind as I struggle to get into first gear. I feel tired this morning, aware of my perpetual anxiety about running out of steam and failing to make our destination. In the paddock beside the road are the pipes of the Morgan–Whyalla Pipeline – long steel snakes crossing the landscape, providing fresh water from the Murray River for the industrial town of Whyalla on the Spencer Gulf.

I think of Stuart's constant search for water as he moved across the continent. After his fourth expedition, Stuart was weak and unwell. He stayed at Montefiore House, the home of James Chambers in North Adelaide, and drank heavily. He didn't drink on his expeditions, but it was known he drank whisky and rum in excessive quantities at other times. Meanwhile the South Australian government insisted that his next expedition get underway immediately.

A dinner was held in Adelaide at the end of October 1860 to farewell the explorers. After Governor MacDonnell's toast to him, Stuart started to speak, but was overwhelmed by calls from the crowd to speak up. He stopped reading and stood silent, staring at the crowd. The chairman of proceedings read the rest of his speech, while Stuart was overcome with emotion at the rapturous applause he received.

On 1 January 1861, Stuart's fifth expedition of 11 men and 49 horses left Chambers Creek, carrying large quantities of arms and ammunition. Stuart rode his beloved mare, Polly, despite her being in foal. They were following the course of the dry Finke River, south of the MacDonnell Ranges, when she came into foal. For hours he rode along the riverbed, looking for water for Polly before discovering a small spring. Her foal was stillborn, and Stuart halted the party for the day to give her time to recover.

Once again he headed north-west towards the Victoria River, as instructed by Governor MacDonnell, but he had to retrace his steps because of lack of water. In search of another route Stuart then led the party northwards, but they couldn't progress through the spiky bullwaddy bush. The horses refused to move and it tore the men's clothes and saddlebags to pieces.

Setting off to the north-west again, they reached a forest of eucalypts and found themselves facing a 150-metre-wide stretch of water, an oasis for brolgas, ibis, ducks and pelicans. The men swam and splashed with delight in the deep water before feasting on mussels and fish. Stuart named it Glandfield Lagoon, after the Mayor of Adelaide, but it was later altered by Chambers to Newcastle Waters.

Stuart made 11 attempts with his team of bushmen to find a route either to the Victoria River in the north-west or the Gulf of Carpentaria in the north-east, but he found no water in either direction. The party was now low on rations and in poor health, so he gave up, despite having pushed only 160 kilometres further north of Attack Creek, which he had reached on his previous expedition. On 11 July 1861, he wrote in his journal:

> *I believe that I have left nothing untried that has been in my power. I have tried to make the Gulf and river, both before rain fell, and immediately after it had fallen; but the results were the same, unsuccessful.*

When he returned to Adelaide, Stuart was invited to visit Governor MacDonnell. While he had been away, the Royal Geographical Society had awarded him the Patron's Gold Medal for finding the route to the Centre on his fourth expedition. Stuart recoiled at the governor's suggestion that he could present the medal to him at an official ceremony. But they did agree – because nothing had been heard of Burke and Wills and the colony still needed to find a route for an overland telegraph line – that Stuart would head another expedition.

***

There is a succession of four-wheel drives pulling caravans on the road this morning, but otherwise it's quiet. A pair of swallows swoop over a Flinders Range wattle with its delicate, pale-yellow puffball flowers and long narrow leaves. We see a sign for the Mawson Trail but decide its big loop before meeting up with the road again is an unnecessary deviation.

At a crossroads, native bees fly in and out of the hole in a farm's sandstone wall and dip into the red flowers of nearby grevillea bushes. Further down the road I'm captivated by the eremophila – a tar bush with bright-red-tongued flowers, and next to it the spiky-leaved emu bush with its deep-pink tongues.

At 11.30 we turn onto the Horrocks Highway. We stop for my mid-morning banana, and as I'm burrowing in my panniers I realise I've lost my mobile phone charger. I empty the contents of both panniers, but it isn't there. In a panic, I try to remember when I last used it. I ring the caravan park in Kapunda and the Rising Sun Hotel, but it hasn't been found. The woman who answers the telephone at the Middle Pub in Clare tells me to ring back tomorrow. There is nothing I can do except turn off my mobile to save the remaining battery.

The only sound is our pedals turning, until the quiet is broken by a loud honk when a double road train comes up behind us and rumbles past. The road becomes clear and still again, and the long view stretches ahead as far as the eye can see.

We stop at Georgetown's general store, a building crowned by an ornate, crumbling green-and-white stone balustrade, with the year '1912' inscribed above the entrance. Going inside is like stepping back into another world. Steve and I bought ice creams here a couple of years ago and I want Fleur to see it. Long counters run down either side of the shop; tables are piled with old newspapers. Caps and stubby holders commemorate the centenary of the shop in 2012, and a couple of bamboo sun helmets are perched beside the ice-cream fridge. Hartmut Tusch, the owner, stands behind the counter. He's intrigued to hear that Bruce and Mim have taken over the Spalding store.

'I might pop over and see them,' he tells us.

Fleur is very patient during my numerous stops to look at birds, plants or buildings. But she also is possessed with a desire to make progress, so most of the time she is a speck in distance ahead of me. But occasionally, now that I've become marginally fitter, I put on a bit of a spurt.

'Why are you so slow?' I ask as I overtake her. That annoys Fleur and usually within 10 minutes the usual order is resumed, with her out in front and me bringing up the rear. True to form, she is ahead when we pass the huge grain silos on the outskirts of Gladstone, a town once renowned for its three-gauge railway junction.

An idiosyncrasy of Australian railways is the different gauges. In 1847 the South Australia parliament passed an Act stipulating the standard gauge of 4 foot 8½ inches between of the rails would be used by the state. A year later the other Australian colonies, NSW – of which Queensland and Victoria were still part – Tasmania and Western Australia also adopted the standard gauge.

However, the private Sydney Railway Company was constructing a line from Sydney to Parramatta and its Irish engineer wanted to use the broader Irish gauge (5 foot 3 inches), so the company asked that NSW legislation change to Irish gauge. A year later the Irish engineer resigned and was replaced by a Scottish engineer who preferred standard gauge, so the NSW government was persuaded to change back to standard gauge.

The other colonies, including the newly formed colony of Victoria, were told of the change, and it was recommended that they adopt the standard gauge. However, when a railway company about to order locomotives and rolling stock from England asked the Victorian government which gauge was preferable the company was told broad gauge. So Australia's first railway line, which ran from Flinders Street in Central Melbourne to Port Melbourne and opened in 1854, was broad gauge.

In 1855 the standard gauge Sydney to Parramatta line opened. But South Australia's first steam-powered train line from Adelaide to Port Adelaide, was broad gauge to maintain compatibility with Victoria.

Ten years later Queensland introduced a narrow gauge, 3 foot 6 inches, believing it could be constructed more cheaply and faster. South Australia adopted this gauge in the 1870s for some of its lines including one from Port Pirie to Gladstone, and another north from Gladstone to Wilmington.

In 1920s the line from Hanley Bridge to Gladstone was converted from narrow gauge to broad gauge. Then in 1970 the line from Port Pirie through Gladstone to Broken Hill was converted to standard gauge, making Gladstone a three-gauge break of gauge junction.

The broad and narrow gauge lines were closed in the 1980s and today only the Port Pirie to Broken Hill line runs through Gladstone. We take the road north that runs alongside the disused railway track to Wilmington. A grey heron stands motionless as frogs croak beneath the Broughton willows. It's half past three and the school bus pulls up ahead of us. A small boy gets off and walks up a track to a farm with a sign at the gate advertising the sale of hay and oats.

Laura is famous for its Golden North Ice Cream, so we stop at Koffi n Kandi Café. Two schoolgirls, in their long, thick tartan skirts and black lace-up shoes, select sweets from the large glass jars of toffee, liquorice, jellies and freckles behind the wooden counter. Susie Higgins, the owner, puts their choices into two small white paper bags.

We head to the refrigerator and ogle the numerous flavours of Golden North, the ice cream made in Laura for the last 90 years. I opt for chocolate, Fleur for boysenberry. We sit at a table outside in the last of the afternoon sun, relishing these treats made with fresh milk and cream from local dairies. I ring Steve's mobile. There is no reply. I know he is at work this evening and probably busy, so I leave a message saying we have reached Laura and I have lost my mobile charger.

I can feel my legs stiffen as we cycle up the street to our accommodation, a three-bedroom house on the main street. It's a large place and the reverse-cycle air conditioning doesn't do much to heat it, so soon after we've eaten we hop into our beds. Wearing my woolly hat and fingerless gloves, I curl up under the blanket with a mug of tea. I open my journal and start to write. I'm tired but happy. It is a joy to be outdoors every day and not cooped up in a vehicle. I adore that pedal power is slowly transporting us northwards.

CHAPTER 11

King Tree and Over the Edge

The following morning I ring the Clare Hotel. To my relief, Deb, who answers, says my mobile charger has been found and she'll send it to me. I offer to pay for the postage, but she says she believes that what goes around comes around and will put in the mail. I feel immensely grateful. But Deb is sceptical about the speed of Australia Post and decides that, to be safe, she should send it to Hawker, where we will be in six days.

My mobile phone is not only almost indestructible but also holds its charge well – the battery is not yet flat. I have been turning it on once a day to check for messages, and I text Steve now and tell him to ring Fleur's number to get hold of me. I have had no mobile reception between towns, but at least until now I've been able to make calls in the evenings. Such irony; following Australia's iconic line of instant communication 150 years after it was constructed and being unable to communicate with the world.

I'm adamant that we get back on the Mawson Trail today. Our destination is Melrose, home of the Over the Edge bicycle shop, and I feel it's a matter of pride that we arrive fresh from the track rather than the tarmac.

The first few kilometres of the Mawson Trail follow the old railway track, which runs beside the Horrocks Highway. From there we bounce along Lynch Road. We cleaned our bikes last night and oiled the chains but, despite the maintenance, Fleur's gears aren't shifting easily this morning. She's stuck in a high gear and needs to be in a low one, as we pedal against the north-easterly wind. I'm elated to be back on the dirt, even though it's harder to cycle over the corrugations.

It's 10.30 and we've covered just over 10 kilometres. But now we're on a muddy track and our tyres are caked in red earth. A pair of kookaburras laugh loud and long as we push our bikes up a hill. At the top, Fleur gets back on her saddle and is away. I'm watching her wobble over a dry, grassy stretch when my gears slip while I'm negotiating a puddle and I promptly fall off my bicycle. The track skirts the edge of a mallee woodland and a flock of Adelaide rosellas fly over. We reach a dip in the track filled with water, so we push our bikes round it, over a bank of mud and between a she-oak and a cypress pine. Bumping over a rocky section, my panniers come off the rear rack. I carefully reassemble them, but five minutes later they come off again. I'm tired and a blaze of anger fires in me, precipitating a torrent of abuse at the panniers and a tirade at myself for not having secured them. While hooking them back onto the rear rack, I break a strap. Cursing and swearing, I secure the pannier to the rack with a plastic tie and hope it holds. I carefully avoid all bumps, but I still catch up with Fleur, who is pushing Sulemon through another quagmire.

The track is too wet to cycle so we push our bikes, their wheels so clogged with the red clay soil they barely turn and climbing a hill is a monumental effort. We make pitifully slow progress as we slip and slide through the mud, like the Burke and Wills' camels when they reached the wet, slippery ground of the northern tropics. In February 1861, two months after leaving Cooper Creek, Burke and Wills had reached the salty mangrove waters of the north coast. Burke had told William Brahe to leave Cooper Creek after three months if they had not arrived back, so this gave Burke, Wills, King and Gray only a month for their return journey. But as the camels' pads were so unsuited to the ground in the tropics the expedition party could travel only seven kilometres a day.

South of the tropics they faced dust storms and the dry heat. Charley Gray began to lag behind, complaining of headaches and back pain. With their supplies running low, Burke killed a camel to eat and several days later his beloved horse, Billy, was their food. Now unable to walk Gray was strapped onto a camel before he died. The other three men spent a day digging a shallow grave and continued south.

On the evening of 21 April, expecting a hero's welcome for having reached the Gulf of Carpentaria, Burke rode his camel ahead of King and Wills into the camp at Cooper Creek to find it deserted. A message was carved on an old coolibah tree:

King Tree and Over the Edge

DIG

3ft, N.W.

And on a low branch was carved

Apr 21 1861.

Brahe and the other men had left that very same day.

The three exhausted men dug and found food in a trunk and a message from Brahe explaining that Wright had never arrived from Menindee with more supplies. Rather than live off these meagre rations in the hope that a search party would soon arrive, Burke decided they should follow Cooper Creek and head to a police outpost at Mount Hopeless in the Flinders Ranges, 240 kilometres away. Wills tried – in vain – to dissuade him. They buried a note under the Dig Tree, but didn't carve a message on the tree trunk. Two days later they set off with their two camels into one of the driest regions in Australia.

A week later Brahe and his men met Wright and the base party making its way north from Menindee. Brahe rode with Wright back to the camp at Cooper Creek, in case Burke and his party had arrived back there. They noticed fresh ash, but thought Aboriginal people must have lit a fire. With no message carved into the Dig Tree, Brahe and Wright thought the explorers hadn't returned. They left without leaving a message on the tree to indicate they had come back to look for Burke and his party.

Meanwhile Burke, Wills and King were only 50 kilometres further down Cooper Creek. Four days after they left the camp one of their camels became trapped in quicksand; unable to free it, they shot it and carved off what meat they could. Soon after, the second camel collapsed, so they stripped its flesh too. They got lost in a side channel of the main creek and spent a month wandering up and down it, while being watched by the local Yandruwandha people, who now and then gave them food, or traded matches for fish, or nardoo cakes for pieces of mackintosh.

They returned to the place where the first camel got bogged in the quicksand. From here Wills walked for three days back to the Dig Tree, hoping someone had come to rescue them. Seeing no evidence, he left no mark on the tree, and returned to Burke and King.

Wills had seen the Yandruwandha grinding the spore capsules of the aquatic fern, nardoo, into flour, so the explorers gathered spore capsules daily and ground them, unaware that the local people's preparation of the nardoo spore cases removed the enzyme thiaminase, which breaks down vitamin B1 in the body. This meant that although the men were eating two to three kilograms of nardoo a day they were growing weaker.

The three men realised their only hope of survival was to find the Yandruwandha and beg for food. But Burke had earlier fired at one of them when he saw him taking an oilcloth, so the Aboriginal people had left the three white men and moved on. Wills was so weak after going to the Dig Tree that he was unable to walk any further, so Burke and King left him some nardoo cakes and water and headed in the direction the Yandruwandha people had gone.

Two days later Burke collapsed and died. King continued searching for the Aboriginal people. He slept in deserted wurleys, Aboriginal shelters made of branches and leaves, found a bag of nardoo and shot a crow. Recovering his strength, he returned to Wills, shooting three crows on the way for them to eat, but Wills was also dead.

Hearing his gunshots, the Yandruwandha came to meet him and took him to their camp. He lived with them for over two months, shooting crows for them, and also curing a woman's ulcerated arm with silver nitrate. She, in return, gave him nardoo every day, until in mid-September he was found by a search party led by bushman Alfred Howitt.

***

The track is so rocky and muddy that we mostly walk, until we reach the wide dirt road heading to Wirrabara Forest Reserve. The strong smell of eucalyptus permeates the air as we cycle past wrinkle-barked gums to the King Tree.

This forest ruler is a 400-year-old river red gum. Fleur stands at the base of the tree with outstretched arms, the rough, grey trunk extending more than twice her arms' length. The circumference at the base is over 11 metres, its height over 36 metres. But it resembles an old man losing his hair. No longer capped with a magnificent crown of foliage, its upper branches are bare and small clusters of leaves grow like sideburns from the thicker, lower limbs.

King Tree and Over the Edge

This colossal trunk of the King Tree stands like a forlorn sole survivor. So many huge old trees were felled to provide timber for buildings, fences and jetties. When the Broken Hill mines were established, the charcoal for the smelters came from Wirrabara Forest. Wirrabara timber was used for poles for the Overland Telegraph Line and for 500,000 sleepers on the Great Northern Railway, running alongside the telegraph line for hundreds of kilometres through the outback.

Appalled by the rapid depletion of South Australia's native forests, the surveyor George Goyder recommended creating forestry reserves to ensure the protection and regeneration of the natural vegetation and a sustainable use of forestry for timber. Wirrabara was one of South Australia's first forest reserves. Today, it is part conservation park and part commercial forestry.

A fire recently tore through part of Wirrabara Forest and the section of the Mawson Trail that passes through it is closed. So we continue down King Tree Road. I glance at the exaggerometer and see that since leaving Laura three hours ago we have cycled only 13.5 kilometres.

We reach a crossroad, where a sign for the next section reads 'dry weather only'. We decide to not take that route and instead head towards Wirrabara town. Several large tree trunks are strapped to the back of a truck that overtakes us. I look at the exaggerometer again. It still says 13.5 kilometres. It's now underestimating our achievements. I give it a jiggle and it gets going again.

My desire to make a grand entrance into Over the Edge after a day on the Mawson Trail has been thwarted. We're back on the Horrocks Highway feeling gloomy, with wheels caked in mud and the wind against us. Juniper is now making a peculiar clunking sound so I stop to look for the problem, but apart from having difficulty getting into first gear, there doesn't seem to be anything wrong. A chirp from a galah, perched on a fence, makes me smile as I get back on the bike.

I'm adamant that we should get off the highway, so after five kilometres we turn onto a road that joins up with the Mawson Trail, beyond the closed section. But looking at the map we decide not to head into the hills this late in the day, where we could find ourselves pushing our bikes through more thick mud. Instead we opt to ride along Dust Bowl Road, which runs parallel to the main road.

Whispering Wire

We stop for lunch and barely talk. I'm very tired and Fleur is despondent that it's half past two already and we still have 20 kilometres to go. But the next hour's cycling is a joy. We weave back and forth across the dirt road, avoiding rocks and puddles, and ahead of us looms the distinctive shape of a mountain known as Wangyarra by the local Nukunu people, and named Mount Remarkable by explorer Edward John Eyre. We cross a couple of shallow creeks. A herd of steers gallop the length of a paddock beside us and two roos take off across the vibrant green grass.

It's only five kilometres to Melrose when we rejoin the Horrocks Highway. I catch the smell of wood fires as smoke curls up from the stone chimneys of a couple of houses on the outskirts of town. A gang of sulphur-crested cockatoos chatters in a tree. It's nearly four o'clock, the underestimator has clocked 46 kilometres, and we're here.

We go straight to the Over the Edge, bursting with pride that we've cycled all the way from Adelaide to here – over 300 kilometres. It is such a significant milestone for me, because I first heard about the Mawson Trail in this bicycle shop, when Steve and I visited Melrose a few years ago.

Richard Bruce, the owner of the shop, opened it in 2008. Since then, 180 kilometres of biking trails have been established in the area, making Melrose a mecca for cyclists. Richard isn't in the shop, but his colleague Dave Hughes gives our bikes the once-over. He says the clunking sound that my bicycle has been making for the last 15 kilometres is due to a lost rack bolt. Like Fleur, I've had difficulty getting into first gear over the past few days, and Dave tells us that our chains aren't clean enough and that we should also keep the small rear chain wheels cleaner.

We're discussing chains and lubrication when Richard arrives, looking incredibly fit. With the build of a whippet and a youthful face, he look to be in his late 20s or early 30s. But actually he's in his mid-40s and has three sons.

'My regular morning cycling circuit is from here to Port Augusta and on to Quorn and back, which is 150 kilometres,' he says casually. When I explain that we are cycling 30 kilometres to Wilmington tomorrow, and it will be three days cycling for us to Quorn, he's obviously nonplussed that we could be so slow. But Kim from North Adelaide Cycles is far more enthusiastic when we send him a text message; he replies with copious congratulations. I think he's amazed that we got over the Adelaide Hills.

We are staying at Bundaleer Cottage next door to the North Star Hotel. It is a four-bedroom single-storey sandstone house. Our room is at the front and tonight Fleur takes the double bed and I have the single on castors, probably more often the bed for a small child.

'Give me your pannier, Rossie, I'll mend the strap for you,' Fleur says. Sitting on the bed she stitches it with strong black thread, while I make us tea. We have dinner at the hotel. The retired couple at a nearby table are on their way home to Adelaide from the Kimberley in Western Australia. In between insisting we taste a piece of smoked kangaroo they tell us about a German cyclist they met on the rough, remote Gibb River Road. He was cycling around Australia and adored by all the grey nomads travelling the track with their four-wheel drive caravans. Not only did they transport his heavy panniers for him, they also cooked him evening meals.

'He had an opinion on everything and could talk the hindlegs off a donkey,' the man says, sounding as if he had tired of the cyclist's loquaciousness. Fleur and I retreat back to our table fearful that he might consider all cyclists overly talkative. We order glasses of red wine from local wineries. Over large plates of food we celebrate our nine days on the road and being halfway through our trip.

CHAPTER 12

Schnitzel or Fish

Having gone to sleep under the window I wake up this morning to find my bed halfway across the room nestled at the foot of Fleur's. I can only assume my tossing and turning during the night set it rolling across the polished wooden floor. After making ourselves baked beans on toast for breakfast we head to the post office. Fleur is sending home two T-shirts, a sports bra and a pair of shorts, and I'm mailing the maps we no longer need, and the pile of pamphlets that I've accumulated like a bower bird since I posted the last lot home from Spalding.

The post office is on Stuart Street, named after John McDouall Stuart who camped at Melrose in 1859 on his third expedition. It was the first time that William Kekwick, who would go on to become Stuart's loyal companion on his future expeditions, was one of his team. Three years later, suffering from scurvy and in poor health after successfully crossing the continent on his sixth expedition, Stuart stayed here again before returning to Adelaide.

Stuart's sixth expedition didn't start well. James Chambers held a farewell lunch for the expedition party at his home in North Adelaide then insisted on buying drinks for everyone at a nearby inn. As Stuart dismounted his horse, his halter got tangled with another horse. One of the horses reared, kicking Stuart in the temple, and the two struggling horses stamped on his right hand. The expedition's leader was taken to Chambers' house; the other members of the party continued on their way. Stuart's wounds became infected and he became seriously ill. But several weeks later, in early November 1861, with his hand bandaged and his arm in a sling he travelled by train to the railhead at Kapunda accompanied by scientist Frederick Waterhouse, who Governor MacDonnell had insisted accompany the expedition. Both men were 46 years old. They were met by William Finke who rode with them to Chambers' property Moolooloo, where Stuart spent a week selecting suitable horses for the expedition, before the pair departed for Chambers Creek. Also that November the telegraph relayed the news from Melbourne of the deaths of Burke, Wills and Gray.

On 8 January 1862 Stuart – on his beloved mare Polly – and 10 men rode out of Chambers Creek. They took 71 horses and pack bags loaded with equipment and food. Several weeks later one man left the expedition. Stuart had instructions to find a viable route to 'the Victoria River or some other place on the north-west coast' for an overland telegraph line. They were to avoid the Gulf of Carpentaria, given that Burke and Wills had already explored that area.

Two months later they were north-west of present-day Alice Springs on the plains near Mount Hay. Having found rainwater in a creek, they stopped to give the horses a drink. A group of Aboriginal men surrounded them, shouting and brandishing spears; Stuart could see more men in the distance in the grass. He ordered his men to fire close to them to scare them off. But the warriors weren't frightened by the gunshot.

'We crossed the creek', Stuart wrote in his journal, 'and had proceeded a short distance across the plain, when they again came running towards us, apparently determined to attack; they were received with a discharge of rifles, which caused them to retire and keep at a respectful distance'. One of the party, Stephen King, gave a newspaper interview 52 years after the event. He said there were 100 warriors.

'The first fire did not seem to disturb them very much; they got down in the long grass. Then we fired lower, and they retreated back into the scrub. Mr Stuart would not let us chase them. He said, "No, we must get on."'

They reached Newcastle Waters and from there Stuart, with a couple of men, set out to find the next source of water and a route northwards. He travelled north-west toward the Victoria River but couldn't find water. In five weeks the party only advanced two days' ride, because he failed to find reliable water sources. But eventually he found chains of ponds to the north that led him to a broad deep creek, which he named Daly Waters. From here Stuart and several men again searched for water. They followed a dry creek bed that Stuart called Strangways River, which eventually became deep clear water. For six days the party continued north along this river, until it reached the Roper River.

Knowing the Roper River flowed into the Gulf of Carpentaria, Stuart looked for another route north. They found a tributary of the Roper, which Stuart called Chambers River, running to the north, and followed that. Stuart thought they had reached the Adelaide River, but it was a river running parallel to, but east of, the Adelaide River; he called it the Mary River. Now travelling through tropical forest and along muddy creeks and marshes, the party was tormented by mosquitoes.

On 24 July the party entered thick scrub. While the men were clearing a way for the horses through the dense network of vines, Stuart walked ahead, stepped onto the beach and stood facing the Indian Ocean at Van Diemen Gulf. He had finally reached the north coast of the continent.

'The sea! The sea!' shouted Francis Thring, the 25-year-old who was first to ride through the gap in the scrub, to the astonishment of the rest of the party who were unaware they were so close to their destination. Stuart dipped his feet, and washed his face and hands in the sea, as he had promised Governor MacDonnell he would do. The following day the men hoisted a Union Jack to the top of a tall tree, a flag made by James Chambers' daughter Elizabeth, with Stuart's name sewn into its centre. Kekwick made a speech, to which Stuart responded, and the party cheered Queen Victoria, Prince Albert and the Prince of Wales.

Supplies were very low, the horses weak, and Stuart's health was failing when, on 26 July, they began the long homeward journey. Stuart's eyesight failed and he had to rely on 22-year-old Pat Auld, who had some surveying experience, to take observations. Five weeks later they reached Newcastle Waters. No rain had fallen on the dry Sturt Plains ahead during the time they had travelled north. Creeks had dried up, and at one point they travelled for three days without water.

Suffering from scurvy and severe malnutrition, Stuart's legs had turned black, his teeth rattled in his bleeding gums and he was feverish. Soon the sick man could ride only limited distances before the pain became too much for him, and he had to be lifted on and off his saddle.

Several times it looked as if he would die during the night. A stretcher was made for him and slung between two horses; he travelled on it for 10 hours a day. He realised the necessity for the party to keep pushing on, because waterholes would continue to dry up as the heat increased with the approach of summer. For the last 35 days of the journey back to Chambers Creek he travelled by stretcher, slowly regaining his health when he was able to eat bush cucumbers and native lettuces. In late November, they reached Mount Margaret Station, which in 1862 was the remotest outpost of white settlement. Here Stuart learnt that his friend and benefactor, James Chambers, had died three-and-a-half months earlier.

On 21 January 1863, the 10 explorers wearing the ragged clothing in which they had travelled across the continent, paraded through Adelaide, cheered by the largest crowd the city had ever seen. On the same day in Melbourne 40,000 mourners watched four black horses pull a funeral car in which lay the bodies of Robert O'Hara Burke and William John Wills.

***

Fleur explores the town and I settle in beside the wood-burning stove at Over the Edge, delectably warm on the sofa. Richard, having barista as well as bicycle skills, makes me a cup of coffee while I use the free wi-fi to check my emails.

Steve and I bush camped just across the creek from the town when we were here a couple of years ago, and we climbed Mount Remarkable. I found a small stone with a thin black line through it, which to me was a symbol of the Overland Telegraph Line. I held the stone in my palm, and walked up the mountain, not knowing then that I would have the opportunity to follow the Overland Telegraph Line and write a book about it. As I sit writing, I remember how near impossible this journey seemed, yet also how determined I was to make it happen.

I could sit drinking cappuccinos in the bicycle shop all day, but Fleur prises me off the sofa and out the door. We cycle out of town at 11.15 on this cold overcast day. Grateful that Fleur has repaired my pannier strap I'm hoping it will hold. Initially, the Mawson Trail follows the Horrocks Highway, but cars are few and far between.

Whispering Wire

Beneath the dappled branches of the river red gums heads of wallaby grass nod in the gentle breeze. One large gum has a long scar near its base where a strip of bark has been removed.

We stop at the monument where the road crosses Goyder's Line. This line – drawn in 1865 by surveyor George Goyder on the map of South Australia from the west coast near Ceduna to the Victorian border – delineated a change in natural vegetation: mallee scrub to the south and saltbush to the north. Goyder believed that the land to the north wasn't suitable for agriculture, only light grazing, because of an average rainfall of less than 250 millimetres a year. Farmers ignored his advice, establishing farms and planting crops north of the line. Then drought hit, and many had to abandon their properties.

The Mawson Trail turns onto a wide, stony dirt road. With the Flinders Ranges a blue silhouette in the distance, we snake happily along, avoiding rocks and following the purple Mawson Trail signs attached to fence posts at junctions. The dirt softens beneath our tyres as we reach a large flooded gully. The water extends to the banks on both sides of the road: should we cycle through this enormous brown pool of indeterminate depth? Or should we wade around the edge and spend the rest of the day with cold, wet feet? Looking at the map, we decide to try a parallel dirt road which might be dry. Thankfully, it is.

The sky has cleared and it's sunny when we stop for our picnic, and with only 10 kilometres to go and all on the flat, today feels like a holiday. This is our last day on the Mawson Trail, because from Wilmington it goes direct to Quorn, but we're cycling via Port Augusta. And from Quorn northwards we've decided to stay on the more direct main road, rather than follow Mawson's circuitous route.

It's just after three o'clock when we hit the bitumen on the outskirts of Wilmington. We cycle down a street lined with kurrajong trees and past children playing in the grounds of the primary school. We're staying at the Wilmington Hotel, a large two-storey 19th-century building on Main North Road. There used to be several large hotels in the town for drovers and travellers to stay before crossing Horrocks Pass to Port Augusta, but this is the only one still operating.

Opposite is the Beautiful Valley Café and Takeaway. When Anne, who runs it, hears we're cycling to Port Augusta tomorrow, she looks up the

Schnitzel or Fish

weather on her mobile phone and announces heavy rain is expected in the afternoon.

Anne and her husband own a property near here. She used to work at the immigration detention centre in Port Augusta, until it shut down earlier this year and she was made redundant. The small café-cum-store had closed and, much to the delight of the locals, she opened it again a few months ago. We buy a loaf of bread, some cheese, a box of crackers and two bananas.

In the hotel, Lindsay, the manager, stands behind the long wooden bar. Along the wall behind him are old fridges with varnished wooden doors and large metal handles. At the far end of the bar, two round men down schooners of beer, overlooked by the stuffed head of a wide-nostrilled black buffalo mounted on the wall.

Lindsay suggests that we take our bicycles up to our room. Having removed the panniers we carry them up the stairs and prop them against the fireplace, beside the small washbasin. Fleur takes the bed by the door and I have the one by the window. Wedged between us is a large wooden 1950s cupboard beside a small chest of drawers.

As there is only a thin doona on each of the narrow, metal-framed beds, I go down to the bar to ask Lindsay for extra blankets. He goes to a back room and returns with a small blow heater, which emits an unnerving burning smell, but at least it heats up the room.

I walk across the street to look at the large building that was once the general store and is now an op shop.

'I've just had a chat with your husband,' Fleur announces on my return.

'What about?'

'He's left Sydney and is in Cobar.'

'But he's not meeting us for another eight days.' Steve is someone who likes to be early, but I wonder what he's planning to do between Cobar and Farina over the next week. Usually I would ring him back immediately, but I don't dare use up my precious mobile battery. Fleur has borrowed the iPhone from a friend and is on a limited call plan, so I don't ask if I can use it. I am about to procure some coins from Lindsay and head to the telephone box on the street when Fleur adds, 'He said he'd ring again.'

We go down to the bar and I ask Lindsay about dinner. 'Schnitzel or fish,' he says, jerking his head in the direction of the dining room.

'Is there anything else?' I ask hopefully.

'It's schnitzel or fish,' he says slower – and louder. 'Ten dollars.' Realising wine is immediately required, Fleur orders a bottle of Mount Remarkable Shiraz. We are the only people in the large, cold dining room. Fleur picks at the fish, and I prod the chicken schnitzel while the waitress and a young girl empty the water out of the bain-marie.

CHAPTER 13

Camels, a Wobbegong and the First Telegraph Pole

A cock crows at 6.20 am. We sit in our beds drinking tea and eating cheese-and-dried-apricot sandwiches before making an early start. Fleur is delighted by my lack of procrastination. But her pleasure is short lived because on the outskirts of town I notice the fine set of testicles added to the black kangaroo on a yellow road sign, and I insist on stopping to take a photograph.

Cycling up Horrocks Pass against the south-west wind is hard. The road is windy and cars – presumably driven by people heading to work in Port Augusta – constantly pass us. Within minutes Fleur is out of sight ahead and my legs and bottom are aching. The clouds are ominously grey and low. Daunted by the steep ascent I forget to smile at the motorists. Prickly hop bushes and paddymelons grow beside the road and smashed beer bottles litter the verge. A she-oak stands beside a ruined sandstone building and the sounds of bleating lambs and baaing ewes ring through the pass.

In my lowest gear I cycle slowly up the pass and after seven painful kilometres, I reach the top to find Fleur waiting for me. She is standing beside a cairn in memory of John Horrocks, who travelled through here just before coming a cropper because of his camel, Harry.

Now it's five glorious kilometres of downhill before we round a corner and see Spencer Gulf below us. We turn off the main road and onto the little-used old Wilmington Road. We're in saltbush country. Native apricots with their small orange fruit stand like sentries surrounded by varieties of bluebush and samphire. Songlarks hover with trembling wings above the low bushes, and white-browed babblers duck and weave among the branches of a needle wattle. In the distance, a train rolls up the coast to Port Augusta. This is still the traditional land of the Nukunu, and Port Augusta is a natural crossroads – the gateway to the west of the continent as well as the north.

It's nearly noon when we pass some old stockyards. I suggest stopping for lunch while we're still in this beautiful open country, but Fleur is keen to press on. We end up on the outskirts of Port Augusta, sitting on the pavement opposite Stirling North Fire Station as we eat our honey-and-cheese sandwiches and fend off enormous ants.

The only consolation is that the first pole of the southern section of the Overland Telegraph Line was planted here in Stirling on 1 October 1870. We ask an elderly couple standing in their driveway about the pole and the Overland Telegraph Line. Eager to help they invite us to sit on a shady bench in their immaculate garden. Their bower looks very inviting, but they can throw no light on the telegraph line, and as Fleur now has her eye on the clouds forming ahead of us she insists we keep cycling.

We stop at the old railway station in Port Augusta. The Pichi Richi railway line from here to Quorn is the last remaining piece of track of the Great Northern Railway, which until 1980 ran from Port Augusta to Alice Springs. Rather than cycling up the steep Pichi Richi Pass on Sunday we have decided to take the Old Ghan steam train. Fleur wanders down the platform, while I study the timetable. 'Fleur,' I say, 'can you look at this timetable?' She walks back up the platform.

'Let me see,' she says.

'Look,' I say jabbing at the board.

'Hold on. Sunday … There's a train at 10.30.'

'That was last Sunday. Trains don't run every Sunday.' Fleur peers at the timetable again.

'There's no train this Sunday,' she says slowly.

The thought of cycling up the steep Pichi Richi Pass precipitates the next nagging worry that we won't actually cover the 42 kilometres to Quorn. It's not helped when we stop shortly afterwards and strike up a conversation with a stout man in his 30s standing on a street corner eating a donut.

'I've tried several times to cycle up the Pichi Richi Pass,' he tells us, 'and I've only ever got halfway.'

Camels, a Wobbegong and the First Telegraph Pole

Fleur has booked us into a deluxe studio apartment at the Oasis for our two nights in Port Augusta. It's near Woolworths, so we head to the supermarket to buy food, then visit the Thirsty Camel, where a surly man with studded lips recommends Over the Edge, a 2006 Shiraz made by Bartagunyah Estate in Melrose. Fleur casts me a doubtful glance, indicating her lack of faith in the pierced man's wine knowledge, but I am so excited that the bicycle shop has its own label that I insist we drink this drop to celebrate making it to Port Augusta.

As we step out of the Thirsty Camel the grey clouds, which have been building all day, burst. We dash across the Woolworths car park and arrive back at the apartment wet through. We turn on the heater, put all our wet and dirty clothes in the washing machine, and prepare chicken and salad for dinner. The Over the Edge Shiraz tastes so good that we drink the whole bottle.

The following morning, while Fleur is cooking bacon and eggs, I go to Woolworths to buy bread rolls for lunch. I'm told brown bread rolls aren't baked on Saturday, but I'm directed to the French bakery on Commercial Road. Music blares out over the deserted mall, and the old town hall is derelict and boarded up. Across the road from the bakery is the nondescript glass-fronted post office. This is the site of the original telegraph station, which in 1870 was South Australia's most northerly post and telegraph office, so it was from here that the Overland Telegraph Line was built to Darwin. But there is no indication of Port Augusta's former telegraphic significance. This is a far cry from Adelaide's splendid General Post and Telegraph Office.

When Stuart returned from successfully crossing the continent, Charles Todd quizzed him for details about the land and its viability for a telegraph line. Stuart outlined where there was timber, and confirmed that there was enough water in the dry centre to sustain men and animals. Todd became confident that a telegraph line could be built across the continent.

In 1863, on the grounds that a trade and communication route had been established between the south and north of the continent, the South Australian government successfully petitioned for the Northern Territory to be transferred from New South Wales to South Australia, giving the young colony an extra 1.35 million square kilometres. A year earlier Victoria had petitioned the British government to annex a new territory on the Gulf of Carpentaria, where Burke and Wills had reached the north coast, but that petition had failed.

By 1870 a transatlantic cable had been successfully laid and plans to connect London to Bombay, present-day Mumbai, neared completion. Attention turned to Australia and the Telegraph Construction and Maintenance Company, which had laid most of the major undersea cable lines around the world, set up a subsidiary company called the British Australian Telegraph Company (BAT). In January 1870, Captain Sherard Osborne, managing director of the company, wrote to South Australia, saying the cable would be brought ashore at Port Darwin, and BAT would construct a line to Burketown on the Gulf of Carpentaria. He asked for permission to cross South Australia's Northern Territory, saying his brother, Commander Noel Osborne, would arrive in South Australia in April to discuss the matter.

It looked as if the line would go to Queensland. Charles Todd now faced seeing his long-held dream of linking Australia with Britain being realised by others but neither he nor the South Australian government gave up. The government replied to the letter, saying that it would give permission, adding: 'This Government, however, would much prefer the construction of a line from Port Darwin to our northernmost telegraph station, Port Augusta.'

When Noel Osborne arrived in Adelaide in April, Charles Todd took full advantage of having his ear before he went to Queensland. Todd told Osborne that a line across the continent was not only possible but would also avoid land that flooded around the Gulf of Carpentaria and be less prone to tropical storms. The South Australian government would also build the line at its own expense and have it completed on 1 January 1872.

The Queensland government officials were furious, pointing out that they were already building a line to Normanton, which would be finished in early 1871, and the remaining 177 kilometres to Burketown could be easily completed. But BAT agreed to South Australia's proposal and Noel Osborne wrote to the government saying: 'The cable will be landed at Port Darwin, if the South Australian Government will pledge themselves to have a land-line open for traffic on 1 January 1872.'

This young colony had committed to completing – in 18 months – the construction of a 3200-kilometre telegraph line through country that had

Camels, a Wobbegong and the First Telegraph Pole

been explored eight years earlier and had not been visited since, and 2250 kilometres of its length had not been settled by the colonists. Charles Todd wrote in his diary:

Then, perhaps for the first time, I fully realised the vastness of the undertaking I had pledged myself to carry out ... It was my life's ambition which I had eagerly looked forward to, but now that its weight really rested upon me, I must confess, at times, it seemed too heavy to bear.

***

I buy the bread rolls and return to the apartment. After breakfast, we ride to the Australian Arid Lands Botanic Garden and spend several hours strolling through the gardens and flicking through the books in the shop, trying to identify some of the plants we've seen over the last few weeks. Sitting at one of the café's outdoor tables, we notice nardoo, with its clover-like leaves, growing in the pond beside us – a reminder of the cruel fate of Burke and Wills.

Cycling back over the old Great Western Bridge, we stop to watch a wobbegong in the shallows. A group gathers to look at the small shark swishing its tail as it makes its way through the water.

'Are you local?' a woman asks us.

'No, we're from Sydney,' Fleur replies. 'We're cycling from Adelaide to Farina.'

'You must visit my sister, Karen,' the woman says. 'She runs the general store in Copley. Tell her Maria sent you.'

The blue western slopes of the Flinders Ranges rise ominously high above a long goods train on the railway to the east. It is up there that we head tomorrow, and I'm having serious doubts about my ability to get up those hills, let alone to Copley, where we are staying the night before we reach Farina.

Near our apartment in Port Augusta is the old wooden wharf, over nine metres wide and stretching 365 metres along the foreshore. A couple of men are fishing from it and several families stroll between the two sets of rail tracks that run the length of it, as swallows swoop and circle over the grey timber.

On a notice board we see a black-and-white photograph of a camel suspended in mid-air as it is offloaded from a ship, while a group of cameleers in their turbans and white cotton shalwar kameezes look on.

Sir Thomas Elder, a Scottish entrepreneur and pastoralist, had ridden camels in Damascus, so he knew they could carry heavy loads and travel long distances without water. He saw them as the answer to expanding pastoralism in South Australia's north. In 1866 he imported a shipment of 109 camels along with 31 camel handlers from a host of exotic locations including India, Persia, Egypt and Afghanistan. Despite their diverse backgrounds, they all became known as Afghans. Elder established a camel stud at Beltana Station, his property in the northern Flinders Ranges, where we are staying in a few days' time.

Fleur nips across the car park to buy another bottle of Over the Edge from the lip-studded man at the Thirsty Camel while I gather up my belongings strewn around the apartment and pack them ready for the morning. I put the numerous pieces of information I've accumulated over the past few days into the large pre-paid envelope I bought in Melrose, so it's ready to post tomorrow.

We eat dinner and sit in the warm studio apartment, drinking wine and discussing the Afghans and their camels.

'It's odd Steve hasn't rung,' I say.

'It is,' Fleur replies. Because he has the number of the Oasis Apartments and Fleur's mobile I assumed he would be in touch when he was in mobile range. Now I realise I have been so caught up with camels and the Overland Telegraph Line I did not think to ring him.

'I'll just check my mobile.' I turn it on. There is still a minute amount of power left in it, and almost immediately the phone starts to beep. I can see Steve has rung numerous times. I dial his number, but there is no answer.

CHAPTER 14

A Visitor and a Phantom

The following morning we go to Commercial Road and I drop the large envelope in the post box. The sun is shining and seagulls circle above us as we cycle back past the mud flats to Stirling North. Looming large in front of us are the Flinders Ranges, their shadowy dips and contours highlighted by the sun. Two lycra-clad cyclists whizz past in the opposite direction. One waves, but they are going too fast for us to ask how challenging Pichi Richi Pass is. Its steepness has been playing on my mind and I am silently panicking that I shall get halfway up and run out of energy to go further.

Charles Todd's plan for the Overland Telegraph Line was to follow Stuart's route north until he reached the Roper River and from there head north-west to Port Darwin. But Stuart had travelled lightly with only horses and a few men. So Todd employed John Ross – an experienced bushman and explorer as well as the manager of Thomas Elder's Umberatana and Beltana Stations – to find the best route for the line. Todd wanted Ross to find a way suitable for heavy transport, with enough water for the working parties and access to timber for the poles. Ross set out in mid-1870 from Adelaide with a surveyor and three men.

Todd split the construction of the line into three sections: southern, central and northern. The southern section ran from Port Augusta to just north of present-day Oodnadatta, the centre section from Oodnadatta to Tennant Creek, and the northern section was to be built from Darwin south to Tennant Creek. The central section was to be constructed by the South Australian government. Edward Meade Bagot won the contract for the southern section, and Joseph Darwent and William Dalwood had the contract for the northern section. Two government overseers were appointed for each of these sections. Todd knew how important it was to keep the men well fed, so every party had to transport tonnes of food in addition to the equipment and materials to build the line.

In Adelaide wagons were built, biscuits baked, harnesses and pack saddles made, and a Port Adelaide timber yard produced thousands of ironbark insulator pins. Todd ordered 100 camels and drivers from Egypt and more than 3000 kilometres of No. 8 galvanised-iron wire was purchased from England.

In late August, the steamer *Omeo* departed from Adelaide for Port Darwin with Darwent and Dalwood's men and supplies, and soon after the parties working on the central section set off. Farewelling one group of men, Charles Todd warned them against the temptations of public houses along the way, adding, amid laughter, that he didn't think for a moment that the idea would ever enter their heads.

Charles Todd was described by his son-in-law, William Bragg, as having 'no commanding personality'. He didn't have obvious leadership qualities, but his son-in-law also reflected:

those who worked for him soon recognised his sense of proportion, his strong grasp of essentials, his acute understanding, and untiring energy ... The whole of his department was infected with his sense of duty and loyalty, his kindly courtesy and good humour.

Over a four-week period the parties of men working on the central and southern sections of the line departed from Adelaide. On 27 September, the last of the men on the southern section left Port Adelaide on a ship for Port Augusta. A day later, the South Australian government received a letter from London saying that the British Australian Telegraph Company had not received the South Australian government's acceptance of its agreement in time for its meeting back in early August – this was because the mail steamer had broken down – so BAT was no longer bound by any agreement with South Australia. Shortly afterwards a message from BAT said that South Australia's commitment to complete the line by 1 January 1872 was a moral obligation and not legally binding. The company therefore required the government to pass a bill binding the colony to the completion date and paying a penalty for every day after that date the line

A Visitor and a Phantom

wasn't completed. If South Australia didn't comply, the British Australian Telegraph Company said it could decide to build an alternative line. South Australia couldn't afford not to adhere to this stipulation, so a bill was drawn up and quickly passed through parliament.

With the amalgamation of the Post Office and the Telegraph Departments, in January 1870 Charles Todd had become South Australia's Postmaster-General and Superintendent of Telegraphs. He now delegated his responsibilities, and in early October travelled by steamer to Port Augusta to concentrate on the logistics for building the line – the supplies of food, the telegraphic equipment and the details of the line's route. He was away for 11 weeks, returning to Adelaide just before Christmas.

***

Both sides of the road are dotted with blue saltbushes. The Pichi Richi rail track is on our left as we face our first major hill. Fleur pushes on ahead and I click into my lowest gear and slowly follow her. I'm overtaking a hairy brown millipede, also heading uphill, when a horn beeps behind me. I look over my shoulder to see a grey four-wheel drive with a green swag strapped to the roof. It's Steve in the Monstermobile.

He pulls up ahead and photographs us coming up the hill. Fleur tells him that she can't stop pedalling because she'll lose momentum, so she cycles straight past him. I reach the vehicle and get the giggles. It is so typical. He is always early.

'Why didn't you answer your phone?' he asks.

'Because I don't have the charger,' I reply, realising he's forgotten. I'm so pleased to see him, even though I don't understand why he is here.

'You'd better keep going,' he says, as Fleur disappears over the horizon. 'I'll see you in Quorn.'

I push on against a headwind to the top of the steep hill where Fleur is waiting.

'I couldn't stop,' she says.

'I couldn't not,' I reply. 'He said he'd meet us in Quorn,' I add.

'We need to press on,' says Fleur. I glance at the exaggerometer.

'We've done 20 kilometres so far.'

We freewheel down the hill to Saltia, a once-thriving township now reduced to just a few stone remains. Cockatoos squawk from the red

Whispering Wire

gums as the wind whistles through the pass. Beside the railway line stand telegraph poles made of segments of railway line. The wire is no longer there, but white porcelain insulators are still perched on the long wooden crossarms. When the Overland Telegraph Line was built in 1870 it crossed the ranges through the Hookina Pass further north. Then when the railway was built eight years later, the line was rerouted along here.

A couple of cyclists in fluorescent green lycra whir past us, as we grind up the steep ascent to Woolshed Flat. This is where the Old Ghan train stops and where we have planned to have lunch. But when we eventually reach it, we find that the gate to the picnic area is locked; obviously it's only for train passengers. If only the train were running this Sunday we would be in there having a leisurely picnic, and my legs would not be burning with the strain of climbing this pass.

We push on a bit further before pulling off the road. Having collapsed on a grassy bank we see two fluorescent flashes as the cyclists speed back toward Port Augusta. Carrying only bum bags and water bottles, they've probably had a cup of coffee in Quorn and are on their way home. I am jealous of the ease with which they cover the kilometres, but much prefer our sedate speed and style, with our focus on the journey not just the destination.

The sky has turned grey, I have a sore bottom and aching legs, and we're pedalling against a cold wind up yet another hill. Finally we reach the top of the pass and I feel so chuffed that I've managed to cycle the entire 35 kilometres, mostly uphill, and not had to push the bicycle.

'We've done it, Rossie,' Fleur says with a grin, and we freewheel most of the last eight kilometres into Quorn.

Lying on the routes of both the Great Northern Railway and the Trans-Australian Railway, Quorn was once a major crossroad for train travellers. Still today there are four hotels on Railway Terrace, and we are staying at the Transcontinental, a huge two-storey edifice on the corner of Sixth Street. I'm standing outside minding the bikes while Fleur is enquiring about our room when Steve pulls up. Fleur returns, saying we are to put the bicycles on the verandah outside our bedroom for the night. Steve carries them upstairs for us and then leaves. He's camped at the caravan park and tells us he will return to the hotel this evening.

A Visitor and a Phantom

Fleur and I sit on our beds. 'I don't want to be the third wheel on this trip,' she says.

'Fleur,' I say, 'we're doing this together. We arranged to do it together.' She looks relieved. Then I remember that telephone call on the third morning when we were still in the Adelaide Hills and Steve said he had rung the Mount Pleasant Police Station and been told that the road between Quorn and Hawker was very busy. He has come early, I realise now, to make sure we're all right.

We walk down Railway Terrace, where people are enjoying a long, leisurely Sunday afternoon in the bars of a couple of the majestic Victorian hotels. An emporium advertising 'Extensive Selection of Travellers Requisites' now houses a second-hand bookshop. Being in the land of the quandong, the little red native fruit, we stop at the Quandong Café and buy a pot of jam and quandong pies to eat on the road tomorrow.

At the old railway station is a map of the Great Northern Railway marking every station and siding between Port Augusta and Alice Springs, including Farina. The railway reached Quorn in 1879 and, built along the route of the Overland Telegraph Line, it reached Farina three years later. It would be another nearly 50 years before the railway extended all the way to Alice Springs. Nicknamed the Ghan the railway line closed in 1980, but Marcia Dahlitz at the information centre tells us that during World War II there were up to 43 trains a day carrying service personnel from here to Alice Springs, and the local Country Women's Association provided hot home-cooked meals – over 360,000 of them – for the troops and for the evacuees travelling south after the bombing of Darwin.

Neatly folded on the beds in our hotel room are face cloths and towels. Clasping our bath linen, we totter down the corridor to the bathroom for showers before heading down to the bar, where Steve is waiting.

He orders a bottle of Shiraz and the three of us sit around the log fire.

'Congratulations for ascending the Pichi Richi Pass,' he says, raising his glass. We regale him with stories of the cycle so far, and he tells us about his drive from Sydney. He says he plans to bush camp around Blinman for the next few days.

'I worry about you two on these roads,' Steve admits later, when we're all tucking into the roast beef special.

'We're fine,' Fleur and I reply in unison.

Whispering Wire

We've finished eating when a tall blonde woman in a red jacket walks over and warms herself in front of the fire. She has lived in Quorn for 15 years and works in the Quorn Hotel further down Railway Terrace.

'I don't believe in ghosts,' she says, as the four of us watch the door to the right of the fireplace open seemingly spontaneously – and then close. 'But,' she adds, 'there's one called Amelia at the Quorn Hotel. I wouldn't sleep in Room One.'

She tells us about her experience while working at the Criterion Hotel. 'I left the door of a bedroom open because I knew I needed to put clean towels on the bed. But when I came back to the room, the door was closed. I went in and the sheets had been folded on the bed, like towels. I thought someone must be playing a joke on me, but the only person in the hotel at the time was the owner, and she swore she hadn't been upstairs.' The door beside the fireplace opens and closes again.

Helen, who's working behind the bar, clears our plates away. The door opens once more.

'Is there a ghost here?' Fleur asks.

'I've only seen him once in the dining room,' she replies. 'He's a dark-haired young man.'

CHAPTER 15

Morse Code, Mawson and Todd

As we cycle past the empty railway sidings and sheds on Railway Terrace the following morning we're overtaken by a long cattle truck. The old railway runs beside the road. Sheep graze the saltbush and a pair of kangaroos bound across the open country. It's 66 kilometres to Hawker, our longest one-day stretch, and it's cold and windy. Steve drives past and stops to take a photograph of us. He says he'll see us in the pub this evening.

The south-west wind pushes us along. In less than two hours we've covered 22 kilometres and by 11 o'clock we're halfway there. The sunlight filtering through the grey clouds catches the soft greens and yellows of the stubbly ground and the blue of the ranges in the distance. A rainbow crowns the corrugated-iron roof of an old stone house as spots of rain start to fall. The busy traffic that concerns Steve consists of an occasional vehicle, usually giving a hoot of encouragement, as we pedal along in the pouring rain.

The rain eases, but there is no shelter from the breeze. We find a culvert, however, beneath the road where it crosses a dry creek lined with river red gums and acacia bushes. On the eastern side we are protected from the cold wind, so we hunker down here to eat our sandwiches and quandong pies.

Getting back on the bicycle after stopping always feels hard. Every kilometre is an effort. Another bank of clouds rolls towards us and it starts to rain again, making this afternoon's cycling particularly arduous. Fleur is in front, as usual. I'm bringing up the rear with my aching, after-lunch legs, counting the kilometres on the exaggerometer. A small white car slows down. The driver, a man in his 30s, leans out the window.

'Do you need food?' he asks with a foreign accent in an earnest tone. I must be looking particularly forlorn.

'I'm fine,' I reply.

'Do you need water?'

'I'm all right for water,' I respond, nonplussed by this attention and concern.

The driver explains that he and the man in the passenger seat – both Italians – have just cycled from Perth across the Nullarbor Plain to Adelaide. They are now having a three-day holiday with their girlfriends before cycling from Adelaide to Cairns. After much, '*Ciao, ciao, arrivederci,*' from me and well wishing and waving from them they drive off, leaving me energised.

The sun comes out again. For the umpteenth time today I'm wobbling on one leg while extracting the other leg from my wet-weather pants, when Steve drives past. Twenty minutes later, when Fleur and I arrive at the Hawker Hotel, the Monstermobile is parked outside. Steve appears from the bar and helps us with our panniers. It's now raining heavily again. I get the key for our room from reception and, much to my delight, I am also handed a package containing my phone charger.

We leave our panniers in the large room at the back of the hotel. I put my mobile, now flat, on charge and we return to the bar. Steve is sitting at a table drinking beer. We talk for 10 minutes and he tells us he has seen mobs of emus near Wilpena Pound. Then he drains the last of his beer.

'I'm leaving.'

'Not in this weather,' I say. But he's adamant he'll be fine. He walks out into the pouring rain and drives off. I imagine how miserable it will be for him, camping in the hills near Blinman on this cold, wet evening. I wish he was staying here in the hotel with us. He's concerned about us, but I realise that he's decided not to get involved in our expedition and won't be swayed from doing his own thing.

Fleur and I head to Hawker General Store to buy food for the next few days. Run by a lugubrious man called Mick, the store has a tired and neglected feel about it. There is plenty of stock but not a great deal we want to eat. But it's a four-day cycle before we reach another store, so we scan the shelves and the freezer for food for tomorrow evening, when we are staying on a property and self-catering, and four breakfasts and lunches. The only tinned fish Fleur likes is salmon, so we buy the last tin on the shelf, as well as half a dozen eggs, a packet of frozen peas, lamb chops, three potatoes, four apples, a loaf of bread, a packet of biscuits and a bar of dark chocolate. To my dismay there are no bananas.

Fleur takes the supplies back to the room while I go in search of Fred Teague's Museum. I ask at Hawker Motors, where I'm directed to some dusty glass cabinets at the back of the shop. There are stones and Aboriginal artefacts, and in one cabinet is a large, white porcelain insulator. Underneath it is a sign typed on white card: 'An insulator first used on the Overland Telegraph Line Port Augusta to Darwin 1872.' This is one of the 36,000 insulators which held the long line when it was first constructed. Beside it is a dark metal insulator. The sign below reads: 'An insulator used to replace original insulator on the Nthn. Section of the Overland Telegraph Line. Original was broken by Aboriginals for tipping spears.' In the early years the linesmen who were responsible for maintaining the line spent much of their time replacing porcelain insulators broken off by Aboriginal people to use for spearheads and scraping tools.

Hawker Motors, unlike the general store, is a hub of activity. People at the counter are buying bread, milk and other groceries as well as their fuel. Books, maps and camping equipment are also for sale. The store was established by Fred Teague in 1952, and he worked here until he died, aged 81. In the 1930s he had been the mailman on the remote Birdsville Track, and he had a lifelong interest in geology, archaeology and anthropology. Now Fred's son, John Teague, together with his wife, Janet, and son, Scott, run Hawker Motors.

When John hears that I'm interested in the Overland Telegraph Line he tells me that Yorkey Thompson lived near Hawker. Yorkey was a wagon driver for the Milner brothers, who in 1870 set out from North Adelaide bound for the Northern Territory with a large mob of sheep to supply 'mobile mutton' to the telegraph working parties.

'He lived four kilometres out of town,' John says. 'It's known as Yorkey's Creek.'

He says that Muriel Chapman, who was the last postmistress at Farina before the post office closed in 1960, was a friend of his mother. When Miss Chapman retired she moved to Hawker.

'Sitting at the table in the kitchen at Hawker Motors one day she said, "I don't know who that is who keeps calling WIL07." It was the ID being constantly repeated on the UHF radio,' John explains, 'and after her years at the Post Office and Telegraph Station at Farina her knowledge of Morse code was so good that she could identify it. But she was very hard to talk to in the end. She got very deaf.'

John tells us that at Merna Mora Station, where we are staying tomorrow, we'll be able to see original telegraph poles.

Back at the hotel, Shaun, the manager, takes the eggs we've bought to the kitchen, to be hard-boiled. Denni, who's running the bar, fills our water bottles with filtered rainwater. It tastes so good after the hard, salty water in Quorn and Port Augusta, and I immediately down a whole bottle and have to ask her to refill it.

The hotel sells Mawson's Far Eastern Party Cabernet Sauvignon, which, being followers of the Mawson Trail, I insist we drink this evening. As a geology lecturer at the University of Adelaide in the early 1900s, Douglas Mawson made field trips into the Flinders Ranges. Finding glaciations in the rocks here ignited his desire to visit Antarctica.

On the wine label is a drawing of Douglas Mawson and his companions Xavier Mertz and Belgrave Ninnis from the Australasian Antarctica Expedition of 1911–14. During their explorations, Ninnis, his sledge, which carried most of their food, and his dog team were lost in a large crevasse. Mawson and Mertz began to kill and eat the dogs, and Mertz became sick and died. So Mawson had to travel alone, without dogs, taking 30 days to cover the 160 kilometres back to the base. Approaching the base, Mawson saw the supply ship leaving the bay, and he and a handful of men had to see out a second perishing Antarctic winter before the ship returned and collected them.

When Fleur and I are back in Sydney she rings me.

'Rossie, the managing director of BackVintage Wines, has just dropped off a case of wine. We were talking about South Australian wines, and I told him about us following the Overland Telegraph Line on our bikes. He's a direct descendant of Charles and Alice Todd.'

Fleur gives me Julian Todd's telephone number and we speak for an hour the following day.

'You should visit my parents in Bowral,' he says, so a couple of days later I take the train to this town about 90 minutes south-west of Sydney. Charles Todd's great-grandson, the 85-year-old standing on the platform wearing a maroon jumper and baggy corduroy trousers, has a discernible likeness to his ancestor, with his piercing blue eyes, bushy eyebrows and similar jaw line, except that he is tall.

Barry Todd drives me past Bradman Oval to where he and Ola, his wife, live on the outskirts of town. He suggests I leave my coat in his office, and walking in there I notice a couple of ceramic insulators sitting on a bookshelf.

In an alcove in the main room is a silhouette of the Bell family – Alice's parents and their 11 children, with Alice, then a young child, prominent in the centre between her mother and father. Also hanging in the alcove is a framed collection of drawings from when Charles Todd and members of the Overland Telegraph Line construction party were stranded on the Roper River.

Next to this hangs an invitation from the government of New South Wales, inviting Charles Todd to 'The State Banquet, to be held in Sydney on Thursday 26th January 1888 in Commemoration of the Completion of the First Hundred Years of Australian Settlement'.

And quietly ticking in the hallway nearby is Charles Todd's grandfather clock. A sailing ship, an observatory and a cottage are engraved on its brass face, and above it is the painted face of the moon, surrounded by golden stars.

Ola makes coffee and we sit by the fire in the main room. On the shelf under the glass-topped coffee table is a newspaper cutting of an article from a 2017 edition of Adelaide's *Advertiser* titled 'On Your Todd, the making of a great man'. It's about the biography of Charles Todd, *Behind the Legend* by Professor Denis Cryle.

Barry's grandfather was Charles and Alice's third child, Hedley Lawrence.

'He left school at 16 and went to work for the stock and station agents, Elder Smith and Co,' Barry tells me. 'Later he had an electrical business and was at the cutting edge of developing electricity to take over from gas, putting street lighting into Adelaide.'

Barry also mentions William Bragg, the Nobel Prize winning physicist, who described his father-in-law Charles Todd as having 'no commanding personality'. Aged just 23, Bragg became a professor at the University of Adelaide and married Hedley's sister, Gwendoline. Ola says that she and Barry were shown his study at the university, a corner of which was bricked up because it was believed to be radioactive.

I mention Douglas Mawson's fascination with the radioactive rocks of the Flinders Ranges and she tells me Lorna, the youngest of Charles and Alice's children, was great friends with him.

'We met Lorna in 1962. By then she was bedridden, but she looked up from her pillow with these fabulous blue Todd eyes,' recounts Ola.

Over lunch Barry tells me the story of his line of the family, and Hedley, who died in 1907 of typhoid, three years before his father, Charles. I remember seeing Hedley's headstone beside those of Alice and Charles at North Road Cemetery. Barry's father, christened Charles but known in the family as Tom, was taken by his mother back to Cambridge, because Hedley's older sister, Lizzie, was living there with her husband, Charles Squires.

'Aged 17, he went to the Royal Military Academy Sandhurst. Being good on horses, he joined the 5th Royal Inniskilling Dragoon Guards, and during the First World War he fought on the Somme. He left the army in the early 1920s, became a tea planter in Ceylon and married my mother, Nancy Burgoyne-Wallace, who he'd met during the war when she was driving ambulances. When the Second World War broke out, my father rejoined the army, and when Colombo was bombed in April 1942 my mother, my two sisters and I were sent back to England. After I left school I joined the Royal Navy and became a signal officer.'

Barry met Ola in Edinburgh and, with a forthrightness similar to that of his great-grandmother, Alice, he declared only the day after they had met that he wanted to marry her. Ola accepted three weeks later.

'These phenomenal blue Todd eyes looked at me, and there was an immediate connection,' says Ola. 'But my dear husband didn't tell me, until we'd been married a fortnight, that he really was Australian, and when my mother found out she was horrified.'

Charles Todd's grandfather clock chimes twice.

'In the early 60s I had an assignment in Australia as the Squadron Signal Officer for the 10th Destroyer Squadron,' Barry continues. 'I was at sea and Ola was in a little flat in Bellevue Hill, but we spent two-and-a-half happy years in Sydney and with our three sons moved to Australia permanently in 1972. I left the Royal Navy and I had to find a job. I worked for Grace Brothers for a few years and spent 20 years as a management consultant with Price Waterhouse.' I'm fascinated that 65 years after his father left, Barry and his family decided to call Australia home.

Barry produces a manila folder of Charles Todd's documents, including his detailed instructions to the Overseers in charge of Works for the Overland Telegraph Line. As well as instructions for building the line and loading pistols and revolvers, it includes the weekly rations allocated to each worker:

Flour	9 lbs
Biscuit	1 lbs
Meat	8 lbs
Sugar	2 lbs
Tea	¼ lbs
Tobacco	¼ lbs
Peas or Oatmeal	½ lbs
Rice or Pearl Barley	½ lbs
Vinegar	1 gill
Lime juice	½ gill
Salt	2 ozs
Mustard	½ oz
Pepper	½ oz
Soap	½ lbs

And each month an allocation of two pipes and two boxes of matches.

An overseer, in addition to making sure men were not idle, had 'to watch over Health and Morals' which included the requirement 'to suppress all gambling, to stop all profane language, swearing and quarrelling, and to endeavour, as far as possible, to promote all rational amusements amongst his party'. Another stipulation was to rest on Sunday.

Horses and bullocks were not to be ill-treated. Exploration had to be made for water before moving camp, and Todd wrote instructions on both finding and saving water. He also gave detailed procedures in the event of a man getting lost in the bush.

Todd included details for encounters with Aboriginal people, stating that 'should any natives be met with, they must be treated kindly but firmly' and that 'no one is allowed to visit the "natives" camp without special permission'. Communication with Aboriginal women was forbidden, the only exception being if the overseer engaged a woman 'in the absence of a man, as a guide to point out the situation of water'. Aboriginal property was also not to be touched. In Todd's final point regarding the Aboriginal people he wrote: 'It is most strictly forbidden to fire upon the natives except in the last extremity, when it may become necessary for the safety of the party.'

Fleur and I clink our glasses of Mawson's Far Eastern Party Cabernet Sauvignon and drink to today's leg of the journey and following the Mawson Trail, while at the next table a group of men loudly regale one another with stories of their intrepid outback four-wheel drive adventures. By the time we return to the room my mobile is fully charged. I ring Steve. It goes to message bank. Probably he has no reception up in the hills.

CHAPTER 16

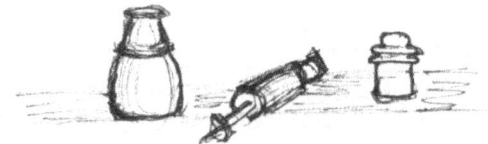

Insulators and Fossils

It's an extremely cold morning, and the four-wheel drivers are shivering and moaning as they pack their vehicles. We stop at Hawker Motors to buy a bag of dried apricots and find it buzzing with people picking up the morning papers and procuring fresh bread. The Monstermobile is parked across the road from the general store, but Steve isn't to be seen. Soon after we set off, though, he drives past us.

There's a low mist this morning and spitting rain. The old railway runs parallel to the road. As we climb a long hill, a triple road train thunders towards us, then a cattle truck rattles past. The other vehicles are Winnebagos towing cars and four-wheel drives pulling caravans, their occupants wave encouragingly as they speed past. But most of the time there's no traffic on the long straight road, just this vast open country, still and soundless, as the morning mist slowly lifts.

A flock of corellas sweeps over the low landscape as we pass several ruined sandstone buildings. We've covered 30 kilometres when we stop at 1.30 for lunch. We sit on sandstone rocks in a dry creek bed, eating our Hawker General Store purchases of tinned salmon, sliced white bread and Nice biscuits. Beside us are two black stumps, the supports for the railway bridge that once spanned the creek. Fleur finds a rusty sleeper pin nestled in the red dirt.

Just before we reach the entrance to Merna Mora Station we turn off the road and follow a track to a surveyor's memorial. Here above the road to the west we see the huge, dry expanse of Lake Torrens. To the east is the wall of Wilpena Pound, the extraordinary natural bowl formed by a large circle of rocky peaks, known as Ikara, meaning 'meeting place', by the local Adnyamathanha people.

On this hill are a surveyor's cairn and three wooden telegraph poles, each with a white porcelain insulator perched on its top, replicas of the original native pine telegraph poles that were used for the Overland Telegraph Line in this area.

During construction, the route of the Overland Telegraph Line was cleared to a width of 10 metres, so the five metres either side of the line was stripped of all undergrowth, bushes and overhanging branches. The poles were about six metres long and made of hard durable timber, bound at the top with an iron strip, as these ones have, and with a hole drilled in the centre to hold the insulator pin. The pole, with the insulator firmly in place on top of it, was raised into position. Poles were erected 12 to a kilometre, and then the wire was strung across the insulators. A length of line wire was attached to every second pole as a lightning conductor, the top extending just above the insulator and the bottom buried a metre underground.

Back on the road after crossing Moralana Creek, we reach the Merna Mora Station gate and take the gravel track up to the homestead. Donald and Kaye Fels and their son Philip and daughter-in-law Sonya are the fifth- and sixth-generation pastoralists on the station.

We arrive to find Sonya cleaning out one of the cabins. As she shows us the two-bedroom stone-built one in which we're staying, she explains that the 526-square-kilometre station is a working sheep and cattle property, although the family also diversified into holiday accommodation in the 1960s.

We're eager to see the telegraph poles that John Teague told me about yesterday, but Sonya isn't sure where they are. Donald, Kaye and Philip are out mustering and won't be back until dark.

In the cabin we unpack our panniers. With my mobile now fully charged I decide to ring Steve and let him know we've arrived, but have no mobile coverage and neither does Fleur's phone. I head to the office to see if I can use the landline, but it's closed, and a sign says to go to the house behind the woolshed.

The door is opened by a young girl with a beaming smile. Her brother, in the background, is wearing a blue shirt with a Merna Mora Station logo on the pocket.

Insulators and Fossils

'Are you just back from school?' I ask.

'We don't go to school,' the boy replies. 'We're at School of the Air and do our lessons at home.' They bubble with excitement at seeing a new person until Sonya comes to the door and takes me down to the telephone. I ring Steve, but there is no reply. No doubt he's out of mobile range too.

We walk to the creek, watching the ringneck parrots flitting through the red gums, and stroll up the hill to the station's airstrip. At one end are disused pieces of equipment – the remains of an old ute, coils of wire and sheets of corrugated iron held down with large stones.

'You never throw anything away on a property,' Fleur says, reminiscing on growing up at Dunmore Park. 'You never know when it might come in use.' Not noticing the 'Keep out' sign, we wander through this treasure trove, pointing out antiquated bits of machinery. I spot some pieces of old porcelain insulators from the Overland Telegraph Line.

'There'll probably be some unbroken ones here,' Fleur says.

'Let's find them,' I say. We see bigger pieces of porcelain and then a pile of insulators still with their wooden pins. We find two in perfect condition and decide to ask if we can buy them. We shake the soil out of them, dust off the dirt, and carry these precious trophies back to the cabin. It is so exciting to be holding one of the original insulators, one component of this long line of communication, it feels like a confirmation of being on track, a sign that this is a journey I should be undertaking.

It's dark when, having been told about my interest in the Overland Telegraph Line by Sonya, Donald Fels drops over to the cabin. In his 60s, this stout man takes off his work boots and stands in his socks near the door, with the look of a busy man popping in for a minute. An hour later we're all still standing and he's still talking.

I tell him I saw John Teague yesterday.

'Hawker Motors is the friendliest service station in the world,' he responds. The original telegraph poles that John Teague mentioned, Donald explains, are back towards Hawker, beyond Ilka Creek, which we crossed five kilometres before turning up to the memorial.

'The stumps are nine to 10 inches in diameter. They're native pines and about 70 yards apart,' he says. 'The telegraph poles in this area were all native pines, and in the areas where there were white ants they were replaced by Oppenheimer poles. They were known as GI poles,' he says, 'because they were made of galvanised iron. They came from England and the three sections collapsed into one another like a telescope. They were carried along the line by camels and then elongated and planted in the ground.'

Donald discusses the construction of the Overland Telegraph Line as if it were yesterday.

'Warwick from Holowiliena Station, east of Cradock, had the contract to provide all the original wooden poles for this section of the line,' he tells us, 'and they were dragged here by bullocks. Between here and Wilpena is the old bullock cueing yard where the blacksmith used to shoe the back hooves of the bullocks.'

He tells us that the three telegraph poles we saw at the surveyor's cairn earlier were erected by Ian Carpenter.

'His grandfather, George Callis, was a ganger on the railway at Mern Merna Siding. My father and Ian's mother went to Mern Merna School together, and Ian spent a lot of time here at Merna Mora as a child.'

As he talks, I'm painfully aware of the two insulators we have extracted from the property dump, which are sitting on the kitchen bench in his direct line of vision.

'The original telegraph line only lasted 12 years in this area. Then the Great Northern Railway – the Ghan – was built and the telegraph was shifted to run alongside it, so my ancestors chopped the old poles down and used them for strainers.

'When the railway line closed in 1980, my brother, who owns a property east of Hawker, and I bought 1150 poles. Most of the poles were made of rail track. They were about 20-foot long and we cut and used them for fencing. But there were also a few GI poles, and few of the old wooden ones,' he adds.

I've been waiting for the right moment to confess our insulator pillage, but the minutes pass, Donald keeps talking and there's no perfect pause opportunity. Fleur is leaning on the bench near the stove, and I notice her inching almost imperceptibly along it. I realise she is trying to hide the insulators from Donald by standing in front of them.

In the last three-quarters of an hour there hasn't been a break in the conversation, let alone an appropriate moment to ask if we could have

Insulators and Fossils

the insulators. He must be thinking that we're a couple of thieves. As each minute passes I feel increasingly embarrassed, until finally I manage to blurt out what we've done and ask if we can have them.

'Oh, yes,' he says, 'you can keep those. They came off the wooden poles.'

I mention that John Teague told us about Muriel Chapman.

'Muzzie was a savage old girl. There's a man called Whitie. He'd be 85 or so now. He used to be a butcher in Adelaide. When he was young he was droving and was meant to be away for a fortnight, but the job took 17 weeks. He got to Farina and needed to call home. Muzzie said he could ring for three minutes and it would cost him three bob. When he went over the three minutes, she let him speak only a fraction longer and then told him that was enough.'

Donald is a trove of local knowledge and has such a deep love of history that I could listen to his stories all evening. But he has to be off at 6.30 tomorrow morning to brand cattle, so he leaves us.

Fleur grills our chops on the barbecue while I cook the potatoes and peas. We spend the rest of the evening dancing with delight at now owning two original insulators from the Overland Telegraph Line.

As we pedal through the morning mist back to the main road, Fleur vetoes retracing our tracks to find the telegraph pole stumps. It would mean cycling an extra 10 kilometres on top of the 50 to Parachilna so I know she's right, but I'm upset about missing the chance to see them, so I'm tailing reluctantly behind her up the highway. Half an hour later Steve pulls up beside us. So much for being independent travellers – we immediately hand him the two heavy insulators and ask him to drive south to Ilka Creek and do a stump search.

The Flinders Ranges are a grey silhouette against the cloudy sky. A spider web in a dead tree holds droplets of dew, and an itchy grub nest hangs like a large, dirty nylon stocking in an acacia bush. A pair of black crows fly into a tree as we pass a freshly killed roo stretched out on the verge. I'm eating a couple of Nice biscuits and a handful of walnuts at 11 am when Steve arrives. He's been unable to find the telegraph pole stumps and says, before he drives off, that he plans to camp on a station near Blinman tonight.

To the left of the road is the Leigh Creek railway line and on the right we can make out the old track of the Great Northern Railway. A pair of plovers skirt a yellow-flowering desert cassia beside a ruined sandstone building. There's no breeze or rain, so it's a dream run of easy cycling.

After another lunch of quandong jam sandwiches – having run out of tins of salmon – we realise, despite our calculations for these days when we are far from shops, that we're also short of bread. Twelve kilometres from Parachilna the north-west wind sets in, and our pace slows as we pedal against it.

The population of Parachilna is three, but it is home to the Prairie Hotel, an oasis in the desert. In the 1990s it was nominated as one of the world's top 100 hotels. It's a unique mix of sophistication and bush congeniality, offering deluxe accommodation. However we're staying in a donga.

'When I'm with Martin I usually stay in five-star accommodation,' Fleur reminds me, as she tentatively opens the door to the converted shipping container. There are two narrow single beds with a couple of square, white bedside tables between them and a single reading light. Neither of us feels inclined to linger in this metal box. First some bicycle maintenance – removing the mud from our chains with a toothbrush before cleaning and oiling them – then a trip to the ablutions block for showers before heading to the hotel.

Behind the bar is Grant Rasheed, who has worked here for 10 years. 'The Prairie Hotel was built in 1876,' he tells us. 'Parachilna was a staging post for the transport of copper from the Blinman Mine. It was also a stop on the Great Northern Railway.' The hotel is renowned for its native and feral food, and a board advertises kangaroo pies and 10-inch camel rolls. But as it's mid-afternoon, we decide on scones with cream and quandong jam.

We have just sat down at a table when Jane Fargher enters the bar. With her husband, Ross, she bought the Prairie Hotel 23 years ago and transformed it from just another isolated country pub to a destination attracting travellers from all over the world. When Grant introduces us, she explains that the dongas and wooden cottages beside them are actually owned by the railway.

'We rent them,' she explains. 'This was a fettlers' camp until the railway line closed in 1980.'

Insulators and Fossils

Ross and Jane also own nearby Nilpena Station, home to two fossil sites dating back 550 million years. These fossils, known as Ediacaran biota, are the first evidence of life on earth, and all living animals are believed to be descended from them. The fossils are of marine animals that lived on the sea floor and had no shells, spines or bones.

Ediacaran biota fossil fields have also been found in Namibia and Newfoundland, but what makes the Nilpena sites so extraordinary is that the fossils found in those places are also found here, but in addition there are ones endemic to this region. Fossilised here in the Flinders Ranges is the first evidence of animal sexual interaction 300 million years before dinosaurs roamed the earth, when the entire area was underwater.

The fossil site at Nilpena is National Heritage listed and not open to the public. Given this restriction, the South Australian Museum has erected a monument at the hotel that shows replicas of the fossils. Here the *Dickinsonia* fossil, with its rippled surface, is imprinted in the rock, and *Spriggina*, resembling a fishbone. Given that *Homo sapiens* is thought to have evolved about 300,000 years ago, and is known to have been in Australia for 60,000 years, the existence of human beings seems like such a short chapter in earth's long history. These soft-bodied Ediacaran biota existed for 40 million years. Dinosaurs were around for about 170 million years. I wonder how long human beings will last.

Contemplating life on such a grand scale calls for a Fargher Lager, the pub's very own beer. Fleur orders a Shiraz and we step back outside and watch the ever-changing orange, pinks and reds of the western sky as the sun goes down. We stand beside a roaring brazier. Sparks fly into the air above the bright flames as the sky slides to a dark shade of blue and the first stars appear.

The front bar is filled with people when we go back inside. We talk to a couple from Hema Maps and a landscape architect from the University of Melbourne, who has carried out a study of the Neales River further along the Overland Telegraph Line. We share a table with one of the three Parachilna residents, photographer Peter MacDonald. Several of his photographs of Kati Thanda-Lake Eyre are hanging in the bar, and one of sand dunes with the Flinders Ranges in the background.

'That took me three weeks to shoot,' he says. 'I had to wait for the light to be right.'

All day Fleur and I have been mesmerised by the light and the blue ranges, but we have failed to capture on camera what our eyes are seeing. I'm guessing now in his late 60s, Peter MacDonald has worked as a photographer for 30 years. His photographic skills and knowledge of and love for this region are evident – as is his sheer joy of having captured an awe-inspiring image.

Sitting with Peter is his friend from Port Pirie, Richard Wickens. He used to do guided tours of this region. They tell us we must turn off onto the Old Stuart Highway to Beltana tomorrow and the following day continue on the old road to Leigh Creek.

'There are very good views along that road,' Peter says.

I've ordered kangaroo, which is lean and delicious, and jealously eyed by Fleur after she tastes it, having chosen the more mundane beef.

'The train is coming,' someone calls from the bar, as we finish eating. There is a mass exodus to watch the freight train rattle past on its 250-kilometre journey from Leigh Creek to Port Augusta. We see car after car, loaded with coal, clattering along the rails. I love trains and standing here under the clear star-studded night sky watching this one pass has a romance to it. But I think of the longevity of the Ediacaran biota and the mining that has taken place in Australia in the last 200 years. Driving a car, flying in a plane, using a computer and a mobile, even riding a bicycle means I play a part in the exploitation of the earth.

I believe I make a difference every time I avoid single-use plastics, buy bulk foods and bring my own containers, and walk rather than drive. And I think those choices often enable me to see further steps I can take to lessen my impact on the environment. But I watch the train wondering what will be needed to ensure clean flowing rivers, fertile land and the protection of native flora and fauna. Minutes pass and the train is still chuntering past until finally we see the last car fade into the darkness. The rattling becomes fainter and fainter until the landscape is again enveloped by silence.

'I counted 155 carriages and three locomotives,' says a man standing next to us.

'It's a long train,' another responds.

CHAPTER 17

Beltana Repeater Station and Telephone Communication

The following morning we toast our last slice of bread. I go to the hotel to see what I can procure. Jane Fargher is at the espresso machine in the bar, making a coffee for Peter MacDonald. I explain our predicament.

'You sound like Burke and Wills,' Peter says.

Coming from Ireland, with a propensity for getting lost and erring on the side of too much baggage, I feel nervy at the mere mention of Burke and Wills. Sympathetic to our carbohydrate crisis, Jane goes to the kitchen and returns with eight slices of wholemeal bread.

We leave Parachilna at five to nine and have cycled seven kilometres when my eye catches a metre-high stump that has been used as a fence post.

'Do you think it was a telegraph pole?' I ask Fleur.

'It's hard to say.' For the next 20 minutes we study several other large fence posts from different angles and are still unable to decide if this one has a telegraph pole provenance.

Further north we pass the remains of Nilpena railway siding – two long, single-storey ruined buildings. The doorways frame the clear blue sky and the scrub, and four emus shake their tail feathers as they prance through the saltbush.

'Telegraph poles!' I shout. We walk over to look at the segments of railway line with their wooden cross poles standing beside the old rail track.

'They're not very tall,' Fleur points out.

'You wouldn't need them much higher than this,' I respond.

'But this looks like a signal of some sort,' says Fleur. 'Or maybe they

Whispering Wire

were for the telephone line.' After further inspection, we decide for the second time this morning there is nothing definitively telegraphic about these poles.

I am photographing a crimson-flowering eremophila bush when Steve drives past. He stops several hundred metres ahead of us next to a large brown fridge just before the turning to Beltana. When we reach him I open the fridge door. It's empty. Fleur and I learn later that it's the mailbox for the pastoral property south-east of Beltana Station.

After a sub-zero night in the hills, Steve tells us he has relocated to the campsite at Copley, where we are staying tomorrow evening.

'What time do you plan to get to Beltana Station?' he asks as he departs.

'Mid-afternoon,' I reply, not giving it much thought.

Further along the dirt road, near an old railway bridge, we find a telegraph pole about which neither of us are in doubt. It is made from a piece of railway line and on its wooden crossbar sit four ceramic insulators. The insulators are smaller and thinner than the ones we found at Merna Mora.

A sign – 'Welcome to Beltana Station' – indicates that we're now on the property, but it's another 12 kilometres to the homestead. A roo and joey hop beside us as we pick our way along the road, avoiding the sharp rocks until we reach a sandy creek bed and have to push our bikes. Walking across the creek we see the track of an enormous snake weaving through the sand. I follow the track to the fence line, hoping to catch a glimpse of the creature, but there is no sign of it.

Soon after we met, Fleur told me about a time in her 20s when she was at Dunmore Park, looking after the property while her parents were away. She heard a rustling sound near the verandah. A black snake with a big green frog in its mouth was making its way towards the house, so she grabbed a spade, intending to kill the snake. But she realised that if she killed the snake, it would let go of the frog and, as Fleur is petrified of green frogs, that was more terrifying. So the snake lived another day. Now, much to my surprise given her willingness to take on a venomous black, Fleur suggests we keep moving briskly onward.

In the creek bed, where we stop for lunch, tiny zebra finches flit from tree to tree, and it's so warm that within minutes we're flicking flies off our food.

Beltana Repeater Station and Telephone Communication

We see Beltana Homestead on a hill, but we head to the historic town of Beltana, a couple of kilometres further on. The flat saltbush landscape gives way to an oasis of river red gums. This is the home of the southernmost of the Overland Telegraph Line's 12 repeater stations, where a Morse code telegraph message would be re-transmitted by the operator to ensure the telegraph signal was strong enough to be read by the operator at the next repeater station along the line. Also, the electrical current was boosted by a large number of Meidinger cells, large glass-jar batteries, each of which produced 1.5 volts of power. Both a communication and a transport centre in its heyday, Beltana had its own brewery, two hotels, a courthouse and a railway station. Today, it's a ghost town with a population of nine.

On a long, faded wooden sign attached to a sandstone building we make out the words 'Telegraph Repeater Station'. Grant Rasheed told us last night that the building belongs to Marion Sheidow, whose gallery is next door. We cycle round to the gallery, where Marion appears in a doorway in a thin cotton skirt and a long-sleeved blue top stained with paint, her white hair pulled back off her wide face. She moves slowly with the help of a long wooden stick.

When I explain that we're following the Overland Telegraph Line, she leads us into the gallery and shows us a couple of large insulators, like ours, with their original wooden insulator pins mounted on blocks of wood. We hadn't realised that both the ceramic insulators and the wooden pins have threads. She shows us how they unscrew.

'My grandfather worked at Beltana Station,' she explains, 'and one of my aunts always yearned to come back to Beltana, so as a family we used to come out here a lot. When the repeater station was up for sale 20 years ago I bought it.'

'Would it be possible to see inside the repeater station?' I ask tentatively. She gives me a wan smile, and I wonder if she's heard me.

'The telegraph room was at the front of the house,' she continues, 'and when I moved in, there were three doors into that room. One from the front of the house, one off the bedroom and one off the sitting room, so a telegraph operator could easily go into the room and send a telegraph whether it was day or night.'

'Would you be able to show us?' I ask. She gazes into the distance and adds, 'At the back of the house was a two-roomed cottage where the linesman lived.'

'How interesting,' I exclaim loudly, to ensure that this lack of communication isn't because she hasn't heard me. 'Can we look at it?'

'It's not there now,' she replies quietly. 'It was pulled down.'

Regardless of the volume of my voice or my enthusiasm, I realise that Marion Sheidow is not going to show a couple of strangers round her home. Nevertheless, she is prepared to chat at the gallery, and she tells us that her granddaughter and her husband and children also live in Beltana.

We stand at the front of the single-storey sandstone building. Hanging near the door is a mobile of a dragonfly that Marion has made from a piece of twisted wood, and laid out in the dirt in front of the building is a labyrinth, a piece, Marion tells us, made by her daughter.

'It's getting hotter and hotter out here,' Marion comments, as she gazes at the labyrinth. 'Temperatures reached 50 degrees a couple of days last summer. But there's nothing you can do about it, so you just put up with it.' On that note of climatic doom, we leave her to explore the rest of the town.

We stop at the Smith of Dunesk Mission Church, a whitewashed stone building with a tin roof. Reverend John Flynn was based here when he was first ordained a minister. The white wooden door is locked. Looking at the church, I wonder if Flynn's dream of creating a 'mantle of safety' for people living in the outback first came to him in this small building. As field superintendent of the Australian Inland Mission, he established nursing homes at Beltana, Marree and Alice Springs, before founding the Royal Flying Doctor Service, which brings the doctor to the patient.

We find a tall galvanised-iron Oppenheimer pole standing beside a native pine telegraph pole, both topped with large ceramic insulators. Next to them is a display of insulators, most of them with the original wooden pins. Some are white ceramic, others brown and green coloured glass; all are coated in a film of red dust. A jagged, weathered sheet of paper stapled beneath says:

> A SAMPLE OF INSULATORS USED ON THE TELEPHONE 'LANDLINE' FOLLOWING THE ORIGINAL 'OVERLAND TELEGRAPH' ROUTE.

Beltana Repeater Station and Telephone Communication

'Those poles we saw this morning could have been for telephone lines,' Fleur says.

Hot on the heels of the telegraph came this new technology – the telephone. Despite this new invention taking revenue from the existing telegraph system, Charles Todd embraced it, saying the telephone 'flashes our thoughts over hundreds and thousands of miles in time inappreciable' and 'will very soon come into extensive use and prove a public boon of great utility and value'.

Initially telephones utilised the existing telegraph wires. A telephone was used to communicate between Beltana's repeater station and the next one 306 kilometres north at Strangways Springs. In 1880, only eight years after the completion of the Overland Telegraph Line, Charles Todd recommended that the South Australian government construct a telephone network that was outside of private property, and also that the government maintain a monopoly on the construction and maintenance of the lines, as well as the management of the telephone exchange. In 1883 the Adelaide Central Telephone Exchange opened in a corner of the Chief Telegraph Office on the first floor of the General Post and Telegraph Office.

It wasn't until 1941 and 1942, during World War II, that a telephone system was added to the telegraph wires, running from Adelaide to Darwin. For the first time it was possible to speak over the entire length of the route.

At 3.30 we're wandering among the ruined stone buildings, imagining what the town would have been like in its heyday, when we step into a spot that has Telstra reception. Fleur's iPhone emits a series of beeps, and several text messages pop onto the screen. They're all from Steve asking 'Where are you?' Fleur hands me the mobile and I ring him.

'Where are you?' he asks, in person.

'We're in Beltana, looking around the town,' I reply.

'You said you would get to Beltana Station mid-afternoon. I've rung there and was told you hadn't arrived.' We have cycled only 12 kilometres from where we left Steve at the turnoff, and the homestead is only a couple of kilometres away, so Fleur and I have been feeling under no pressure to hurry there. I didn't think Steve might be worried.

'We're going there soon,' I say.

Whispering Wire

The sun is going down by the time we cycle up the hill and into the station's yard. It was here that Thomas Elder and his manager, Samuel Stuckey, established a camel-breeding program in the 1860s and set up a transport company. The camel strings transported goods and materials to remote stations and returned with wool bales.

In the old woolshed, a woman cooking dinner introduces herself as Helen.

'Someone rang earlier to find out if you had arrived,' she tells us.

'Steve,' Fleur and I reply in unison. We both feel at ease cycling through this increasingly remote country, so we find Steve's concern difficult to understand. He, on the other hand, is aware of the need to check we've reached our destination for the night and haven't run into trouble.

In the woolshed we see shelves of ceramic and glass insulators, and an old camel saddle made of sticks and held together with rope. Half-a-dozen broad-brimmed Akubra hats are for sale. Helen explains that Akubra has stopped manufacturing the favourite hat style of Graham Ragless, Beltana Station's owner. To have it made, he had to order a minimum of 25 hats – all the same size – which he did, and some of those are now for sale.

We have a room in the shearers' quarters, a long, single-storey whitewashed stone building from the 1860s. We shower and change and head back to the woolshed to find several people standing outside around a brazier. The resident llama is also enjoying the warmth of the fire.

Eleven of us sit at the long table in the woolshed for dinner. The only other guests are a couple in their 70s, who are staying for a few days. The rest are working at the station, including a retired couple, Mick, who was in the navy for 44 years, and his wife, Lyn. They have been travelling for the last 18 months, working in different places. Helen and Dean are from Gosford in NSW. Helen tells me they both worked full-time in their own business, and had a house with a large mortgage and their children in day care and after-school care.

'We suddenly thought *for what?*' Helen says. 'So we bought a bus and are travelling around Australia.' They are working here for a few months, while their two oldest offspring attend school at Leigh Creek. Another couple have been doing volunteer work here for a couple of weeks and are off tomorrow to a paid job.

At the head of the table is Graham Ragless, who has just returned

Beltana Repeater Station and Telephone Communication

from a cruise with his wife, Laura. Moulded by the country, he looks as if he would only exist under a large Akubra, and I can't imagine him on a cruise.

He tells me that the 1876-square-kilometre Beltana Station is bigger now than it has ever been, after he amalgamated it with adjoining Puttapa Station, where he grew up. Traditionally, Beltana was a merino station, but Graham explains that he is moving away from the wool-producing merino to the dorper. He is delighted with the cost saving because this fast-breeding meat breed sheds its fleece naturally, avoiding the need to be shorn.

We tuck into roast lamb – a dorper – with carrots, broccoli, pumpkin and potato dauphinoise cooked by Helen. It's delicious and, having insatiable cyclists' appetites, Fleur and I both have second helpings. But the *pièce de résistance* for me is the quandong pie made by Marion Sheidow. I savour every mouthful of the culinary delight baked inside the Beltana repeater station.

CHAPTER 18

Wind, a Dead Roo and Celebration

We sit eating the last of our Weet-Bix at one end of the very long wooden table in the shearers' dining room. On the wall hangs a map of Beltana and Puttapa stations. The adjoining property is Moolooloo, which James Chambers owned and where John McDouall Stuart stayed on his northerly expeditions.

As we attach our panniers to our bikes, Graham Ragless, under a scruffier Akubra hat this morning, pulls up on his motorbike. He's hooting with laughter.

'How far do you reckon you'll get today?' he roars.

'Copley,' Fleur replies.

'You should go all the way on the old road,' he says. 'Just get over the fence where it meets the highway and continue along it. Good luck,' he chuckles. I can't understand why he doubts our cycling ability – until we set off. The wind is coming directly from the north, and that's the direction we're heading.

In Beltana town, Ron Tarr stands outside the old railway station. He tells us that he and his wife bought the station in 1979. They operated a general store – which also sold alcohol and fuel – from the railway station, until three years later when the main road was rerouted, bypassing Beltana. So they built the Beltana Roadhouse on the new road and ran that for 30 years, until they closed it 18 months ago.

'We're trying to retire,' he explains, 'but no one wants to buy out here. We may just have to walk away.'

We follow the Old Stuart Highway from Beltana cycling directly into the howling wind. I tie my large red-spotted handkerchief over my nose

Wind, a Dead Roo and Celebration

and mouth as protection against the dust and proceed, bandito style, before skidding in the bulldust and nearly falling off.

Hills that we would now usually sail up are today forcing us to walk. We pass a native apricot, a solitary sentinel surrounded by saltbush, its small orange fruits buffeted by the relentless wind as we push up towards Puttapa Gap. I have doubts whether we'll make it to Copley.

At 11.30 we stop for a biscuit break. We've covered only eight kilometres since we left Beltana town. We pass ruined fettlers' cottages. There's another hill, and at the top of that we have a glorious view of a mountain. We're on a delicious downhill stretch when the older couple, who were at dinner last night, pull up beside us on their way to Leigh Creek to do some shopping.

'You're doing terribly well,' the man assures us, and his wife coos with encouragement as we bemoan our slow progress.

Ten minutes later, as we're pushing our bicycles through a stretch of sand, Steve drives along.

'You haven't got very far,' he says. 'How are you going to reach Copley at this rate?' We quickly wave him on his way.

He's barely out of sight when we reach a culvert under the road protected from the wind. We're ensconced there, drinking tea and eating the last of our supplies – nuts, chocolate and bread spread with quandong jam – before we notice the head of a dead roo dangling between the bars of the cattle grid only a couple of metres from us. There is a pool of fresh blood directly below it.

This young animal was probably hit by a vehicle last night, becoming one of the estimated four million Australian mammals killed on the road every year. I think of the many wombats I saw dead beside the road before the captivating moment I caught my first glimpse of one alive. I'm so wind-worn and weary that I haven't the energy to move away from this macabre spectacle. We sit in silence.

'Luckily it died recently and it doesn't smell,' says Fleur.

Usually by lunchtime we've done most of our cycling for the day, but today we've covered only 15 kilometres and have another 22 to go. Soon after we get back on our bikes, the couple pass us on their way back from Leigh Creek, now looking doubtful about our progress.

At quarter to two we reach the main road and make a definite decision not to continue on the old road, which Graham Ragless suggested. For once, anticipating easier progress, I'm happy to see the smooth bitumen. But almost immediately we're facing a steep hill. Fleur cycles up it and I push my bike behind her.

'This too will change,' I repeat to myself over and over, as the agony seems interminable. And it does change. We get a reprieve from the relentless northerly when, for a short distance, we're not heading directly into it. My heart sinks at a sign – 'Windy Creek' – but today the creek proves no windier than everywhere else. Two enormous haul-truck tyres indicate the turn-off to the coal-mining town of Leigh Creek, and we cycle the final stretch to Copley. After 36 windswept kilometres I'm utterly exhausted.

At the caravan park, the owner, Shirley Mills, shows us into a spacious two-bedroom cabin. At the other end of the park, in direct line with the cabin's front door, Steve has pegged the swag.

'It's because they care,' Shirley says with a smile and sweeping hand gesture, to explain the protective behaviour of husbands with adventuring wives.

There is no sign of Steve, so we walk down the road to the general store to buy supplies for tomorrow.

'I know you two,' says the owner, Karyn Ridsdale, as we walk in. She tells us her sister, Marie, who we met on the bridge at Port Augusta while looking at the wobbegong, emailed her about us.

There is no tinned salmon, so Fleur agrees to tinned tuna for tomorrow's lunch. We also buy nuts, a tomato and a tin of baked beans for breakfast, and Karen gives us a couple of ripe bananas. From Shirley Mills we buy four freshly baked quandong pies for our celebratory dinner with Steve and Martin in Farina.

The temperature has plummeted and the daylight is fading when Steve arrives at the door. I suggest he shares the double bed with me tonight, but he's adamant he's sleeping in the swag. The three of us walk to the Leigh Creek Hotel, where we are joined by Brian, a 20-something from Adelaide. He has a long-term plan to build an eco-house in Nicaragua, but he is currently earning several hundred dollars a day driving a group of Chinese men with exploration rights around the area. It's 65 kilometres to Farina tomorrow, so Fleur and I turn in early.

Wind, a Dead Roo and Celebration

The following morning – both wearing scarves bandito style over our faces to protect us from the dust – we cycle as fast as we can along the 33 kilometres of bitumen to Lyndhurst. For the first time, we're travelling light today. Steve is transporting all our clothes, and we're carrying only what we might need – wet-weather gear, spare tyres, spokes and equipment required for repairs and maintenance.

A family of roos bounces across the road. An eagle coasts on the thermals above us. The sun is shining and now the breeze is behind us.

'I feel like Priscilla, Queen of the Desert,' shouts Fleur, with her scarf flying out behind her.

We pass an open-cut coal mine, a swathe of country cut so bare it looks like a wasteland, and once again I long for a third way, a way of life which doesn't decimate land. I think of how the Aboriginals existed for so many thousands of years because they saw themselves as part of the land, rather than regarding the country as a resource. Running beside the road is the embankment of the Old Ghan, and half-a-dozen donkeys trot along the fence line beside us.

Mid-morning we reach a large, blue painted sign – 'Lyndhurst / Population 30 (most days)'. Today the town is deserted. The corrugated-iron door of the public toilet clanks open and shut, and the roof of a shed rattles in the wind. The roadhouse is closed up with a 'For Sale' notice on it.

The outback can be an elusive place, although a local will usually tell you if you've reached it or not. But even they have differing opinions. Lyndhurst is deserted today, so there's no one to ask. But as we roll off the bitumen and onto the wide dirt road stretching into the distance, I'm certain we've now reached the outback. Fleur and I, on our bicycles, seem very small in this vast open land.

Soon after we leave Lyndhurst we're overtaken by Steve. A road train thunders along this wide dirt highway, leaving a cloud of dust in its wake. All falls silent, and we're alone on the road again. The wind is hooting, but fortunately it's not on the nose today.

We scour the country for a gully out of the breeze where we can eat lunch. On a hill overlooking the road we see a tall Telstra transmission tower and a tin shed. In front of the shed we're protected from the wind, so we unpack our panniers. But the shed sits six inches off the ground and the wind whistles underneath it. In an instant, my mug of tea has blown over, and the bread rolls are flying across the gibber, chased by sachets of butter. So we use the panniers as wind blockades. Then we sit up here enjoying our last lunch, watching the four-wheel drives – loaded with jerry cans, swags and firewood – driving along the dirt highway below. I think back to the day we left Adelaide, not knowing if we would make it to Farina. Now, in less than 20 kilometres, we'll be there.

A couple of hours later we reach the turn off to Farina. We prop our bicycles against a large sign advertising the deserted town and its campgrounds and photograph each other grinning in front of it. According to the exaggerometer we have cycled over 800 kilometres.

Up the dirt track we come to the ghost town. A solitary red-brick fireplace and the crumbling sandstone buildings are timeless, but seeing a rusty car with its driver's door hanging open is a stark reminder that 60 years ago this town was home to a community.

One of Fleur's conditions before agreeing to sign up for our epic expedition was that we would end our cycle with a visit to Farina's underground bakery. For several weeks every winter, a baker stokes up the ovens of the old Farina bakery to coincide with the Farina Restoration Group volunteers' annual working bee. But there is no aroma of freshly baked bread, no meat pies, sausages rolls and not a whiff of warm jam doughnuts wafting through the stone shells of the deserted buildings.

However, we do find the shell of the post and telegraph office. The roof is long gone, but the sandstone walls are still standing. Two galahs sit side by side, preening themselves on the back wall of the four-roomed building. The front room, which would have been the telegraph office, has three doorways, the same layout as the Telegraph Repeater Station in Beltana. There's a door from the front corridor, one into the sitting room and another to the bedroom. This is where Muriel Chapman lived until 1960, when the post office closed. Three times a week at 2.15 am, accompanied by her dog, she would take the mailbag to the station and wait for the train. Occasionally she would still be waiting at seven o'clock in the morning. I wonder if she used to wash in the cast-iron enamel bathtub, now sitting in the dust behind the building.

Between the ruined sandstone buildings, we can't find either the homestead or the men's quarters, where we are staying. Having cycled in every direction, we realise both are down a track beyond a sign that says 'No access beyond this point'. The Monstermobile is parked outside a small, two-bedroom metal-clad hut. It isn't romantic or glamorous, but it provides a welcome refuge from the wind.

Our next concern is how Martin will find the place in the dark. Fleur wants to call him, so we go to the homestead to ask if there's mobile reception anywhere in Farina. Martin is probably out of mobile range most of the time, so we can only hope he'll stop somewhere with coverage and pick up a message.

'The best place for reception,' says Kevin Dawes, who with his wife Anne, bought the pastoral lease on the 286-square-kilometre Farina Station in the early 1990s, 'is the war memorial.' We walk up there, but the strong wind prevents Fleur from picking up a signal, so Kevin lets her use his landline. She leaves Martin detailed directions, telling him to turn in when he sees her fluorescent trousers attached to the fence post – and to collect them on his way through.

'The underground bakery is being set up next week when the school holidays begin,' Kevin tells us.

It's seven o'clock and pitch-black when Martin pulls up outside.

'I thought I was going to have to turn back,' he tells us. 'The Quorn fuel station was closed. I didn't realise there was one at Hawker, and if I hadn't managed to get fuel at Leigh Creek, I wouldn't have had enough to get here and back to Port Augusta.'

We light the kerosene heater, which makes the no-frills hut feel like a haven. The four of us sit at the small round table in the kitchen, eating, drinking and talking. Between the laughter and elation at having actually managed to cycle from Adelaide to here, I feel sad that this segment of the journey is over. Fleur and I have become so close, and I've loved these days of cycling.

CHAPTER 19

The Twin Tub and the Railhead

Fleur's parting gift is to make a batch of scones, which we eat hot from the oven. Then, having sat and talked for too long, Martin and Fleur have to leave quickly. I give Fleur a big hug and watch the hire car, with her bicycle in the back, drive away.

When I ask Kevin where I can do a load of washing, he leads me into a small shed next to the men's quarters. Pointing to an old twin tub, he gives me explicit instructions on how to operate it.

'Clean it first,' he says. 'It hasn't been used for a while.' I look inside and see it's coated with a thick layer of red dust.

I put all my cycling clothes in one tub, fill it with water, then put the machine on a four-and-a-half-minute cycle. This is not a set-it-and-forget-it machine. There's a hose outlet for emptying the tub, but the water doesn't drain out if I put the end of the hose into the sink. So I place a bucket on the ground, and when it fills with water empty it into the sink. I repeat the wash cycle, then fill the tub a third time to rinse the clothes, before I put them in the second tub, place a piece of red rubber over the lid – obviously the original lid either broke or was lost – and set the spinning process in motion.

Steve sticks his head into the shed a couple of times during the procedure. But he gets bored and takes off in the Monstermobile to set up at the campsite, where we are staying this evening.

Finding pegs in a rusty tin, I hang up the clothes. The wind has already whipped up and is whirling the Hills hoist around, so it's a perfect day for clothes drying. While that's happening, I cycle to the town.

Initially known as Government Gums, when the railway reached here

The Twin Tub and the Railhead

in 1882 it was optimistically renamed Farina, Latin for 'wheat', in the hope it would become a prosperous agricultural region. Dry conditions meant that wheat didn't flourish, but it became a service centre for outback pastoral stations.

I cycle to where stock was once loaded onto the rail trucks. Beside a loading ramp stands a two-level rail truck for carrying sheep. After the Overland Telegraph Line was built, many pastoralists acquired leases here and further north. But the town's heyday was over when the railhead was extended north to Marree, and Farina's population began to decline.

Beyond the campsite up a hill is the cemetery. Most of the graves are marked only with simple wooden crosses and a rectangle of stones collected from the surrounding area. It's an austere sight. In the far corner, away from the Christian burial grounds, are five Muslim graves, a reminder of the Afghans, whose camel strings carried supplies to all the remote districts not reached by the railway line, and their families who lived in the town.

By mid-afternoon the washing is dry, and I cycle back to the campsite with it. I pack into the panniers the bicycle spare parts and clothes that I won't need for this next leg of the trip, and Steve puts them on the roof rack. Then we attach the bicycle to the rear rack.

Near where we are camped, enclosed by high wire, is an artesian bore well. For a couple of months during the construction of the Overland Telegraph Line, two men had the job of drawing water from this well with a bucket and transferring it to a large stone holding tank.

The sun has gone down and it's cold. Steve lit a fire earlier, and we sit watching the flames licking a long piece of wood until it finally lights. I pick up the pin from the old red-gum sleeper he has broken up for firewood to take back to Sydney for Fleur. She wanted one but said it would be too heavy to take on the plane.

Steve cooks sausages and a couple of pieces of lamb over the fire and I make a salad. Back in Sydney we talked about not rushing this section of the journey to Alice Springs and enjoying being in the outback. But I can sense Steve is unsettled. As we eat, he admits that when he was camping alone in the Flinders Ranges he not only worried about Fleur and me on our bicycles, but also about his job; there has been talk of another round of redundancies.

I fill the billy can with water and nestle it into the fire's red embers. When the water boils, I throw in a handful of tea leaves and allow the tea to boil for a couple of minutes before taking the can off the fire and swinging it three times. I rest the billy at the edge of the fire and wait for the leaves to settle before pouring the tea into our tin mugs.

Steve turns in soon after 8 o'clock. I sit mesmerised in front of the fire, listening to the low conversation and occasional laughter from the nearby campers and the sound of snoring from the swag.

With a stick, I move the half-cooked sausage from the ash into the hot embers so it burns. The temperature has dropped, so I put a couple of small pieces of wood on the fire to keep it alive a little longer as I sit writing my journal.

Not long after I crawl into the swag beside Stephen and gaze up at the stars through the mosquito net. Stephen gives a soft grunt as I turn over and wrap myself around his warm body. Through the thin foam mattress I can feel the hard ground against my hipbone, but I know that in a couple of days I'll be used to sleeping in the swag again. I love that feeling of lying on the earth, enveloped by this huge country.

CHAPTER 20

The Afghans and Hunting for Reg Dodd

A solitary telegraph pole – a piece of rail line – stands in the gibber, and a pair of emus prance across the flat country. The road runs through Mundowdna Station, the property Sidney Kidman acquired in 1906. For the cattle king it was an ideal location close to the railway and at the southern end of the Birdsville Track. He used it as a fattening depot for stock that had been walked from his properties in the Channel Country and the Northern Territory before they were sent by rail to Port Augusta and on to Adelaide, Melbourne or Sydney.

Driving into Marree, we pass the impressive two-storey sandstone hotel. Opposite is the old railway station, and beside the high platform sit old engines and a rusty steam locomotive.

When I visited the State Library in Adelaide, I was given a book about the town's first post and telegraph master, James Arthur O'Brien, written by his son. The post office, which opened in 1884, the same year the railway reached here, was in a cattle truck, and every evening O'Brien had to disconnect the telegraph wires because during the night the cattle trains would be loading and shunting. By morning his post-office truck was usually at the other end of the railway yard, and he had to call for volunteers to help push the truck back to the connecting pole.

O'Brien sent telegrams for Sidney Kidman about his stock. He also patrolled the line when it broke. On two occasions the line was cut by men in trouble. They knew if the line was broken a telegraph man would set out to find the fault and fix it. O'Brien saved the life of the first one, reaching him in time, but the second man was dead when he found him.

Steve needs a Ventolin inhaler, so we stop at Marree Hospital. We're talking to the nurse, Sister June, when a man comes in who looks remarkably similar to the photograph of the person who runs Arabunna Tours, who I've been trying to contact.

'Are you Reg Dodd?' I ask. He doesn't reply.

'Ron is Reg's brother,' Sister June says. When I explain to Ron that I hope to talk to his brother, he tells me he saw Reg earlier this morning on his way to the Arabunna Community Centre.

We're staying in Marree tonight, so we check into the Oasis Caravan Park before I go looking for Reg Dodd. In the communal cooking area are eight pieces of white bread laid out on a table. Next to them is a man with a long beard and a bald head wearing a skin-tight nylon camouflage-print outfit and bright green shoes. I notice a bicycle carrying four panniers beside a small tent, and a pair of socks drying on the fence. He's not talkative, but he lets drop that he's cycled here from Newcastle, just north of Sydney. I glance at Juniper riding on the back of the Monstermobile, and Fleur and my journey seems a comparatively unimpressive endeavour.

We leave the cyclist to his bread, and I walk over to the Arabunna Community Centre. On an exterior wall is a mural that depicts life in the Hermit Hill Springs Complex, a wetland region of mound springs near here. Underneath is written:

The GREAT ARTESIAN BASIN underlies nearly a third of the Australian continent. Water enters it from the high country at the basin fringe in particular the Great Divide in Queensland. At an average flow rate of about 1 cm per day water travelling 3000 km across the basin from the recharge beds in Queensland to springs in South Australia takes 822,000 years to complete the journey.

Inside I find Jan Whyte, who works here as a volunteer. She tells me Reg hasn't been in yet today, so I wander over to the Lake Eyre Yacht Club. Established in 2000, the club sits, complete with its boat ramp, 100 kilometres from Australia's largest lake. The lake has water in it every eight years or so, has filled to capacity just a few times in the last 160 years, and is usually a shimmering dry salt pan. These conditions sound to me most inauspicious for the average yachtsman. But its doors are open and inside is the commodore, Bob Backway, waxing lyrical to Steve about the club's sailing program. It transpires the recent regattas have

The Afghans and Hunting for Reg Dodd

been on the Coongie Lakes, in the Cooper Creek area north-east of here.

I leave them to discuss sailing and head back to the Arabunna Community Centre. Stepping onto the wooden verandah, I push open the flyscreen door.

'He's still not back,' Jan says.

Originally from Melbourne, Jan Whyte first came to Marree as a member of the Friends of the Earth Anti-Uranium Collective and has lived here for over 20 years. She talks about the discovery in the mid-1970s of one of the world's largest copper deposits and the world's largest known single uranium deposit at Olympic Dam, south-west of here, and the opening of the mine in 1988.

'In the mid-1990s, when Western Mining Corporation expanded its production, the South Australian government issued a licence to extract up to 42 million litres of water from the Great Artesian Basin every day at no cost,' she says. 'Olympic Dam is owned by BHP. It uses an average of 35 million litres of water from the basin each day, and the station bores and the mound springs are losing pressure.'

Water rising from the mound springs in this region sustained the Aboriginal people for thousands of years. It was the water in these mound springs that ensured the survival of John McDouall Stuart and his exploring parties when they travelled through this country to the north of the continent.

The first bore was sunk into the Great Artesian Basin at Bourke in Western NSW in 1878. And as more bores were drilled thousands of square kilometres of country were opened up for pastoralism. But only a few years after the bores were sunk they started to corrode and became free-flowing; up to 95% of the water was wasted to evaporation and seepage. It wasn't until the 1990s that the capping of bores and the piping of water was implemented, radically reducing water wastage.

The Great Artesian Basin is one of the largest and deepest underground reservoirs in the world. It's believed that the giant aquifer is topped up by rainfall, particularly on the slopes of the Great Dividing Range, but it's estimated that the time the water takes to travel from there to the most distant parts of the Great Artesian Basin can be up to two million years. Extracted water takes hundreds of thousands of years, if not longer, to be replenished. Jan Whyte and Reg Dodd are just two of many people across the country raising awareness of this valuable water and the need to preserve it for future generations.

Jan turns on the lights of the museum section of the centre so I can look around. There's a photographic and narrative exhibition by Reg Dodd titled *Working Together, Stories of Aboriginal involvement in the Overland Telegraph Line and the old Ghan Railway*.

In 1863 John Warren – Reg Dodd's great-grandfather – took up a large pastoral lease at Strangways Springs, west of here. He later established a partnership with Thomas Hogarth and extended their property to Anna Creek Station near today's tiny township of William Creek. John Warren was able to establish a working relationship with the Arabunna people. When the head station was moved from Strangways Springs to Anna Creek, the Arabunna men – who also worked as sheep herders – helped to build the Anna Creek Homestead. With their knowledge of the country, they were able to find the best stock routes across the land, and they showed the white men where to dig wells and set up stockyards. John Warren provided rations for crews during the surveying and construction of the Overland Telegraph Line, and the Arabunna showed them sites with drinkable water.

John Warren returned to Adelaide, leaving his son, Francis Dunbar Warren, and Thomas Hogarth to run the property. Francis met an Arabunna woman, Nora Beralda, and they had seven children together. Unlike most white men at the time, who neither acknowledged their Aboriginal families nor lived with them, Francis Dunbar Warren remained with his family for the rest of his life. In 1911 John Warren, then a state MP, argued vehemently in the South Australian parliament against removing Aboriginal children from their families. Francis Dunbar Warren sold his share of Anna Creek Station in 1918, and the family moved to Finniss Springs, 60 kilometres west of Marree, where Reg grew up.

There is still no sign of Reg.

'He's busy at the moment,' Jan says. 'It's NAIDOC Week and also the Camel Cup.' She shows me a poster for the Camel Cup this coming Saturday. 'People and camels come from far and wide for it,' she says. 'For many years the champion camel was Dish Dash from Coward Springs, just up the Oodnadatta Track. Last year a camel from Boulia, in Central West Queensland, took away the trophy, and in 2012 Rodney Sansom came all the way from Newcastle in NSW with his camels.'

The Afghans and Hunting for Reg Dodd

I tell Jan I'm eager to find out about the cameleers, so she directs me to the telecommunications centre on the other side of the railway line, where she says I'll find Irene Zada.

I pass the large, camel-shaped sundial made of railway sleepers, and the old mosque. The mosque has clay walls a metre high and tree stumps support the frame of long branches that form the pitched roof, which is covered in a thin reed thatch. When the Overland Telegraph Line was being constructed, a maintenance camp was established here for the workers and the Afghan cameleers. Later the town became known as 'Little Asia', because of the number of cameleers operating out of the town. Then there were two mosques in the town, and this is a replica of one of the originals.

I find Irene Zada and another woman discussing the Camel Cup over mugs of tea. Irene is stout with dark curly hair and flamboyant gold earrings. I ask about the Afghans.

'My mother could have told you plenty,' she says, 'She was the daughter of a cameleer, but she died a couple of months ago.'

'I'm sorry,' I murmur.

'She was 102,' Irene adds.

'That's a good age.'

'Yes,' she reflects, obviously still raw from the loss. She points out a small, white tin house.

'Go over there and talk to Raymond Moosha.'

On either side of the wooden door are two large pieces of quartz. A Persian carpet hangs over the fence to air. A white plastic chair sits in the dirt in front of the small corrugated-iron building. Raymond is standing outside the back of the house. He is a small, fit-looking man with olive skin.

'This house is 100 years old,' he says. 'I was born here, and I'm 79 now.' He drove here this morning from his home in Adelaide for the Camel Cup. He's staying with his niece, Karen Moosha, who now lives here; she is the daughter of his twin brother, Raz.

'Father and Grandfather and my uncles all had camels strings,' he reminisces. 'There were camel yards in this whole area,' he says, pointing to the open space behind the house. 'And the mosque used to be beyond them, not where it is now, near the railway. When Raz and I were small, the camels were still around. And I remember Grandfather wore a turban. That was my mother's father, Dahleh Balooch. He died when I was seven.

'But Raz and I weren't interested in the camels. We were chasing the horses. I left school at 14 and went to work on the stations. I worked at Coward Springs, making saddles and bridles and looking after the animals. I was a bit of a drover. I spent five years working on the stations and then worked on the railways for a couple of years, as a porter and in the goods shed. After the camels, my father and uncles worked on the railways too. For a while I was on the transhipping platform. Marree was as far as the standard gauge came from Adelaide, so we carried all the goods across the platform and loaded them onto the narrow-gauge train.'

His tale now finished, he tells me he worked for a rennet company in Adelaide for 39 years. All I can think of is the junket, sprinkled with nutmeg, Marabella used to make. My father was allergic to milk, but could eat junket due to the enzymes in rennet.

I walk back to the campsite, and Steve and I take our food over to the large open fire at the camp kitchen. The cyclist is there, and more forthcoming than he was this morning. Evan is 49. He has cycled from his home town of Newcastle up to Byron Bay – Australia's easternmost point – and now he's heading to Australia's westernmost point – Steep Point in Shark Bay. Having travelled through Cameron Corner before coming down the Strzelecki Track, he's already well adapted to the remoteness.

A family from Sydney and several other campers have gathered around the fire. We listen as Evan recounts how he recently lost the bolt that holds his bicycle seat in place.

'I didn't have a replacement,' he says. 'But, fortunately, a passing motorist had a cordless drill and drilled out the old bolt and put in a new one.'

Evan is following the Oodnadatta Track to Marla then going to Uluru and following the track from there to Western Australia.

'I do about 100 kilometres a day,' he says, explaining that he gets up in the dark and walks until dawn, when he starts cycling. He attempted this trip earlier in his life, but he didn't get all the way, so before he turns 50 he's making this second attempt.

CHAPTER 21

Precious Water

The task this morning is to find Reg Dodd. Steve and I go to the Arabunna Community Centre. Jan Whyte tells us that Reg said he'd be back shortly. We wait for a while, but there's no sign of him, so we drive across the railway to the general store.

Lyle Oldfield, the owner, is behind the counter. I explain that we're looking for Reg Dodd.

'There he is,' he says, pointing to a ute turning down the street beside the hotel on the other side of the railway. We leap into the Monstermobile and catch up with him outside the Marree Aboriginal School.

'Go back to the community centre and I'll be there shortly,' he says.

I am standing outside the centre waiting for Reg when I notice, across the road, a man sitting on a white plastic chair outside the old butcher's shop. Yesterday Jan told me this is where the Afghans sit soaking in the sun every morning. I walk over and introduce myself. He is Max Dahleh. His father, uncles and grandfather were all cameleers, he tells me.

'I'm younger than Raymond,' he says, 'so I don't remember much. The cameleering came to an end in the 1940s.'

While we're talking, Raymond and Irene arrive and sit on chairs beside Max. Prompted by my interest in Marree's history, they reminisce about the days of kerosene fridges. 'There was no electricity until the standard gauge reached here in 1957,' Raymond says. Conversation turns to working on the railway.

'I started work at 14,' Irene recounts, 'and I cleaned the Ghan for 12 years. One Christmas Day we all got drunk and we still had to clean the train. It must have been okay, because no one complained.'

Whispering Wire

The Afghans are joined by Paulo, a man from the former Czechoslovakia, who takes his place on the empty plastic chair next to the others.

'I've been in Marree 52 years,' he says. 'I worked on the railway as a foreman, until I had an accident.'

'Paulo's a star now,' Irene chips in. 'He was in the film *The Rover*.'

'I had two days filming on it,' he explains in his thick Eastern European accent, 'and I was invited to Adelaide for the premiere.' I leave them enjoying the morning sun and head back to the community centre.

'You missed him,' says Jan.

'What do you mean?'

'He popped in, and now he's gone off to Alberrie Creek.'

Steve pulls up outside, and I can't hide my disappointment.

We drive back to the general store and buy bread, beer and fuel. I'm climbing into the passenger seat when Steve points out Reg Dodd, who is filling his truck at another bowser. I go over and he tells me he's very busy because of NAIDOC Week and the Camel Cup. He doesn't have time to meet. But he gives me his card and suggests we speak on the telephone. There is nothing else I can do, so Steve and I start down the Oodnadatta Track.

Steve enjoys driving. Only when he's very tired or has had a few drinks can he be prised off the wheel. I like being a passenger, so it's a perfect arrangement – as long as he can be persuaded to stop occasionally. About 20 minutes out of Marree he pulls up for me to take a photograph of a railway bridge spanning a salt-crusted creek. At that moment Reg Dodd overtakes us, his red cattle dog hanging its head out of the passenger window.

We stop again at the Dingo Fence and marvel at this six-foot-high construction. Designed to keep dingoes out of south-east Australia it stretches over 5600 kilometres from near Dalby on Queensland's Darling Downs, where Fleur grew up, to the Great Australian Bight.

We roll across the cattle grid into dingo country. Our next stop is Mutonia Sculpture Park. It's the work of Robin Cooke, a conservationist who took part in a protest rally about the millions of litres of water being extracted from the Great Artesian Basin for the Olympic Dam mine in the late 1990s. After the protest he camped at Alberrie Creek, and seeing old machinery lying about he asked Reg Dodd if he could use it to make sculptures. Since then he has returned on a regular basis to create more pieces.

Two aeroplanes, their tails planted in the ground and their wings overlapping form the entrance to the collection of sculptures, all made from discarded materials, dotted across the desert. An old windmill has been painted green and pink and transformed into an enormous metal flower. Large rusty wind chimes sway in the breeze. A chain of one of the chimes is broken and gives out a low, mournful, monotonous clang as it hits the chime next to it. The sculpture that particularly captivates me is known as Dottie the Dingo, its body a huge water tank, its head an old car. We pull into Alberrie Creek Siding at the far end of the park so I can photograph it.

Reg Dodd's ute is also at the siding. I walk over to apologise, thinking maybe we are trespassing on Aboriginal land. He is with another man, Vincent Warren, and he tells me they are off to collect firewood as they are bringing schoolchildren out here tomorrow. I ask him about the large wooden building here at the siding.

'It was built in the 1940s as fettlers' accommodation,' he says. 'It was here when we were kids.' A track runs down from the siding to Finniss Springs, where Reg was born. Reg's mother, Amy, daughter of Francis Dunbar Warren and Nora Beralda, had nine children with Tom Dodd, before she met Arrernte man Alan Buzzacott, and had five sons, the oldest of whom is Reg.

'I'm certified a Dodd, but really I'm a Buzzacott,' he says.

Reg grew up on the Finniss Spring Mission and Finniss Springs Station, which his grandfather owned, until he was 13, when he started working as a stockman on Anna Creek Station. Around the same time Reg's father got a job working on the railway, and his parents and four younger brothers moved to Marree.

It was probably because of the influence of his grandfather, Reg says, that the railway employed Aboriginal people. Initially hired as fettlers, they worked here at Alberrie Creek and at nearby Curdimurka, before taking up positions as foremen, train examiners and stationmasters in Marree. Reg worked on the railway for 26 years, and for 20 of those he was a train examiner, until the last freight train left Marree in 1986.

Whispering Wire

After Francis Dunbar Warren died in the late 1950s, his family members, including Reg, continued to run the pastoral property. But lack of management skills, disputes and difficulties made them look at how they could manage the land differently. They surrendered their pastoral lease and began planning with the state government to run it as a jointly managed national park. But with a change in minister and, Reg says, pressure from Western Mining Corporation, the national park did not get the go-ahead. So in the late 1990s Reg submitted a native title claim for this area, and in 2012 about 300 Arabunna people gathered at Finniss Springs to receive the native title for more than 70,000 square kilometres.

'Would you like to see some stumps of the original Overland Telegraph Line poles?' Reg asks casually. Having tried to track him down for the last 24 hours, I am ecstatic that he now not only has time to talk but is also going to show us these – especially as Fleur and I didn't see the ones near Merna Mora.

'You'll see us parked down the track,' he says. The ute disappears in a cloud of red dust.

I photograph Dottie the Dingo before we follow them. Vincent and Reg are standing a short distance from the road. When we walk over to them Reg points out a collection of stones of different sizes and shapes. 'These are Aboriginal tools,' he says, 'this used to be an Aboriginal camp. Near here is a natural stone table used for thousands of years for men's ceremonies, until the Overland Telegraph Line came, and John Warren, my great-grandfather, suggested it would be best if the ceremonies were held in another place. This area we're on is called Well Field A.' It was from here that the Olympic Dam mining operation at Roxby Downs first started extracting water from the Great Artesian Basin.

'Around this area are about 300 to 400 natural springs. In the past, the water went for 20 to 30 feet in the air, because there was so much pressure. But not now. There has been a hell of a decline, but people don't seem to care. They used to have rallies and that, but not now.'

As we walk across the gibber, Reg points out the hardy acacia known as dead finish, the cane grass and the mulga. 'And here is an original Overland Telegraph Line pole,' he says. The 60-centimetre-high native pine stump is still firmly embedded in the ground, and I dance around it in raptures. Eighty metres further on Reg points out a second stump.

Precious Water

It's far more weathered than the first but just as firmly planted. I try to imagine the telegraph poles every 80 metres and the wire between them stretching for kilometre after kilometre across this dry, stony country.

I could happily spend the day listening to Reg's stories about the telegraph line, his family and his lifetime on this land. But we are aware that he and Vincent have a busy day, so we don't take up any more of their time. Since this meeting, Reg Dodd's book, *Talking Sideways*, which he co-wrote with Malcolm McKinnon, has been published, a fascinating insight into this place. A combination of history and memoir, it also highlights the complexities of Aboriginal culture in modern times.

Fifteen kilometres further along, the Oodnadatta Track skirts the edge of the dry Kati Thanda-Lake Eyre. When Steve and I saw it for the first time in 2006 it was the accomplishment of a long-held dream. Once again, I'm mesmerised by the seeming infinity of stark shimmering salt, stretching as far as the eye can see. Steve stands taking in this vast white expanse, and I walk down to the shore and cross over the old railway line. The rails have been removed, but the sleepers are still here. The dry, salt-crusted mud glimmers in the sunlight, creating a mirage. I wonder when the lake will again fill with water and transform into a feeding and breeding ground for multitudes of pelicans, terns, egrets, ibis and black swans.

At Curdimurka Siding, a few kilometres farther on, a lopsided Oppenheimer telegraph pole stands beside the single-storey whitewashed stone railway building. It reminds me of an Irish cottage, with its huge stone fireplace and wooden-beamed roof. The railway siding is named after Kuddimuckra, a giant snake, believed by the Arabunna to live in Kati Thanda-Lake Eyre. There is a story that tells of those who first saw the Ghan travelling along the shores of the lake fleeing in terror, thinking it was the great serpent.

Just beyond the siding, a long railway bridge crosses Stuart Creek, and there is a track down to Stuart Creek Station. John McDouall Stuart had originally named this land Chambers Creek. It was here that he was granted a pastoral lease by the South Australian government for his exploration endeavours, and from here that he set off on his northern expeditions.

It was also near here, on his second expedition in 1859, that Stuart and his party came across a group of Aboriginal people. An old man approached the exploring party, intrigued by Stuart, who was smoking his pipe. So Stuart gave him a pipe and showed him how to light it. Using sign language, Stuart asked the man where the party could find water. He and a group of men led them a short distance.

'I expected they were going to take us to springs, and was disappointed when they showed us some rain water in a deep hole', Stuart wrote in his journal. The horses drank the hole dry, while the Aboriginal men looked on in astonishment. Stuart then asked where more water could be found. 'They would go no further with us, nor show us any more, and in a short time after, left us', Stuart wrote. Over tens of thousands of years, the Aboriginal people had evolved a method of surviving in this dry Country. They knew where to find water, but they also realised that others would require this precious resource, and therefore it was necessary to use it sparingly. The white men with their thirsty horses didn't share this understanding.

On a stony ridge here at Stuart Creek a 45-million-year-old fossilised gumnut was found. Other fossils found in the rocks here include araucaria and cypress pines, casuarinas, flame trees and kurrajongs. As Steve and I rattle along the track, I marvel at the continual pulse of life on this old land, how human beings are such small players in the life of our planet. Yet how we live each day, the choices we make, our emotional states and ambitions, our acts of selfishness or kindness, all make a difference – either positively or negatively – to our families, friends, communities, countries and environment.

A deviation down a rough track brings us to the Wabma Kadarbu Mound Springs Conservation Park. We walk around Thirrka, also known as Blanche Cup, a white carbonate mound with a reed-fringed, dazzling blue pool of water at its centre. In a nearby mound the water ripples and emits small squirts and then a large bubble gurgles to the surface. This is Pirdalinha, the Bubbler. Here in the dry desert these two springs are truly an oasis.

We stop for the night at Coward Springs, once a railway siding, now a campground run by Greg Emmett and Prue Coulls.. We set up near a couple of 100-year-old date palms. 'They were part of a government experimental date plantation,' Greg tells us, as he cycles up to collect our camping fee. 'The dates taste very good, and I'm propagating more.'

Precious Water

Coward Springs is another oasis. In the 1880s, a bore was sunk here and millions of litres of Great Artesian Basin water flowed across the dry gibber plains, creating a wetland. The bore flow rate has been controlled and reduced since the 1990s but, deemed to be of value to the many birds, plants and small native animals which exist here, this area continues to be a wetland.

We take ourselves off for a soak in the spa, a small, bubbling pool edged with railway sleepers. The artesian water is naturally warm and we sit submerged – watching tiny birds flit in and out of the wetland reeds – until the air temperature drops. Steve takes the timber we collected earlier in the day off the roof and lights a fire. Before leaving home, I cooked and froze half a dozen meals, which Steve stashed in the Engel fridge-freezer before setting off from Sydney. I heat up the chilli con carne that has been defrosting on the dashboard all afternoon. After we've eaten, we study the map. Steve, agitated, admits he's worried about work. He spoke to a colleague a few days ago and says there is talk of major changes and redundancies.

Steve heads to the swag and I sit gazing at the fire overwhelmed with doubt. His restlessness derails me, making me question whether this quest to follow the telegraph line to Darwin is mere self-indulgence. I adore the slowness of the journey and the stillness here, but I sense he is itching to keep moving and cover the kilometres. Dingoes yowl in the distance, and a large log glows red with the faint breeze.

CHAPTER 22

Unlikely Cameleers and the William Creek Hotel

We get out of the swag to see several humps protruding above the saltbushes, over the fence from where we are camped. A large camel stands with head erect and eyes closed, absorbing the first rays of morning sun. Maybe this is the Marree Camel Cup champion, Dish Dash.

I am admiring the porcelain insulator doorknobs of the ablutions block when I see Evan filling his water bottles from the rainwater tank. He tells me he slept near Curdimurka last night, and at nine in the evening he was woken by a young policeman asking him what had happened at the tennis courts in Marree. Evan appears shaken as he explains how he was accused by a girl of grabbing her arm when he was in Marree. He says two policemen asked him numerous questions before eventually leaving him alone.

Greg and Prue operate camel safaris from Coward Springs, and as we drive away a dozen camels, herded by a border collie, are padding down the Oodnadatta Track. We cross several salt pans before stopping to collect firewood among the clumps of poached egg daisies sprung up with the recent rain.

'God be with you,' says Evan, as he cycles past in his nylon camouflage outfit, bright green shoes and matching green helmet plus fly netting over his face.

Just off the Oodnadatta Track is Strangways Springs, the second of the 12 original Overland Telegraph Line repeater stations. It was also once the pastoral property of Reg Dodd's great-grandfather. The dry-stone walls of the stockyard are still standing, as is a large stone water tank. All that remains of what was the homestead and, from 1872 to 1896, the Overland

Unlikely Cameleers and the William Creek Hotel

Telegraph repeater station, are a few walls. In the mound of stones beside them grows pink-flowering hop bush, the seeds of which, Reg Dodd told us, came to Australia in the saddlebags of the Afghans.

An original native pine telegraph pole protrudes from the saltbush into the clear blue sky and I keep turning to catch another glimpse of it as we walk to the cemetery. A grave is marked only by a rectangle of stones and a wooden cross lying on the sandy soil inside it. Nearby a marble headstone commemorates Mary, the wife of telegraph linesman Albert Hewish, who died from complications after childbirth. It's a stark reminder of the extreme isolation of the telegraph workers and their families.

There's no wind and not even the sound of a bird. We walk from mound spring to mound spring, some now extinct because of loss of pressure caused by bore drilling into the Great Artesian Basin. Others, though, are still pushing up water to the dry surface. I'm captivated by these mounds caked in white salt – one covered in pink samphire bushes, another with saltbush, and some topped with reeds and sedges.

Forty kilometres along the Oodnadatta Track is William Creek. A handful of buildings mark South Australia's smallest town, with its population of only two to four people in summer and swelling to about 10 in winter with the cooler weather and the tourist season.

We pull up at the William Creek Hotel, a low, single-storey building with a green corrugated-iron roof, built in 1887 as a support station for camel drivers working on the Overland Telegraph Line. Inside there is a long bar and a row of shabby swivel chairs. Down one end are four high wooden stools around a large barrel, at the other a dartboard and an ice-cream fridge. A payphone sits in the middle of the bar. Every inch of the ceiling is covered in business cards, greeting cards and banknotes from around the world.

Trevor Wright's mop of grey hair appears. He mutters that he needs to avert a fuel bowser crisis and darts outside. For over 25 years Trevor Wright has lived in William Creek, operating his company, Wrightsair, from here, making scenic flights over Kati Thanda-Lake Eyre, as well as flying to remote communities and doing cattle spotting work. Behind the bar is a more relaxed young bush pilot called Rev, who tells us he's working here for the season to get up his flying hours.

Whispering Wire

When Steve and I first visited William Creek Hotel in 2006, Trevor flew us in a four-seater Cessna over the nearby Painted Hills – a range of rich red, yellow and white sandstone mounds and monoliths shaped by wind and erosion, they look as if an impetuous painter has taken to them with a large brush. We also met another of the town's residents, Phil Gee, who ran camel treks and camel-training courses. Soon after, Phil moved to Adelaide to work for the SA government on the feral camel management program. He had just helped a Melbourne antique dealer, Flynn Moustafa, and his friend, Dave, train three camels. When we met Flynn in the hotel, he told us he was married with three children and had a successful antique business in Melbourne. But he had sold the business, along with his house, and he and his family were moving to the Whitsundays, where he planned to run camel rides along Airlie Beach.

'You can be a sheep in life, but I want to be a coyote,' Flynn had said when I questioned the feasibility of this project. He added, 'If one business doesn't work out, another will. Camels are also good at land clearing, especially lantana, and the meat is good.'

'I had camel steak here for dinner this evening,' chipped in Dave. 'Very tasty, like beef.'

The following day they had set off in an old red Dodge truck with a large irascible bull camel called Shrieky, and two smaller, more docile ones.

Steve and I pay Rev to stay at the town campsite for the night. As we're setting up, I wonder what happened to those two unlikely cameleers and their camels.

Steve lights a fire and we watch a Cessna roll down the runway behind the pub and take off – a scenic flight over the lake. He places a couple of potatoes wrapped in foil into the fire, and while they're cooking we sit and watch the sky turn red and the sun set, before grilling lamb chops with zucchini and capsicum. After we've eaten, I return to the hotel to ring Marabella in Ireland. It's quarter to eight. Rev and Louise, an English backpacker also working here, are the only people in the bar.

'Why is it so quiet?' I ask.

'Everyone is in the Dingo Café having dinner,' Louise replies.

I pick up the receiver of the payphone on the bar, feed in five $2 coins and dial the number. Unable to get through, I try again. After several

Unlikely Cameleers and the William Creek Hotel

attempts, Louise tells me international calls can't be made from this telephone. So I dial our friend Kelly Rae in Alice Springs, but that call doesn't go through either. Having resorted to the hotel's wi-fi, I'm sending an email on the iPad when Trevor enters the bar.

He tells me that as business owners have left, he's acquired more and more of this tiny town. Several years ago he bought the Dingo Café and the camping ground. Bruce Ross and Mim Ward – who Fleur and I met in Spalding and who now run the general store there – sold the lease for the William Creek Hotel to a couple whose dream was to own an outback pub, Trevor tells us.

'Realising after three months this wasn't their dream at all, they put it back on the market. But after three years of water in Kati Thanda-Lake Eyre, the lake was now dry, and travellers were no longer flocking in their hundreds to see it. Interest in this isolated pub dried up along with the water. As the success of the town depends on the success of the pub, my hand was forced and I acquired the lease of the hotel.'

'It's a bit like playing Monopoly,' he adds, 'and the greatest amount of time is spent maintaining services, like water, power and sewage.' But Trevor has big dreams for this little town.

'We've gone from eight generators back to one and put in a town power grid, and cut diesel usage by 50 per cent. The next plan is to add solar power to the grid, and then run a desalination plant so the town has potable water.' I'm remembering the mug of tea I had at the hotel back in 2006 – which was so salty it was undrinkable – when the payphone on the bar rings.

Trevor picks it up. It's Mick at Leigh Creek Police Station. Trevor blinks as fast as he talks. He says there's been a request by some of the William Creek residents that a policeman come here. They're concerned about Evan's imminent arrival, having heard about an incident in Marree. Trevor transfers the call and disappears through a door behind the bar.

'He's only a few kilometres away,' Louise tells him when he returns. I am ignored when I point out that a heavily loaded bicycle is not the best getaway vehicle and suggest that maybe he's not a threat.

Suddenly the bar fills with people, and Trevor introduces me to Bobby Hunter, a tall man in his 60s wearing a wide Akubra hat. I also meet Bobby's friend Hobbsy, who sports a smaller, jaunty trilby. Hobbsy is visiting from Port Broughton for several days; he used to work as an engine driver on the Old Ghan.

'I drove the train from Port Augusta to Alice for seven years,' he tells me, 'and from Marree to Alice its speed was only between five and 10 kilometres an hour. We used to carry a gun, and on one trip, going around a big curve, I got off the train and shot two wild turkeys and plucked them in the engine room. Sir Reg Ansett was a passenger and he saw this trail of feathers floating past the train window. When we reached Alice Springs, he asked, "Are you giving me a turkey for dinner?"'

Bobby Hunter manages Stuart Creek outstation and has worked for nearly 50 years on Anna Creek Station, the 23,677-square-kilometre property that covers an area larger than Belgium.

'I moved to Anna Creek Station at the age of 11. My parents were friends with the Nunns, and Dick Nunn managed Anna Creek Station. Father came as a handyman,' Bobby explains. 'Before that we lived in Oodnadatta and Dad worked at the aerodrome.

'My father's family were Poms. My mother's father was Irish, and my mother's mother was a full-blooded Kokatha woman. Mum died several years ago. She had 11 kids and I was number four. I was a bit of a show-off. From the age of 11 I was rounding up cattle in the school holidays, and I started working full-time at 14. From a young age I loved riding horses, and then we mustered on horses, but it's by plane and motorbike now.'

Hobbsy and Bobby Hunter finish their beers and head off. I start talking to Janelle, a New Zealand cook who's been working at Anna Creek Station for several months. On this winter's evening in 2014 it is still owned by S. Kidman and Co, and Janelle tells me there are currently 16,000 head of cattle and 13 people working on the station.

'Some are camping out at the moment because they're mustering.' I have visions of them huddling around a fire while a stew simmers in a large camp oven.

'Oh, no,' she says, dashing my romantic impression of the stockmen's life. 'They have a big truck with a table and kitchen inside, and I send them off with cold meats and a ready-made meal they can heat up.'

In April 2015, S. Kidman and Co, owned by the Kidman family for over 100 years, put all its 11 cattle stations, covering 100,000 square kilometres, up for sale. When the sale was announced, the company had 155,000 branded cattle and 30,000 calves to be marked. It employed 170 staff and on average produced 15,000 tonnes of beef a year.

In 2016, Gina Rinehart's Australian–Chinese consortium, Australian Outback Beef, took over all the Kidman properties except Anna Creek Station, because of its defence sensitivity on account of its proximity to the Woomera military testing range. The Anna Creek lease was purchased by the Williams Cattle Company of South Australia.

Janelle looks at her watch and says she must go, she has an early start. So at 9.40 pm I am completely alone in the William Creek Hotel. I walk out into the cold night air and discover Louise smoking a cigarette.

'It's an odd evening,' she muses.

CHAPTER 23

The Peake

The following morning Evan's bicycle is leaning against the wooden rail outside the hotel. Inside I find him sitting on a bar stool, eating a packet of chips. Rev is standing behind the bar. It appears that the panic about Evan coming to town has passed.

We buy fuel and ice before continuing along the Oodnadatta Track. Just before the entrance to Anna Creek Homestead we pass a mob of horses, and three roos sit motionless with paws poised, staring at us.

We turn into a 13-kilometre-long rough track to the Peake Telegraph Repeater Station. We saw an occasional vehicle on the Oodnadatta Track, but now we're alone. With fierce concentration Steve negotiates the Monstermobile around rocks and sudden dips and troughs. Grey-trunked gidgee grow in the dry creek beds, and beneath them are lilac baubled silver-tails and red desert fuchsia. The isolation is exhilarating as we move slowly through this desert country, dotted with yellow-flowering sandhill wattles. But it's also unnerving. We are utterly reliant on the vehicle and always in our minds is the thought that we could break down. I imagine how remote it must have felt to the telegraph men when the repeater station was first built.

Eventually we reach the wetland area with its clusters of rushes and patches of white salt. These springs, which run even in times of drought, are called Yardiya by the Arabunna people. Reg Dodd explained to us that the Arabunna had a duty of care for the land, which continued after white settlement. He described how the Arabunna Elders he knew straddled both the new colonial world and their age-old traditional way of life. 'Old fellas used to catch the train at Alberrie Creek when I was a kid at Finniss

The Peake

Springs. They'd get off at Peake and head into the hills for six weeks or so, supposedly prospecting around the old gold and copper mines. Their real reason for being there was to fulfil their responsibilities as Elders, checking on sites and looking after country.'

When Stuart came across Yardiya in 1859 he wrote in his journal that they were the largest springs he had seen, with an immense flow of water. It seems like an oasis even now, as we walk along the stream lined with red gums, willows and gidgees. I imagine the significance for the Arabunna of this abundant water in the middle of the dry desert country and why they continued to camp in the area after the telegraph station was built.

When construction of the Overland Telegraph Line began in 1870, the Peake Telegraph Repeater Station on Mount Margaret Station, which had been a pastoral lease since the mid-1860s, was the farthest outpost of settlement in South Australia. There are several ruined whitewashed buildings, but the high chimneys and walls of the seven-roomed repeater station are still standing. In one room the plaster is still on the wall, and in the corner is the rusty broken frame of a brass bed. I look out through the hole in the wall – once a window – at a couple of date palms swaying in the breeze.

I walk to the nearby deserted copper mine and peer into a couple of mineshafts, before clambering up the hill beside it. I look down at the remains of the telegraph station and the pastoral settlement buildings, and at Steve's small figure walking between them.

The Peake Telegraph Repeater Station closed in 1891 when the telegraph operations were moved to the new township of Oodnadatta on the recently completed railway. In 1903 Sidney Kidman bought the property, and the Peake became part of Kidman's chain of stations across the interior of Australia.

As we inch slowly back along the rough track in the Monstermobile, a willy-willy spins the red dust into the air ahead of us, before whirling off across the gibber plain. Soon after rejoining the Oodnadatta Track we stop to gather firewood. Above us a pair of wedge-tailed eagles ride the thermals, spiralling higher and higher into the cloudless blue sky.

It's half past two when we pull up beside the Neales River at Algebuckina Bridge. We set up camp on the dry part of the riverbed close to the water's edge. Clumps of deep-pink samphire bush grow on the salt-crusted red sand, and a pair of dragonflies dance above the water.

Steve opens a bottle of cold beer, pleased to be able to finally relax. Within seconds he's covered in bush flies. Leaping up, he grabs the insect repellent and liberally sprays every bit of exposed skin. But it's no deterrent to the flies. After attempting to drink beer and eat slices of cheese through clenched teeth to avoid swallowing flies, we decide that rapid movement is the only remedy to escape these creatures. Steve abruptly sets off, walking briskly up to the railway bridge while I follow, counting 44 flies on the back of his shirt.

The impressive steel Algebuckina Bridge is nearly 600 metres long, and sits high above the river. A gate prevents people from walking across it, but the tracks and sleepers are still there.

Several years ago I met John Moriarty AM, one of the Stolen Generations. His mother was a Yanyuwa woman, from Borroloola in the Gulf of Carpentaria, who spoke eight Aboriginal languages. His father was Irish, from Blennerville in County Kerry. When John was four years old his mother took him to the Roper River Mission, a couple of hundred kilometres away, for schooling.

'We stayed with relatives in the camp at the mission,' he explained, 'and in the morning she took me to school and picked me up when the school day was over.' He had been attending the school for several days when she came to collect him one afternoon, only to discover that he had been taken away in an army truck along with a number of other Aboriginal 'half-caste' kids and some adults.

The truck drove them to Alice Springs Telegraph Repeater Station, which was then an Aboriginal children's home. They stayed there for several days, before being put on the train to Adelaide and on another to Sydney.

John grew up in homes in NSW and Adelaide. Charles Perkins, who would later become a well-known Aboriginal rights activist, and his brother, Ernie, had been sent from Alice Springs to St Francis House in Adelaide by their mother to ensure they received a good education. The brothers lived in the same children's home as John. John and several other boys who had been removed from their families stayed in a hostel in Alice Springs during school holidays, where they spent time with the

The Peake

Perkins family. John described the trips the boys took on the Ghan from Adelaide to Alice Springs.

'The train travelled slowly at times, and we used to get off and collect bottles and rocks, and then throw the rocks to smash the bottles – not a good thing to do, when I think about it nowadays,' he adds. 'One of the boys was a very slow runner and the train was about to cross the Algebuckina Bridge. The rest of us were sitting on the train, watching him running to catch it. He just made it onto the last carriage before the bridge.'

As Steve and I stand looking at the bridge, with the gaps between the sleepers and the long drop to the river below, I realise it would have been impossible for this slow runner to have caught the train once it started crossing the bridge; I imagine his relief when he boarded it in the nick of time.

From the age of four until he was 15, John Moriarty didn't see his mother. He had, though, written several letters and tried to connect with her through the welfare department of the Northern Territory government. Having finished school and about to start a fitter and turner apprenticeship, he was on holiday in Alice Springs.

'I was wandering around the streets with my cousin Boofa,' he says. 'We looked across the road and saw this Aboriginal woman looking at me. She strode across the road and said, 'Where are you from?'

'I'm from Borroloola.' I responded.

'What's your name?'

'John Moriarty.'

'I'm your mother,' she said. We sat down in the gutter with Boofa and she told me about the family and that my grandmother, who had looked after me, had died.'

John describes himself as 'one of the fortunate children', because he reconnected with his mother and extended family, whereas some of the other boys never did. He went on to become the first Indigenous player to be selected for the Australian national soccer team, South Australia's first Indigenous university graduate, as well as an Aboriginal rights activist. In the 1980s he founded Balarinji Design Studio with his wife Ros Moriarty and they achieved national and international fame with the designs of the Wunala and Nalanji Dreaming Qantas aircraft. John and Ros have three children, and his family is all-important to him.

His son James got the idea to set up a soccer program at Borroloola for young boys and girls from the age of two to 16 years. So the family established John Moriarty Football, promoting good health and wellbeing, as well as supporting young athletes to achieve their soccer potential. Now the program operates in the Northern Territory, Queensland's Kuranda region and the Dubbo region of NSW; it coaches 1400 kids a week.

Back at the camp, Steve opens the bonnet of the four-wheel drive. A couple of days ago he noticed a crack in the radiator firewall support. He is concerned that it may have become longer, but after careful studying he decides it hasn't.

'But,' he says, 'if it gets significantly worse, we can't continue along off-road tracks all the way to Alice Springs. We'll have to get back on the bitumen.' Given he's a trained motor mechanic, I don't argue. Now that we've followed the Overland Telegraph Line this far, it doesn't bear thinking that we could be thwarted by this crack. But it hasn't increased in size – after all the rough tracks we've been on so far – so hopefully it isn't a cause for concern.

CHAPTER 24

Oodnadatta, the Angle Pole and Eringa

Two black swans fly across the red dawn sky. It's cold this morning and my fingers are so numb that I struggle to dismantle the swag. By quarter to eight we're back rattling along the track. Coolibahs and gidgees cast their long shadows across a creek in the lemon light, and saltbushes dot the flat country.

At Oodnadatta we pull up outside the Pink Roadhouse – aptly named because the main building, the adjoining fuel station and garage are all painted pink. An old Volvo estate – also pink – is parked out the front. Inside, behind the post-office counter, is Adriana Jacob, who is sporting a pink shirt and a matching pink hair tie. Adriana and her husband, Neville, once had the lease on the William Creek Hotel.

'We've gone pinker,' she says with a laugh, explaining that since they bought the roadhouse they have painted it a slightly deeper shade of pink.

The Pink Roadhouse was opened in the mid-1980s by Adam Plate and his wife, Lynnie. The couple arrived in Oodnadatta after following the railway from Alice Springs with a collection of camels, donkeys and horses 10 years earlier, and they stayed. In 2012, Adam died competing in the Adelaide Targa rally. Lynnie sold the roadhouse the following year to Neville and Adriana.

Beside Adriana, also in a pink shirt, is Hayley Nunn. Her grandfather, Dick Nunn, was a friend of the parents of Bobby Hunter, who I met at the William Creek Hotel. Hayley's father, Eddie Nunn, grew up at Anna Creek Station with Bobby Hunter, and he now manages Macumba Station, another Kidman property, just north of Oodnadatta.

We're tucking into egg and bacon rolls when Steve suddenly remembers the Monstermobile's third-party insurance and registration are due today. As there is no mobile reception we spend the next 15 minutes squashed in the telephone booth outside, feeding one- and two-dollar coins into the payphone while talking to the insurance company and Roads and Maritime Services. We return inside to drink our now lukewarm coffees, and Steve embarks on a lengthy discussion with the two men at the next table about suitable tyre pressures for the tracks. It is as if the spirit of Adam Plate is hovering above them. Passionate about vehicle safety on these outback roads he had printed a handwritten leaflet about optimum tyre pressures on dirt tracks, and when we were last here Adam and Steve had a long talk on the topic.

I get a key from the front counter to the Oodnadatta Museum, which is housed in the old railway station. For nearly 40 years, until the rail line was extended to Alice Springs in 1929, Oodnadatta was the railhead for goods and people travelling to Central Australia and a hub for the Afghans. There are photographs of the cameleers and their strings, and also ones of Ned Chong, who worked on the Overland Telegraph Line, before establishing extensive market gardens at nearby Hookey's Waterhole.

Today, over half of Oodnadatta's population of 200 is Aboriginal, consisting mostly of Arrernte and Yankunytjatjara people. I walk around the town and past the Oodnadatta Aboriginal School, empty because of holidays. A white girl and a black girl walk arm in arm down the street, and a woman stands in front of a weatherboard house, calling in language to her young son.

Back at the Pink Roadhouse, Steve is talking to Adriana. She looks so much happier now than I remember her when she worked at the William Creek Hotel. She says she found the long hotel evenings very hard, combined with having few places to go in that tiny isolated town when she had time off.

'Now I have my evenings, and I love it,' she smiles.

Adriana points me to books about the area compiled over 30 years ago by Adam and Lynnie Plate. I find some neatly typed pages about the Oodnadatta repeater station, established here in 1891 with the arrival of the railway, when the original Peake repeater station was closed. There is a black-and-white photograph of the repeater station. When I show it to

Oodnadatta, the Angle Pole and Eringa

Adriana she doesn't recognise it, but Hayley tells me where to find it. She adds with a grin: 'It's owned by Adriana and Neville.'

Steve and I find the old timber weatherboard building in a severe state of disrepair. Most of the paint has peeled off the wooden cladding, and the corrugated-iron verandah roof is sagging. There isn't much left to indicate that it was once a telegraph station. But walking round the building, much to my excitement, I come across a pile of old ceramic insulators. I pick up a long, thin porcelain insulator. Unlike the ones Fleur and I found at Merna Mora, it doesn't have an inner skirt, but the wooden pin is in far better condition. On top of the insulator FB41 is printed in black ink. Holding it, I feel I've unearthed another piece of forgotten history. I later discover that FB41 indicates it was made by the Melbourne's Fire Brick and Tile Company in 1941, so it would have been purchased for the Overland Telegraph Line upgrade during World War II.

Returning to the roadhouse, I ask Adriana if I can buy it.

'Just put something in there,' she says, pointing to the Royal Flying Doctor Service donation box on the counter.

Several kilometres north of Oodnadatta we reach the Angle Pole Memorial. It's marked not by a telegraph pole, but by a long, curved tree branch, enclosed by a wooden fence. It marks the point that the Overland Telegraph Line changed direction and headed more northwards. Attached to the fence is a pink-and-white sign handwritten by Adam Plate, explaining the significance of the site. When the railway was first extended here, the line was known as the Port Augusta to Angle Pole line.

The Oodnadatta Track continues westwards, but we take the less well-travelled track to the north, following the railway and the Overland Telegraph Line.

'What's that sound?' Steve says, as we sail over a sand dune before bouncing onto corrugations. We both listen intently. It's a rattle, but what's causing it? For the next 10 minutes we try to discern the source of the sound. Eventually I discover that the toolbox, which Steve carefully stowed behind his seat, is dislodged, so I jam it in place with a jumper.

The track becomes rough and rocky before metamorphosing into smooth red sand, as we cross Fogarty's Claypan. Then we're back, shaking across stony gibber country until suddenly the road changes back to sand. Steve pulls up on the crest of a dune, beside a rattlepod grevillea bush with its clusters of long, creamy flowers. As he gets out to check that the firewood on the roof rack is secure, I realise that we need something to eat this evening. But the meals I pre-cooked before leaving Sydney are all frozen solid in the freezer. I grab a packet of kangaroo sausages and put them on the dashboard, hoping the heat of the day's remaining sun through the windscreen will defrost them.

After a turning to Dalhousie Hot Springs we pass a couple of four-wheel drives travelling south, the first vehicles we've seen since turning off the Oodnadatta Track over 100 kilometres back. We are back on the gibber and the stony track is so rough that Steve slows to a crawl. After passing timber post and rail stockyards, we reach a large waterhole. A rope hangs from a coolibah at the edge of the water, and black embers in the sand indicate several recent fires. It's the perfect spot to camp for the night.

As the sun goes down a flock of corellas flies over the water, and a pair of galahs nudge back and forth along a branch of the coolibah. Studying the map, we conclude we must be at Eringa. This waterhole and the cattle yards are part of Eringa Station, the first property Sidney Kidman bought on his own after his brother and business partner Sackville died in 1899. Purchasing this lease was of such significance to Sidney that he gave the name Eringa to both his home at Kapunda and later his house in Adelaide. But Eringa Station wasn't one of his most successful properties; it suffered several severe droughts during the time he owned it.

Sidney Kidman continued to buy properties. His method was to put down a deposit, muster the fat cattle on the new place, and head to the nearest telegraph station to sell them 'over the line' so he could immediately begin paying off the balance. His assets grew, but his lifestyle didn't change significantly. He was mostly away from home, usually in the saddle somewhere in the outback visiting one of his properties. He worked hard and alongside his men rather than sitting in an office, and he preferred sleeping in a swag beside a campfire to the comfort of a bed. He drank and smoked, but in moderation, and apparently he never swore. His expletive for a particularly troublesome steer was 'jolly tinker'.

By the early 1900s this cattle king's empire was well established and, in 1908, 51-year-old Sidney Kidman took his first overseas trip. He travelled to England with Isabel and their three daughters, Gertrude, Elma and Edna, and young son, Walter. Sidney Kidman's interactions with London's

Oodnadatta, the Angle Pole and Eringa

bus drivers caught the eye of the English press and caused an uproar in the Australian media. He used to sit up the front of the omnibuses, preferably next to the drivers and close to the horses, bombarding the drivers with questions and tipping them when they let him hold the reins. Discovering the drivers were worried about their futures, as horse-drawn buses were being phased out and replaced by motorbuses, he asked them if they would like to work for him. Kidman saw how well they treated their horses and believed they would make good stockmen. Kidman offered to pay the passage to Australia for the driver and his family. About 25 bus drivers took up his offer, and two of them went on to become station managers.

When Sidney Kidman was knighted in 1921, the English newspaper *The Times* described him as 'the largest landholder in the Empire', owning 'over 32,000,000 acres which carry some quarter of a million cattle and many thousand horses'. If his partnerships in properties had also been taken into account, those figures would have been doubled – 64 million acres or 259,000 square kilometres, an area larger than the whole of the United Kingdom.

Ringneck parrots fly in and out of the red gums overhanging the waterhole. We cook the sausages on the fire and eat them with salad, then I fill the billy can with water for tea and place it in the hot embers. Steve makes tea and pours it into our tin mugs.

As I sip my tea and Steve points out the first stars of the night, I imagine Sidney Kidman – whose favourite drink was tea – and his men camping in this exact same spot. I also think of John McDouall Stuart, who had camped here many years before Kidman, and the English tea lover, Charles Todd, who built this long telegraph line through the heart of the continent and started work at the age of 15. With his aptitude for mathematics, he was employed at the Royal Observatory in Greenwich as a human calculator, under Sir George Airy's plan to advance British astronomical science. He worked an eight-hour day in winter and a 12-hour day in summer, earning sixpence a day. I imagine what it must have been like for Stuart to lose both his parents when he was only 10 years old, and for Kidman with no memory of his father, who had died when he was not even a year old. He was five when his mother remarried the drinking, brawling farmhand Stephen Starr, who constantly ran up debts. Long before young Sidney left home at the age of 13, his childhood would have been marred by his stepfather. I wonder if these three men would have made such an impact on the continent if, in their early lives, fate had dealt them a different hand.

A wind in the early hours of the morning wakes me up. Steve is sound asleep, but I'm worried that the fire could reignite. Flames are licking the half-burnt timber, and the embers are glowing, so I make several trips back and forth from the waterhole with buckets of water and douse the fire pit. When I get back into the swag I lie awake, aware of the spirits of this magical place.

CHAPTER 25

Chambers Pillar

I fill the bucket with water from the creek and wash. Steve reckons it's too early for breakfast, but I devour the two cold sausages left over from last night in a slice of buttered bread.

Back on the rutted track, we pass an abandoned upturned car before pulling into Abminga siding. The long, single-storey buildings, constructed in the late 1920s when the line was extended from Oodnadatta to Alice Springs, are now empty shells. The ground is littered with pieces of corrugated iron that once made up the roofs. A large, elevated water tank stands beside the rusty rail tracks together with the remains of a wooden coal bin, a sign that this forgotten siding was once a major coaling station for trains.

We're bouncing along, listening to Bruce Springsteen and the Sessions Band's rendition of 'Further On (Up the Road)', when we reach the Northern Territory border. We hurtle northwards, before I look at the map and realise we've passed the next repeater station.

'We've missed Charlotte Waters,' I say to Steve.

'What?'

'We need to turn around.'

'*What*?' he says, in a tone that suggests my lax map reading is an inexcusable error. But eventually I persuade him to turn tail, and we retrace our steps to the few pieces of rubble – the remains of a stone wall, a rusty square tank and the remnants of some corrugated-iron tanks. This is all that's left of Charlotte Waters repeater station. Sitting on the stark and treeless gibber plain, it was nicknamed Bleak House. The original sandstone building had eight rooms and a 9000-gallon stone water tank in the courtyard. There was a blacksmith's shop, a cart shed and harness room, a paddock and stockyard and a second large water tank with a 20,000-gallon capacity. But in 1930, soon after the railway had been built, the telegraph station moved to Finke, north of here, and it was abandoned.

While we're walking around the desolate site, two white Toyota Landcruisers pull up, followed by a Hilux ute towing a large caravan. We've spent most of the last 24 hours alone, so the sudden appearance of these people is a jolt. Watching the drivers and passengers get out of the vehicles and walk across the dirt to read the faded information signs, I'm acutely conscious that they, like us, are travellers passing through with little or no connection to this country. Admittedly there is not much to see, but as they cast their eyes, with scant interest, over the remains, I find myself doubting my own journey. To me, travelling is a gift of discovery, not only of the place but also of the self and I hope that I never lack appreciation for what I find. But seeing these other four-wheel drivers stopping for a cursory look before driving on makes me dwell on what gives a journey significance. It is the places and people along the way and the final destination, but also it is the time – this segment of time out of everyday life – which makes it so precious.

The track becomes rich red sand, and signposts direct us to Finke, even though since the 1980s the town has been called Aputula. We fill up with fuel at the general store. Several dogs are lying outside, and zebra finches with their distinctive red beaks hop around a puddle of water under a tap. This remote community began as a railway siding in 1929. Most Europeans left the area after the major floods in 1973 and 1974 caused extensive track damage and the railway line was rerouted to the west. Today the population of Aputula numbers 200, consisting of Lower Southern Arrernte, Luritja, as well as Pitjantjatjara and Yankunytjatjara people.

Four kilometres out of town we cross the wide sandy bed of the Finke River. We alternate between following the route of the Finke Desert Race, the annual off-road motor race, and the Old Ghan railway track. Spinifex, creamy-coloured mulla mulla and paddy melons grow in the red sand, and a single desert oak stands on a dune.

We pass a couple of rusty upturned cars. Desert oaks pepper the

Chambers Pillar

landscape – thin young ones that look like old men, and the more mature ones with their broader branches. Steve negotiates a plethora of sleeper pins as we shake along what was once the railway track. The track passes through a rock cutting before Bundooma Siding, where 'Fuck You Buck Rogers' is written in large letters on the huge, elevated water tank.

On the track to Maryvale Homestead, much to my delight, we pass several Oppenheimer poles, one of which still has its ceramic insulator. Apart from the odd solitary one, until now we've seen Oppenheimer poles only at telegraph stations or the odd railway siding; I wonder if these Oppenheimer poles had been part of the original line. We don't stop at the homestead to ask, because we're taking a 45-kilometre deviation along a rough track on Maryvale Station to visit the rock called Idracowra by the Traditional Arrernte Owners, and later named Chambers Pillar.

We cross the wide, dry bed of the Hugh River and follow the track over the rocks and through the sand bowls. Brahmin cattle, with their long ears and humped backs, roam the paddocks. Between the cushions of spinifex are spreads of silver tails and among them blue and pink eremophila. A swallow swoops across swathes of Mitchell grass and lilac and pink mulla mulla.

With the light fading, we realise we're not going to reach our destination before dark, so we start looking for a place to stop for the night. Fences on either side of the track mean there's nowhere to pull over – until we reach the top of a high ridge. Here we can see in every direction. In the distance, across the plain ahead of us, is the distinctive finger of rock, silhouetted against the darkening blue sky.

Steve brings the vehicle to a stop and turns off the engine. I look for the least stony piece of ground on which to set up the swag. We decide not to light a fire this evening and instead warm up the lamb curry I've defrosted on the gas stove. The temperature has plummeted with the setting sun, so I put on my thermals, three jumpers and a jacket, then can't move my arms, so remove two layers.

This is our last night of camping, as tomorrow we'll be in Alice Springs. It's been so special to move slowly across the country and sleep on the ground over the last week. We sit gazing at the clear night sky and the Milky Way blazed across it. Then we climb into the swag leaving the canvas open at the top so we can see the stars through the mosquito net. I lie on my back taking a last lingering look before falling asleep.

It's still dark when we wake up and Steve sees a shooting star as he clambers out of the swag. I wiggle into my clothes under the covers and rise to see the first pale hint of dawn below the morning star.

The eastern sky metamorphoses from burnt orange to a bluish yellow as we drive down the steep, stony track. Mesas with their flat tops are silhouettes on the dawn sky and ahead is the pillar of rock. Rolled out along either side of the track are carpets of wildflowers – native fuchsia and white flowering tobacco, alongside long tails growing like grass across the sand, and clumps of yellow billy buttons.

At the entrance gate to the Chambers Pillar Historical Reserve are instructions to use UHF Channel 10 while travelling through the eight kilometres of sand dunes to the pillar itself. So at every bend and crest I announce our approach, only to be met with stony silence, except for interjections from Steve on my radio communication style. I'm adamant that I'm being friendly, while he claims I'm imprecise, to which I take umbrage. We drive most of the way without a word, except for my radio calls. But our disagreement dissolves when we catch our first sight of the rock up close.

The handful of campers near the pillar aren't yet up, so we're alone at this sacred site. In Arrernte tradition, this sandstone monolith is Itirkawara, a knob-tailed gecko spirit ancestor. A huge, powerfully built man of superhuman strength, Itirkawara had a violent temper and killed several ancestors. He disregarded the strict marriage code and took a wife from the wrong skin group, so his relatives banished the couple. The pair went into the desert. Itirkawara was raging with fury, and his wife shrank from him in deep shame. Here, among the dunes, they turned into stone – Itirkawara into the pillar, and his wife, still turning her face from him in shame, into a nearby rock.

John McDouall Stuart saw this remarkable rock for the first time on his fourth expedition. Travelling in 1860 with only William Kekwick and 18-year-old Ben Head, he was on his second attempt to reach the north of the continent and find a route for the Overland Telegraph Line. Stuart described it in his journal as having the appearance from a distance 'of a locomotive engine with its funnel'. Although Stuart named landmarks and rivers left, right and centre as he crossed Central Australia, he

Chambers Pillar

didn't name this one. But when his journal was published in Adelaide an addition had been made, saying that Stuart had named it Chambers Pillar in honour of James Chambers. Apparently Chambers, as Stuart's benefactor, had a tendency to alter names in Stuart's journal to those of his own choosing, so it could have been the doing of Chambers.

Steve walks around the mound on which this magnificent tower of sandstone stands, while I gaze at the red rock. James Chambers and his wife, Catherine, were granted a free passage to South Australia in 1836 because he had been an agricultural labourer in England, and farm labourers were considered essential for the success of the new colony. But Chambers wasn't settling for the life of a farmhand. He was a natural entrepreneur, and soon after disembarking the ship he saw a need for wagons to transport newly arrived settlers and their possessions in the young colony. So he built a cart and became a carrier before establishing a transport business. By the end of the 1850s he and his two brothers were among the largest landowners in Australia.

Like Stuart, Chambers had also lost his parents at a young age and both men were heavy drinkers. When Chambers transported gold from Victoria to Adelaide with the Commissioner of Police, Alexander Tolmer, he fitted the cart with a false bottom and filled it with brandy. Every few miles he would stop the cart and have a nip and give one to each of the constables on the escort. But whereas alcohol charged Chambers up and drove him to accomplish, Stuart was described by one of the stockmen of William Finke, his other benefactor, as the 'beastliest drunk'. Alcohol made him loud, emotional and sometimes morose. And while James Chambers had wealth, a wife and children, John McDouall Stuart had none of these.

The 50-metre-tall rock stack is a captivating sight. Its top has an iron-rich hard red cap, which protects the paler softer sandstone below it, and it stands on a mound of mustard-coloured sulphurous sandstone. I climb the steps up the mound to the base of the pillar and here, carved in the pale sandstone are 'J Ross' and nearby 'A G 1870'. 'A G' probably stands for Alfred Giles, who was second-in-command to John Ross in the Overland Telegraph Line exploring party, sent out by Charles Todd ahead of the construction crews to survey the route and find water as well as timber suitable for poles. But the country surrounding the pillar lacked both timber and water, so the Overland Telegraph Line was built 30 kilometres to the east near the Hugh River and Maryvale Homestead.

Also carved in the rock are the names of William Hayes and his wife, Mary, who came through here in 1884. Hayes worked at dam sinking and fencing for Sir Thomas Elder, who had recently acquired Mount Burrell, the name at that time for Maryvale Station. In 1890, with their bullock teams and wagons, William and Mary brought a consignment of Oppenheimer poles to Alice Springs to replace the wooden ones on the Overland Telegraph Line. The couple took up land around Alice Springs, and 20 years later they had established themselves as successful Central Australian pastoralists. The Hayes family purchased the leases for Owen Springs, Undoolya Station and Mount Burrell, which was renamed Maryvale after Mary Hayes. Mary and the Hayes daughters shared the station work with William and the sons; the women mustered, branded, drove and slaughtered as well as any man.

Among the other names engraved in the stone are those of R.E. Warne and W.D. Randall, who both worked on the Overland Telegraph Line, and that of P. Cheeseman. A.P. Cheeseman was a haulage contractor on the telegraph line. I'm torn between being fascinated by these names, which capture the early moments of the telegraph line's history, and the sense that, regardless of their historical significance, these names are graffiti on a sacred site. Metal steps and viewing platforms have been built beside the rock so that visitors can see these carvings up close. But to me they also seem like scars on this magnificent monolith.

I look down at the red sand below, peppered with spinifex and swathes of long tails catching the morning light as they shimmer in the slight breeze. As I walk down I meet a relief ranger who tells me the wildflowers are so abundant here because a fire recently came through and there was rain in the summer. I walk away from the pillar and a magpie, perched on a dead tree, stares at me with its dark, soul-piercing eyes.

CHAPTER 26

Halfway and Nowhere to Stay

I find Steve with his head under the bonnet of the Monstermobile, studying the crack in the radiator firewall support.

'It's longer,' he says gloomily. Not wanting to exacerbate the problem, he drives very slowly back to Maryvale Homestead with both of us praying the crack won't lead to a break.

On the wall of the homestead shop there's a map of the area showing the original Overland Telegraph Line running past here. Wanting to find out if the Oppenheimer poles we saw yesterday were on the original route, I ask a woman in her 20s behind the counter. Her name is Rebecca; she's a northern English backpacker working here for just a few months, so she has no idea about the poles and the station owners aren't around.

As there's no mobile reception here, Rebecca lets me use the landline to call our friend Kelly Rae to let her know that we'll be in Alice Springs this afternoon. Kelly has been living in Alice for the last couple of years and invited us to stay with her. But now she tells me she's about to leave Alice and has sublet her house and moved in with friends, so we'll have to find alternative accommodation.

Leaving Maryvale Homestead, we pass more Oppenheimer poles beside the track. I later learn that these and the ones we saw yesterday are originals from the Overland Telegraph Line, and I wonder if they were from the consignment that William and Mary Hayes brought in their bullock wagons to the Centre in 1890.

Thirteen kilometres north we reach the derelict Rodinga railway siding. The Old South Road runs alongside the old railway track, and the country on either side of it is dotted with young deserts oaks and towering ghost gums. We're enveloped in a cloud of dust as an old Ford sedan whistles past. Approaching the East MacDonnell Ranges is a line of telegraph poles. Some are Oppenheimer poles and others are pieces of railway line with wooden cross bars supporting the ceramic insulators. In some places the wire is still running through the insulators, in others it's broken. We roll onto the bitumen after eight days of dirt tracks. And as we drive through Heavitree Gap we pass the new Ghan train – the camel logo on the side of its carriages – as it moves slowly over the rail track beside the road heading south.

John McDouall Stuart crossed the MacDonnell Ranges 45 kilometres west of here, but Overland Telegraph Line surveyor William Mills discovered this pass, a sacred throughway known by the local Arrernte people as Ntaripe. Mills named it Heavitree after his school in Devon. Initially the Overland Telegraph Line ran through Temple Bar, now known as Honeymoon Gap, further west, until it was rerouted through here. The Gap heralds our arrival in Alice Springs. It feels such an achievement to be here, and I can see Steve's relief that the Monstermobile held together. We drive along Telegraph Terrace and see a road sign; it's 1515 kilometres to Darwin. I'm over halfway along the Overland Telegraph Line.

We drive to a campground near the town centre where we stayed a few years ago. I can't wait to walk to Todd Mall and have a coffee at a café. But we arrive only to be told that the campground is full. So I start ringing hotels in town, thinking what a treat it will be to have a long shower and sleep in clean crisp white sheets. But the hotels are also full as the Alice Springs Show is on this weekend. The other campsites I contact are booked too. So we end up back at Heavitree Gap Caravan Park, the only place that can accommodate us. Here we're corralled to a small patch of grass by a wiry, grey-haired man who tells us he used to be a cook on the Old Ghan and also worked as a fettler.

Kelly pulls up in a dark-blue four-wheel drive with an Aboriginal dot design along the side. She works for the Central Desert Shire Council as a counsellor in remote communities north of Alice Springs. Sporting bright pink lipstick and dressed in layers of lilac, maroon and magenta wool, she leans out her window.

'You only come to Alice if you're a missionary, a mercenary or a misfit,' she says with a laugh, before getting out of the vehicle and giving us a hug. Now in her 40s, Kelly was born and bred in Sydney and had a very urban existence. Neither Steve nor I could imagine her living in Alice Springs, but she took to the outback town from the moment she arrived.

Kelly and I worked together on a health program at Sydney community radio station 2SER. She was doing a communication degree and I was learning the ropes in journalism. She then lived in the same block of units as us for several years. Despite loving the Red Centre and her work, Kelly finds the isolation hard, so she has decided to head back east. She arrives with her existential problem of belonging and life purpose and a pot of coleslaw. Steve makes a call to a work mate while Kelly and I are talking; he's thinking about the redundancies the company is making and wondering if he still has a job.

It's nearly dark when he finishes the call, so he fires up one of the gas barbecues and cooks patties while I make a salad. Kelly has to leave soon after we've eaten. The campsite feels decidedly gloomy. We're not allowed to light a fire, but it's too cold to sit outside without one, so Steve suggests we go to the nearby Heavitree Gap Tavern and have a drink. Inside, a large screen is showing a football match and people press coins into pokie machines. But it's warm in here. Steve orders a beer and I have a glass of red wine and we perch on high stools at a small table.

'To reaching Alice Springs,' I say, as we clink glasses.

'I can't keep travelling north with you,' Steve says. 'With the uncertainty at work I need to get back to Sydney.' I can fully understand his desire to get home as soon as possible, but it's a surprise as he's always so keen to explore new places. While I am assuring him that whatever happens with his job we'll be fine, whirling around in my head is the dilemma of getting from Alice Springs to Darwin.

It's minus two degrees the following morning. I'm adamant, after our early starts for the last week, that we should have a leisurely cooked breakfast. Steve lights the barbecue and the gas hob next to it, but because of the wind the bacon doesn't cook and the billy doesn't boil. I collect a couple of wheelie bins and position them to create a breeze barrier, and the bacon starts to slowly sizzle as a family of five from Lithgow in NSW surround us, hovering around the flames to get warm.

Steve scours the campsite and finds a less breezy barbecue, one that is not only protected but also in a sunny spot. We relocate there and cook bacon, eggs, tomatoes and toast. We are sitting having a leisurely breakfast in the sun when an Aboriginal man approaches us.

'Did you complain about me being noisy last night?' he asks.

'No,' Steve replies.

'We didn't hear any noise last night,' I add. We were exhausted and slept like logs.

'Someone said the noise came from Site 23, my site.'

'Well, it definitely wasn't us,' says Steve. The man is clearly agitated. Steve is trying to reassure him when a white woman in her 70s who, like the man, is also a caravan park permanent resident, comes up.

'There was a group of students who were very loud last night,' she says.

'I suffer from anxiety,' the man mutters. 'I don't need this. I'll just move out.'

'Come with me to the office,' she says to him, 'I'm going to report this.'

Ten minutes later the pair return, having resolved the issue, and soon after I'm dancing around the barbecue to the strains of Dire Straits pulsing from Site 23's caravan as its resident tinkers with the engine of his old BMW. But the greatest treat is having a hot shower and feeling clean again. I throw all our dirty washing into a couple of large machines and buy pegs from the supermarket while Steve checks over the vehicle before the long drive back to Sydney.

Kelly has the day off work, and pulls up in her troopie at 9.30. We leave Steve with his head under the bonnet of the Monstermobile and head into the centre of town. She takes me to the Red Dog Café on Todd Mall for a treat, large mugs of coffee and almond friands. We sit in the sun and discuss how I can get from here to Darwin.

I decided before leaving Sydney that cycling the 1500 kilometres of bitumen road between Alice Springs and Darwin wasn't possible because the distance between roadhouses is often 100 kilometres and sometimes more than 130. Taking a bus is an alternative, so we go to the Greyhound bus office. The woman there says I can take my bicycle, and get off at towns along the way. Kelly says she drives every week to Ti-Tree, 200 kilometres north of Alice Springs, and she could ask her boss if I could travel with her. I like that idea; I could take the Greyhound bus north from there. But the downside is that the bus leaves Alice Springs every evening, so I would be arriving in some towns in the middle of the night and boarding the bus again in the middle of the following night. Another option is to hire a car, so Kelly takes me to the tourist information centre, where a woman named Julie kindly takes a lot of time to explain the places she thinks are safe to stay when travelling alone. After intensive fact-gathering and more cups of coffee, I'm still no nearer to formulating a plan, as neither of these options feel right. Eventually I decide that the best course of action is drive back to Sydney with Steve tomorrow, and once there work out how I'll complete this journey.

CHAPTER 27

Back to Alice Springs

I stare out of the small window at the ground thousands of metres below with its red ridges and gullies and occasional pockets of water – lakes held in the redness – and wavering lines of long, dry creek beds. The plane touches down. It is seven weeks since Steve and I left Alice Springs.

As we drove down the Stuart Highway on our way back to Sydney, Steve had suggested we could fly back to Alice Springs and drive to Darwin together. But once we returned to Sydney and I started planning the final stage of the journey, he was unable to get time off work. A friend, Alison Martin, wanted a holiday in the Northern Territory, and she agreed to drive with me from Alice Springs to Darwin on the proviso that we go swimming in the springs en route.

Another friend told me that his sister and her boyfriend had a week's holiday delivering a campervan from North Queensland to Brisbane. I found the company on the internet and rang the telephone number. The woman at the other end of the line said she would ring me if a vehicle needed to be delivered from Alice Springs to Darwin. I never heard from her again, so I booked us a hire car and accommodation along the way.

Kelly Rae has left Alice Springs and Alison has suggested we stay at the YHA. I'm apprehensive that I'll be dossing down in a dormitory full of drunken backpackers. But I need to save money, and as I'm on my own in Alice Springs for four days before Alison arrives, I decide to brave the YHA at least for one night.

The airport transfer bus stops on Leichhardt Terrace, and the driver tells me the YHA is around the corner. There's an old reel-to-reel projector at its front entrance, a nod to the art deco building's previous incarnation as the Pioneer (Walk-In) Open Air Theatre.

Back to Alice Springs

Amy at reception gives me a key card to a four-bed dormitory and tells me to take a pair of sheets and a pillowcase. I walk through to the open-air central area. At the far end is the original projection house with its tiny high windows, and on a wall is a black-and-white photograph taken in the 1940s, when the theatre was filled with lines of deckchairs. Now there are only a few rows of deckchairs and much of the courtyard is taken up by a swimming pool.

I gingerly open the door to the dormitory. 'Hello,' says a New Zealander with grey hair lying on a lower bunk, 'I'm Lesley.' While I make up the top bunk opposite, Lesley tells me she has been in Alice Springs for a couple of months but is now on her way out. 'I'm helping at a wildlife care centre with the joeys' evening feed. I just wish my grandchildren could see the creatures,' she adds. 'They're beautiful.' As the door closes behind her, I realise my roommate is a far cry from the type of backpacker I was expecting.

I head off to visit the old telegraph repeater station, walking the four kilometres from town up the dry bed of the Todd River. Ringneck parrots peck the ground between the yellow billy buttons. The riverbed changes from rock to sand, and in some places to a moist and sticky mud. Initially there are houses on either side of the river, and a girl cycles along the path on the bank above me. But soon I leave the town behind and am completely alone.

Bluebells grow in the sand and daisies protrude from a bed of dry leaves. On the banks are river red gums and red rocks rise beyond them. A dingo pads onto the riverbed ahead and stands, staring at me. We hold each other's gaze as I walk past. I look back over my shoulder. It's lying down but still holding me in its sight.

As I see two men walking ahead of me – wondering if they are Eastern Arrernte, the people who have inhabited this area for over 20,000 years – I catch my first glimpse of the telegraph station. The Overland Telegraph Line surveyor, William Mills, the first European to find Ntaripe/Heavitree Gap, was also the first white man to find the springs here, which the Arrernte call Atherreyurre. Mills called the main one Alice Spring which, he recounted, 'I had the honour of naming after Mrs Todd.'

I climb onto the bank and follow the telegraph wire running from Oppenheimer pole to Oppenheimer pole toward the telegraph station.

Steve and I first visited here eight years ago, but at the time we knew very little about the Overland Telegraph Line. Now, having seen Beltana, Strangways Springs, the Peake and what's left at Charlotte Waters, I'm struck by how well preserved the Alice Springs Telegraph Station buildings are.

The telegraph station is now a museum and historical reserve. I pay the entrance fee and head to the barracks. Erected in 1871, this combined telegraph office and men's quarters was the first colonial building in the area. It has a gun hole in its thick stone wall, as it was designed to be defended if required, although that was never the case.

It was from here that the first telegraph message from Alice Springs to Adelaide was sent on 3 January 1872, carrying the news that C.W.I. Kraagen had died of thirst 100 kilometres down the line. He had been travelling to Alice Springs to take up the position of stationmaster. He was accompanied by two operators, Mueller and Watson, and the three of them had gone ahead of the slower main party with its loaded bullock teams. Three days out from Charlotte Waters they were unable to find water. They searched unsuccessfully for two days until Kraagen, who had the best mount, rode on alone in search. For the following two days Mueller and Watson continued to search for water. In desperation, they killed one of their horses and drank its blood to survive. Having energy to continue, they found water that day. Several days later Kraagen's body was found near an angle pole by a linesman. He had died of thirst. Ninety years later Kraagen's grandson found his grave and headstone – a piece of tin – and punctured with a nail the message 'perished here for want of water'. Mueller took Kraagen's place as the first stationmaster of Alice Springs.

The other sandstone buildings – including the stationmaster's residence and its separate kitchen, the battery room and post and telegraph office – were constructed later. In the barracks is a display of a dozen Meidinger battery cells, each about 25 centimetres high. A glass jar containing copper sulphate was upended into a jar of water to create a copper sulphate solution. At the bottom of the solution was a lead plate electrode. From this an insulated copper wire ran through the solution and out of the jar, which stood in a larger jar containing a solution of magnesium sulphate, with a zinc cylinder as an electrode.

Back to Alice Springs

Each battery cell created about 1.5 volts of power, so it took a great many cells to produce the 120 volts needed for the telegraph line to operate. These battery cells had to be maintained, so in addition to all those in use there were others being cleaned and recharged.

Beside the telegraph office is an Oppenheimer pole on which are eight large ceramic insulators with a line attached to each one. The lines, which run down to a grooved wooden board inside the telegraph office building, carried the power from the battery room to boost the line voltage so the signal was strong enough to reach the next repeater station. On the table in the telegraph office is the repeater, used by a telegraph operator to retransmit all the Morse code telegrams and press messages coming in, before sending them south to Adelaide or north to Darwin.

Walking outside, I notice a circular evaporation tank built into the ground nearby. Not only were the telegraph staff transmitting messages, they were also collecting weather data. Every four hours the temperature, air pressure and wind strength were measured and telegraphed to Adelaide. Rate of evaporation was measured daily, as was rainfall when it occurred. With the Overland Telegraph Line repeater stations stretching the length of the continent, and numerous telegraph stations throughout South Australia, Charles Todd was collecting meteorological data for a huge land mass.

I walk from building to building, imagining life here in the early years. The station was staffed by six men: the stationmaster, an assistant telegraph operator and four linesmen. The linesmen were responsible for maintaining 290 kilometres of line, which ran halfway to Charlotte Waters southwards and halfway to Barrow Creek northwards. From a lonely outpost, this telegraph station grew into a small village, home to many telegraphists and their families and linesmen. Many local Arrernte people worked as housemaids, child carers, labourers and stockmen.

The discovery of gold in the East MacDonnell Ranges in 1887 brought hundreds of men north along the telegraph line to seek their fortunes. The Alice Springs Telegraph Station was the only colonial settlement in the area, and the staff couldn't provide enough food and medical supplies for these gold-diggers. So a year later the South Australian government gazetted the town several kilometres south of the telegraph station, and although John McDouall Stuart hadn't travelled through this region – the closest he got was 45 kilometres to the west – it was named Stuart.

In her book *Alice on the Line*, Doris Blackwell describes the nine years of her childhood, from 1899 to 1908, when her father, Thomas Bradshaw, was stationmaster at the Alice Springs Telegraph Station. Her mother, Atalanta, was 33 years old when she took the train from Adelaide with her four children and a young governess. Aged eight, Doris was the oldest child; the youngest was her brother at only 18 months. Thomas Bradshaw met them at the railhead at Oodnadatta, and from there they made the 18-day buggy journey to Alice Springs.

In the upstairs room of the Adelaide Post and Telegraph Office on King William Street, Thomas Bradshaw had been in charge of the night telegraph staff. But here in isolated Alice Springs he was not only stationmaster but also a Special Magistrate. On court days, the staff dining room at the telegraph station was transformed into the courtroom where Thomas Bradshaw administered justice. Numerous cases of cattle spearing by Aboriginal people were brought before him. He was 'eminently fair', his daughter writes. 'He even tried to extend justice to the Aborigines and temper it with mercy; at the turn of the century in Central Australia that was not at all an everyday occurrence.'

World news passed through Alice Springs Telegraph Station on its way to Adelaide. But Thomas Bradshaw scrupulously observed the rule of not divulging information, and he never imparted news to his family, even though it would be published in all the Australian papers the following day. The only concession to this principle of secrecy was international tragedy, so he did tell his family the news of Queen Victoria's death in 1901, the end of the Boer War in 1902 and the San Francisco earthquake of 1906.

Atalanta gave birth to three more children while the family was in Alice Springs, and each time she was assisted by Annie Meyers, the only other white woman in the area. Rations were delivered to the telegraph station once a year. For months, Doris would watch her parents making long lists of what was needed, from food to fabric and replacements for cups and saucers that had been broken. The lists were sent on the mail coach to Adelaide merchants who supplied the goods. Then one day a long string of camels, each loaded with large, creaking wooden packing cases, padded into the station compound. School and work would stop with the yearly arrival of supplies.

Back to Alice Springs

Doris Blackwell reminisces about the mob of 60 horses at the telegraph station that grazed along the riverbank. Every day 30 horses were brought into the yard. The following day they were released and the other 30 horses were brought into the yard. The horses had to be ready at short notice in case there was a break or a fault in the line. When that happened, an Aboriginal rider and an operator left from each of the two stations between which the fault had occurred. One pair rode north and the other south until the problem was found.

The Alice Springs Telegraph Station stopped operating in January 1932, when the new post and telegraph office opened in Stuart. The following year, due to popular demand, Stuart was renamed Alice Springs.

The telegraph station grounds and the surrounding area were made an Aboriginal reserve, administered by the federal government's Department of Native Affairs, to provide a home and school for mixed race Aboriginal children. It's heart-wrenching thinking about the period from 1932 to 1942 when the telegraph station became 'The Bungalow' and was home to these children, most of whom had been forcibly removed from their Aboriginal mothers.

In 1914 an Arabunna woman, Topsy Smith, arrived in Stuart from the Arltunga goldfields after the death of her husband, Welsh miner Bill Smith. She came with seven of their children and a large herd of goats, which the family grazed on Akeyulerre. It became known as Billy Goat Hill. A shed was constructed opposite the Stuart Arms Hotel and the Smith family lived in the shed. Under the *Aboriginals Ordinance Act 1911*, part Aboriginal children were removed from their families, so they were brought to The Bungalow, and Topsy Smith took them in and looked after them.

As the number of children grew, Ida Standley, was appointed matron. She had been appointed by the South Australian government as Alice Springs's first schoolteacher and had ruffled white parents' feathers by suggesting that white and part-Aboriginal children should attend classes together. The white parents objected so she taught their children in the mornings and the part-Aboriginal children in the afternoon. She insured that the mixed race children grew up with both self-esteem and a basic education. By 1923, 60 children were living in two iron sheds, tirelessly cared for by Ida Standley and Topsy Smith. Five years later overcrowding forced The Bungalow to move to Jay Creek, 50 kilometres west of Alice Springs, and then in 1932 to the Alice Springs telegraph station.

Alec Ross grew up at The Bungalow and now conducts tours of the telegraph station. He is a great-grandson of John Ross, who was commissioned by Charles Todd to lead the exploring party to find the best route for the Overland Telegraph Line and select suitable places for stations. Sadly, Alec has recently had a stroke, so I don't have the opportunity to talk with him. His mother lived a traditional life on Neutral Junction Station, near Barrow Creek, where Alec was born, and worked for his father. Aged three, Alec was taken away from his mother because he was unwell. After a spell in hospital he came to live in The Bungalow and he did not see his mother again for 46 years.

In 1942 Alice Springs became the supply base for the war effort on Australia's northern shores. Trains carrying thousands of troops would arrive each week. From here the troops and their supplies travelled in military trucks up the recently bituminised road to Darwin.

The telegraph station was used to accommodate what were known as the Native Labour Gangs – the Aboriginal people recruited to help the war effort. So in early 1942, Alec Ross and most of the other children at The Bungalow were moved to a Methodist mission on Croker Island, northeast of Darwin.

Three weeks after the children arrived on the island in February 1942, the Japanese bombed Darwin. As the bombing persisted, a message was sent to Croker Island saying a boat was being sent to evacuate the Europeans. But the 95 children were to remain there until after the wet season. Three young women missionaries – Margaret Somerville, Jess March and Olive Peake – stayed to look after the children until April, when a boat arrived to take them all back to the mainland.

Guided by two Aboriginal trackers, the missionaries and children walked 500 kilometres through Arnhem Land to Pine Creek, where they were loaded onto a cattle rail truck and then onto army convoy trucks heading south. When they reached Alice Springs, the children stayed at the telegraph station for a few days before taking the Ghan to Adelaide, and from there they went to a children's home near Sydney.

The Department of Native Affairs resumed control of the telegraph station reserve at the end of the war. Aboriginal people who visited Alice

Back to Alice Springs

Springs were allowed to camp at the old telegraph station. By the end of the 1950s there were 400 people living at the telegraph station, and in 1962 all permanent residents were moved to a new site at Amoonguna, 14 kilometres south-east of the town.

***

I climb up nearby Trig Hill. From the top I can see bushland in every direction, the only buildings in sight are those of the telegraph station below, with the MacDonnell Ranges rising behind them. I walk to the small telegraph station cemetery and back to the station, my head buzzing with its history.

At the telegraph station I find a tall grey-bearded man I saw earlier in the YHA. A pair of binoculars hangs around his neck, and he has a long-lens camera trained on a white-plumed honeyeater drinking from a dripping tap. His name is Jack, and he's about to spend three days with a local 'birding expert', he tells me. We walk together back along the river path to the hostel.

It's dark by the time we get there. I go to the supermarket to buy food. Back in the hostel kitchen, a couple of women show me where to find the pots, pans and utensils, and I make myself a bowl of pasta. A young couple are sitting down one end of the long table, and the women who helped me earlier are deep in conversation at the other end. Feeling slightly self-conscious, I sit on my own. Back in the room getting the teabags and chocolate I brought from Sydney, I see that Lesley is already asleep. She doesn't stir later as I pack and unpack bags to search for my pyjamas, thermals and beanie on this sub-zero night. Nor does she wake in the middle of the night when I descend from the top bunk, scramble around looking for my boots and clomp along the verandah to the bathroom.

At seven o'clock in the morning Lesley's alarm clock goes off, and she leaves to assist with the joeys' morning feed. I'm left in bed thinking how lucky I am to have her as a roommate. In the kitchen this morning, a woman in her 60s, who introduces herself as Joy, is at the stove making a feta cheese, spinach and sweet potato omelette. Sitting on the sofa and sipping tea from a porcelain mug is an immaculately turned-out woman called Rose. She tells me she's doing volunteer work for the Alice Springs's Desert Festival, which opens in a couple of weeks. I'm eating my boiled egg and toast when Lesley returns from feeding the joeys and cooks herself eggs and bacon. As she sits down beside me with a pot of freshly ground coffee, I decide I definitely want to stay here rather than sit alone in a hotel.

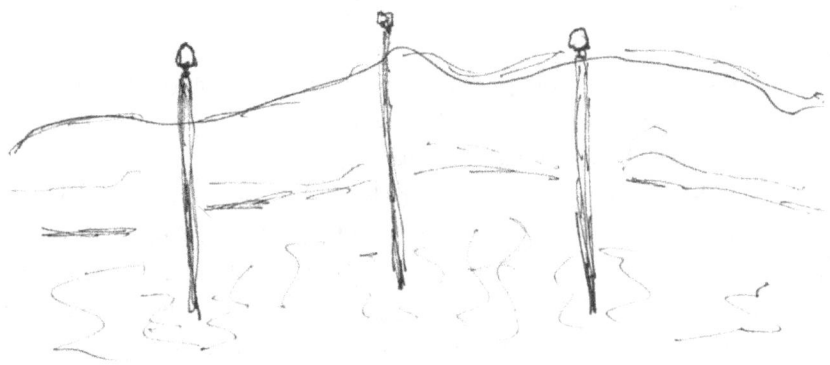

CHAPTER 28

M.K. Turner

I sit in the courtyard looking again at Margaret Kemarre Turner's book *Iwenhe Tyerrtye: What It Means to Be an Aboriginal Person*. Written partly in Arrernte and partly in English, it's about Aboriginal connection to Land, each other and the importance of language to identity. It also talks about the changes since the arrival of non-Aboriginal people in Australia. I first came across this book in my local library. The construction of the Overland Telegraph Line brought colonial settlers to Central Australia, and it changed the Indigenous way of life forever. I am fascinated to talk to Margaret Kemarre Turner, known as MK, because she has experience and understanding of the traditional Aboriginal way of life as well as the non-Aboriginal way. Kelly Rae put me in touch with Jodie Clarkson, who has arranged for me to meet MK.

I change into a skirt so that I look respectable for this esteemed Elder and leg it down Leichhardt Terrace. Jodie is waiting for me there, outside the Aboriginal Interpreter Service office where she works. We climb into her four-wheel drive. She turns the ignition but it doesn't start.

'It's just been serviced,' she says plaintively.

Neither of us verbally acknowledges that vehicle idiosyncrasies must sometimes just be ignored, but as we sit and discuss a bean pod on the dashboard, it's apparent we agree on this. Jodie, in her early 40s with long, strawberry blonde hair, tells me she has lived in Alice Springs for 18 years, and has a six-year-old son, Jacob.

Five minutes later Jodie turns the ignition key again and without a cough or splutter the engine starts. We drive toward Heavitree Gap, turn into a residential area and stop outside a single-storey house. MK and her daughter, Amelia Turner, are sitting in the shade drinking mugs of tea. Two little boys run around the garden, playing with a toy trailer filled with mud.

We sit and Jodie, always eloquent, discusses the children's language book that Amelia has written, launched at Alice Springs Public Library earlier in the week. MK, in a black shirt, long brown skirt and black plimsolls, is in her late 70s, her face unlined and youthful and her hair hardly grey.

There is no babble of introduction. We sit in silence, sometimes punctuated by a sentence or two.

'MK met the Queen,' Jodie says.

'Oh,' I reply, unsure of what to say.

'When the Queen came to Alice Springs in 2000.'

Jodie tells me later that she was very nervous when she asked MK if she would like to meet the Queen, not knowing MK's feelings on the matter. But she was keen, and took the opportunity to give the Queen a videotape of local Aboriginal people pleading for the abandonment of the Northern Territory's mandatory sentencing legislation.

It is decided that Jodie will take MK and me to the Aboriginal Interpreter Service to talk. As we drive back to Leichhardt Terrace, MK tells Jodie that her Centrelink payment has been stopped and that she needs to go to Anglicare and get help to sort this out. So we head to the Anglicare centre on Bloomfield Street.

The three of us go in, and at reception MK asks for Deng, who has previously helped her with Centrelink issues. When Deng, a Sudanese refugee, arrives the four of us go into a small room. There are significant numbers of Sudanese in Alice Springs, Jodie tells me later. She says the population of Alice Springs is roughly one-third new immigrants, one-third white Australians, and one-third Aboriginal First Australians from many language groups.

Deng dials the Centrelink number and puts the telephone on speaker in the middle of the table. 'Hello, this is Mrs Turner,' MK begins. MK explains that the payments she received for appearing in a film were one-offs rather than a regular income, so her Centrelink allowance is restored and we're on our way.

We pull up opposite the Aboriginal Interpreter Service. MK walks over to a river red gum on the edge of the car park and shows us white flakes on its leaves. '*Ilperlatye* – snowflakes,' she says with a smile that lights up her face. 'We put them in a cup for the children. They're formed by tiny little black insects, and you blow the insects away,' she instructs. Jodie and I scrape the flakes off the leaves and follow MK's instructions before popping them into our mouths. They are sweet and delicious.

Inside, Jodie makes mugs of tea for MK and me and leaves us together in a meeting room. An Akarre woman, MK was born in Atitjere, the Harts Range area, about 130 kilometres north-east of Alice Springs. She tells me her parents moved to the goldmining town of Arltunga in the East MacDonnell Ranges, and from the age of 10 she lived in a dormitory at Arltunga Mission with the Catholic nuns. She learned her traditional songs and law from her seniors. In 1953 the mission was moved to Ltyentye Apurte, 80 kilometres south-east of Alice Springs, and was renamed Santa Teresa Mission. MK was in her mid-teens when her parents sent her and her sister to school there.

'We didn't go home for most holidays because it was too far for my parents to come, as they only had camels. They only came at Christmas time.'

In 1955 she was married in the Catholic Church to an Arrernte man. MK continued her education in Darwin and Alice Springs, where she qualified as a language interpreter. She taught language and culture and cross-cultural courses at the Institute for Aboriginal Development, and was one of the founders of Irrkerlantye Learning Centre, which focuses on intergenerational learning for Arrernte people. In 1997 she was awarded the Medal of the Order of Australia for service to the Aboriginal community of Central Australia, her interpreting work and for preserving language and culture. She was also nominated as 2022 Mparntwe NAIDOC Elder of the year.

She tells me her book took seven years to write with the assistance of her friend Barry McDonald and her niece, Veronica Perrurle Dobson. She starts talking about being part of the Land.

'We are the Land,' she says. 'The Land where I'm from in Atitjere owns me. I am part of that Land. As Aboriginals we feel that the Land belongs to us, because we are the Land. We are the trees. We are the creeks. The Land is our creation.'

She talks of being on her Homelands and describes that sense of belonging to the Land.

'Our skin name is in the Land, and that's part of us. We eat from our own Country, eating fresh kangaroos and drinking beautiful kangaroo blood. We sleep under the stars from our own Country and read the stories in the sky.'

As she talks about belonging, I ask her what place Deng, the recently arrived Sudanese refugee, will hold in this country he now calls home. Or Fleur, whose descendants arrived in Sydney 200 years ago.

'They are part of this place but they do not belong to this place.' She is quick to tell me that I am an Irish indigenous person, because that is where I come from. She looks at me squarely: 'You can own land, or a house, but you don't really belong to this place. It's not really yours. Like this table. This table didn't grow from the ground here. It was just put here, so people can talk around it, and food can be placed on it, but it's not from here. In the same way new people are here, but not from here.'

The conundrum that pops into my mind is that this fake-wood-topped table and I are here now – for better or worse. Australia is home to us both, so if we don't belong here, where do we belong?

MK says she regularly visits her Homelands, and she laments the changes she's seen in her lifetime. '*Alangkwe* – wild banana – used to grow on the ground on the Homelands at Atitjere, but they don't grow as much now. Pigweeds used to be big, and spread with flowers popping out,' she reminisces, 'but they don't grow like that now. The pigweed's big long seedpods were full of seeds, and I remember seeing grinding stones left by the old people near the plants, but I don't think we'll find any pigweed seeds now to grind up.

'The native grasses have been overtaken by buffel grass. The water in the rock holes isn't good water now, because introduced animals have got into the waterholes. The soil today is not the same as it used to be, because it's been destroyed by cattle hooves and the topsoil has blown away. The richness of the soil is not there anymore.'

MK speaks Akarre, her father's language; Alyawarr, the language of her mother's Country; Arrernte, her husband's first language and the language of the people in the Alice Springs region, and English. She can also understand Western Arrernte and Anmatyerr.

'Every Aboriginal language is sacred for those that speak it. Words are given to us by the Land, and these words are sacred,' she tells me.

I know from learning Irish that language is held in the Land. There are words in Irish that capture a place or a situation in a way that the English language can never do, even though it's now Ireland's primary language.

Arrernte is spoken by about 3000 people in Central Australia. It's taught to students in the primary schools of Alice Springs and is an optional subject at the public high school. Some employers in Alice Springs encourage their employees to learn basic Arrernte.

MK stresses the importance of maintaining language. 'If you lose your language, you're not anybody. You'll be lost and your children will be lost too. I tell my great-grandchildren, "No English."' She is worried that many Arrernte people are either not speaking their language to their children or they are not speaking it properly, so a new mixed language is evolving.

Not being from Alice Springs, MK does not hold the local stories, but she does tell me that the Central Arrernte people say the river red gums alongside the Todd River that I passed yesterday are young men travelling. She also says that Billy Goat Hill, called Akeyulerre, is where two sisters travelling from Port Augusta to the Top End stopped. It is a sacred women's place, she tells me, and men shouldn't 'sit down' there.

'Those two women travelled all around Mparntwe, and Billy Goat Hill is one of their special places. Two Women Dreaming,' she says.

I am intrigued by this long Dreaming track, extending from Port Augusta to the northern coast of Australia thousands of years before the telegraph line. 'The ladies were travelling this route, and the line came after them,' MK says with a smile. 'That Stuart,' she adds, 'he's a Johnny-come-lately.'

She tells me that some of her cousins were 'line bods' on the Ghan railway. 'They cut timbers and laid the line, and used to look after the camels. The railway picked up a lot of Arrernte people from here to work on the line. Some people from here worked at Oodnadatta, and they got married and remained there,' she explains.

In the final chapter of *Iwenhe Tyerrtye*, MK talks about not having 'blaming business', holding both English and Arrernte languages in Alice Springs and holding both cultures. It's similar, she explains, to being a Catholic and holding that faith along with her traditional culture and beliefs. I so admire her for this conciliatory attitude.

She finishes talking, and I thank her for taking time to talk with me.

'Say *kele mwerre*.'

I copy her pronunciation as best I can. '*Kula mora*,' I say slowly.

'It means "thank you" in Arrernte.'

Despite her belief about the two cultures holding one another, she now admits she's furious about the recent erection in Alice Springs of a statue of John McDouall Stuart. It was given to Alice Springs Town Council by the local Freemasons' Lodge to commemorate the 150th anniversary of the explorer reaching the area. It was originally unveiled in 2010 but immediately removed and put into storage because the council's Public Arts Advisory Committee considered there had been insufficient consultation with the local community about the piece.

But recently the four-metre-high statue of Stuart was placed in Stuart Park. It depicts Stuart holding a rifle, which is historically accurate, but it has incensed MK and many other people in the local community.

'I think the man standing in the middle of the park is very racist. I feel like throwing a big rock at it. Many Aboriginal people were killed by guns and that's why a lot of people are very angry.'

When Jodie, MK and I get back into the four-wheel drive MK insists that I should be shown the recently erected Stuart Memorial. Five minutes later we pull up in front of the large statue of John McDouall Stuart with his long, shaggy beard and broad-brimmed hat, holding a rifle. A temporary fence has been erected in front of it.

'He was an explorer, and although in his journal he apparently never mentioned killing Aboriginal people, he represents the people of that era who massacred many Aboriginal men, women and children. He could have been depicted carrying a compass, not a rifle. It is blatantly offensive,' Jodie says.

As we drive back to MK's house, she asks Jodie to stop at Piggly's Supermarket so she can buy groceries. On an A-frame stand in front of the building is a dot painting of a black crow with 'WARNING' written above it in large red letters. And underneath – 'Drinking alcohol in restricted or alcohol-protected areas is an offence'.

'The black crow,' Jodie explains to me, 'is considered unlucky, and using it in this way is inappropriate.'

Jodie ducks into the takeaway next door to buy something for her son, and I go into the supermarket with MK. Recent legislation stipulates that no one is allowed to consume alcohol within a two-kilometre radius of where they purchased it, and a policeman is standing in the aisle checking purchasers' ID.

I pick up a red plastic shopping basket and follow MK down the aisle. She points out the vegetables she wants, and I put them in the basket – pumpkin, half a cabbage, a cauliflower, carrots and green beans. She selects some meat and adds several yoghurts to the basket. MK stops at a long, low freezer and looks at the kangaroo tails. She picks one up several times but puts it back.

'Why don't you get one?' I ask, as she eyes it longingly.

'The neighbours don't like it if I have too many fires,' she replies.

We pull up outside MK's house. No one is in the garden now, but voices can be heard inside. MK tells Jodie and me to leave the groceries by the front door. As we drive off, she knocks on the door and gives us a smile and a wave as she waits to be let in.

CHAPTER 29

Ngangkere Frank Ansell

Rose sits at a long table in the kitchen, sipping tea from her porcelain cup. I make breakfast and join her. She tells me about when she was employed by the government at Manus Island Regional Processing Centre to organise recreational activities for asylum seekers. This was before the controversial offshore immigration detention facility closed in 2017. She cries as she talks about the old Afghan Hazara men held there day after day, forever hoping they would be reunited with their close relatives who were now living in Australia. She's just applied for a position with a not-for-profit organisation called MoneyMob. If she gets the job, she'll be working in a remote Aboriginal community, helping people manage their money.

Jack joins us at the table. He opens a bird book on his iPad featuring the tweets of different species and plays the chirp of the red-browed pardalote. This particular pardalote, he tells me, can be found at the old telegraph station.

This morning I've arranged to meet Frank Ansell, who is a *ngangkere* – a traditional medicine man and healer in his 60s. He combines ancient Aboriginal healing and teaching with modern coaching techniques, and in 2011 he gave a TED Talk in Brisbane. I find him standing outside the hostel at 8.30 wearing jeans and a broad-brimmed black hat, and missing a couple of lower front teeth. I'm intrigued by his long fingernails, particularly his nearly inch-long thumbnail. I discover later from Sue Gregory, an executive leadership coach with whom Frank Ansell runs retreats, that he has been up most of last night with a local Arrernte woman who was unwell.

Ngangkere Frank Ansell

We walk up to the Todd River and sit under the shade of a river red gum. He lights a cigarette and tells me he was born in Alice Springs, describing himself as a 'half-caste' – half Aboriginal and half white European. His parents were of mixed race and spent time at the telegraph station when they were children.

'My dad came from Undoolya, 15 kilometres from here, so he was still on his own Country with his family around. My mum was stolen from Ti-Tree and brought there. My nanna followed her tracks and lived around the telegraph station, so she could be close to her daughter. She never went back to her own Country.' The name Ansell is of German heritage, and Frank says he also has French heritage; his mother's father was Eugene Nicker.

'He was a miner working out at Arltunga and met Nanna when she was a young girl.'

Frank explains that he grew up feeling that he didn't belong to either the white man's world or – because he didn't know the laws – the Arrernte one. In his adult life, until the age of 30, he was an alcoholic. He describes being continuously drunk and living with seven or eight other alcoholics under one of the Todd River bridges; jail was part of his existence.

He moved to Katherine and appeared in court, having been caught drink driving for the fifth time. The judge gave him the option of one month in a rehabilitation centre or 18 months in jail. He chose rehabilitation and was taken to a centre by two men.

'Those two gentlemen changed my life,' he admits. 'Something happened in that month of sobriety. In the AA program they say you need a spiritual awakening to be able to combat the spirit in the bottle, and somewhere along the road it happened to me. My mind cleared and my life started to get better.'

He was employed at the rehabilitation centre and sent to Brisbane to do his counsellor training. He became a program manager for the Foundation of Rehabilitation with Aboriginal Alcohol Related Difficulties (FORWAARD) in Darwin.

'I wanted to tell everyone about alcohol and not to use it. I wanted to warn others: "Don't put it inside of you. It's a spirit, and at a point where you're not prepared for it, it will take you for a ride."' He was highly commended for his work with the foundation in Darwin but admits that he was still trying to discover who he was. He found it difficult to live away from his own Country without a strong support network of family and friends.

He came back to Alice Springs, where he worked as a mental health worker. He was chair of Lhere Artepe Aboriginal Corporation, the town's native title organisation, and was on the board for the Institute for Aboriginal Development. He was seemingly a pillar of society. Then he thought, *What the hell am I doing here? I'm on this treadmill, and I've been conditioned to believe it's right.*

'I started to go crazy and wanted to kill myself. Doctors recommended drugs and rehabilitation centres, but my uncle, whose father is an Arrernte man from near Santa Teresa, stepped in. In Aboriginal culture my uncle is my dad too – my old man – and he said to the doctors, "You mob give him to me for a couple of weeks. If I can't do nothing, I'll give him back to you."'

He took Frank down to the bend in the Todd River, near Frank's birthplace, and sang to him. 'It was like someone had lifted all the crap off me in 10 minutes. "I've got to learn this," I told him. He said, "Everyone needs to learn this. They need to get in touch with their spirit." So I went and lived with him for a year on his homeland in the Santa Teresa area south-east of Alice Springs.'

Now under the guidance of this old man, he underwent a 12-month intensive traditional mentoring in healing, which began with truly healing himself. He learned the important songs and he learned about bush medicines.

'After my old man healed me, he said, "You go out now and start healing the world. I'm behind you, and if you ever feel in trouble, come back to me." Then he got all the old men together – the leaders and Elders. They all sat in a circle around me, and he got them to sing me.'

As he's talking, Frank points out a police vehicle on the other side of the dry riverbed. Three men and a woman are being moved along, and they walk our way. One man stops and he and Frank talk in Arrernte.

'They're drunk, poor things,' Frank says, when the man has gone. He lights another cigarette and gazes at the dry riverbed. 'In white man's world they split your mind, they split your body. They split your soul, they split you up from who you are. It's day and night, good and bad. No, it's all

Ngangkere Frank Ansell

one. It's all God.' I feel he has read my mind. My head is spinning with the stories of injustice I've heard, and I feel confused and fragmented.

'Stop splitting yourself up and come back to one,' Frank says. 'Don't beat yourself up. Don't lessen who you are. It's important what you think of yourself, because you change the vibrations within your body with your thought. Just do good and you can't be bad, and be at peace with yourself. You are Spirit. Spirit is you. You can't split from that.'

Frank starts to sing a song. His voice is quiet, and the words and sounds are strange, but when he stops, my confusion has fallen away. I smile. I feel I've remembered who I am.

He gives me a pot of ointment made with olive oil, beeswax and pintye-pintye, a plant that grows in gorges and along watercourses. He tells me it's good for women's problems and also alleviates tension and stress.

'Spirit is in everything,' Frank continues. 'Spirit is in water and we are made of water. In Aboriginal culture, what we call water is the rainbow serpent. The rainbow serpent is everywhere and in everything, and we use that power for healing. The rainbow serpent is not only our spirit, it's your spirit. It's in everybody.

'White people come up to me and say, "How come you are healing us and giving us this information when we did all this stuff to you Aboriginal mob?" I say, "Well, if we want to change our situation we've got to change your situation." The Aboriginal system looks after this earth, and I want everyone to look after the earth first, because if there's no earth, there's no us.'

We walk down Todd Mall, where Frank is greeted by every second person, and stop for a coffee at Alice Plaza. On the way back to Leichhardt Terrace, he pauses outside the council chambers. Growing out of the paving stones, next to the modern building, is a magnificent river red gum.

'This was where I was conceived and also born,' Frank says.

Behind the fence, in a courtyard on Leichhardt Terrace, are four elderly Aboriginal men sitting on white plastic chairs. On the street outside, a distressed white woman and a young Aboriginal woman surrounded by five police officers shout about land rights. Frank walks up to the group to see what is happening, but decides not to get involved.

We reach Frank's sporty white MX-6, and with a wave he drives off. I walk back to Todd Mall to meet Jodie Clarkson for lunch at the Red Dog Cafe. I tell her about the scene that Frank and I witnessed.

'There is the traditional governance system,' she explains, 'and our whitefella law is imposed upon the traditional governance system. Many younger Aboriginal people have grown up under the white governance system. Under the traditional system, everyone knew who was responsible for what country.'

She talks about Mparntwe, the Country around Alice Springs, which extends approximately 10 kilometres to the east, west and north of the town, and one kilometre to the south.

'Mparntwe *apmereke-artweye*, the traditional owners, are responsible for the sacred sites on this Country. Since colonisation of this area, many sites have been damaged or destroyed to make way for roads and buildings. It is very hard for *apmereke-artweye* to fulfil their cultural obligations to their Country and ancestors with pressure from government and developers,' she says.

'The *apmereke-artweye* have *kwertengwerle*, who are like their offsiders, helping them look after Country. *Kwertengwerle* are from the adjoining Country. So you are the caretaker of your neighbour's Country. You don't make decisions about it, but you help look after it and hold part of the story of the Country. An Ampetyane and an Anale person, who are *kwertengwerle*, each sing part of a song for the Country in a ceremony; they each hold part of the story. One would never sing the other's part of the song, but if the other one made a mistake, they would pick it up, because they know it. It's a way of double-checking, backing up and repeating to make sure the story is straight. It's a wonderful model of sustainability.

'But,' she adds, 'since the whitefellas arrived here that system has got completely messed up, and that's why it's difficult for people to follow that old way, because it's often no longer there.'

Jodie came to Alice Springs 18 years ago when her now ex-husband got a job at the casino. 'I had this weird feeling when the aeroplane was landing that I was arriving home,' she recounts. 'It was extraordinary, as I'd never been here before, but I looked out of the window and couldn't stop laughing with excitement.

'They say you're either a misfit, a missionary or a mercenary when you come to this place,' Jodie says. I remember Kelly saying the same thing. 'I grew up in Newcastle and felt like I didn't fit with my family, the town or the community. And when I came here, it felt like being a misfit meant that I fitted. It was really cool.'

At that moment, our conversation is drowned out by the sound of Elton John and Kiki Dee's 'Don't Go Breaking My Heart' at high volume, as a group of dancers shimmy down Todd Mall in a 24-hour dance marathon. All we can do is smile and watch as the gyrating figures prance past.

'Another thing that makes this town so awesome,' says Jodie when she can make herself heard again, 'is that we have the biggest gay and lesbian population per capita in the country. I've got an Aboriginal mate who is a cross-dresser, and he can walk up and down town wearing his big wigs and people are just like, "Hey, how you doing?" I think that makes this town really special.'

Jodie was employed at the Alice Springs Desert Park for 18 years and worked closely with the Arrernte Elders, particularly the women, establishing the park. She also managed the team of guides, 70% of whom were local Aboriginal people, and was instrumental in developing an effective apprenticeship program. She has recently started working as an interpreter trainer at the Aboriginal Interpreter Service, set up by the NT government to support the basic human rights of first-language speakers so that they can fully understand and fully express themselves when dealing with professionals in the legal, health and social services sectors.

What strikes me most about Jodie is her calmness and aura of peace. In my short time in Alice Springs, I feel overwhelmed by the politics of the place.

'If you want to make the world a better place, it starts with you. It starts with your attitude and your compassion,' she says with a smile. 'You need to stay in the place of compassion even when you feel you've been shat upon from a great height. You can't afford to get angry, because as soon as you get angry you become irrational. The Dalai Lama has been telling us for years to stay in the place of compassion, to think from a place of love, not from a place of hate.'

CHAPTER 30

Gillen, the Ghan and *First Citizen*

Jodie heads back to her office and I walk down Stott Terrace to Akeyulerre, aka Billy Goat Hill, the significant Dreaming site for the two women who travelled from Port Augusta through here to the north coast.

During World War II water tanks were built on the summit of the hill, and there is a road to the top, but I climb a path. Empty beer bottles and water bottles lie abandoned in tussocks, and just below is the Stuart Highway with its constant stream of vehicles. But this still feels sacred. At the summit stands a desert bloodwood, and clumps of pink hop bush grow among the boulders. As I walk to the north side of the hill I see Anzac Hill straight ahead of me on the other side of town. Known as Atnelkentyarliweke in the Arrernte language, it's another sacred site of Alice Springs. On the south side of the hill I'm looking directly through Ntaripe/Heavitree Gap. The MacDonnell Ranges stretch along the horizon, and there is Alhekulyele, the peak, also called Mount Gillen, after telegraph stationmaster Frank Gillen.

In 1867, Frank Gillen, aged only 11, left school and got a job as a telegraph messenger with the Clare post and telegraph office. He later worked in Adelaide's main post and telegraph office before being posted to Alice Springs for three years in 1875, followed by 12 years at the Charlotte Waters Repeater Station. In 1891 Charles Todd appointed him stationmaster at Alice Springs.

The congenial Frank Gillen was known for his concern for Aboriginal people. As a senior government official and a justice of the peace, he was asked in 1891 to investigate the deaths of two Aboriginal men on Tempe Downs Station. He questioned the native police and, as a result of their statements, police officer William Willshire was charged with the shootings. A court case was held in Port Augusta, but Gillen wasn't summoned there to give evidence. The native police also retracted the statements they had made to Gillen, so Willshire was found not guilty.

But Gillen's reputation was enhanced with the Aboriginal Elders. The government also decided to establish a court in Central Australia. In 1892 Frank Gillen was appointed a special magistrate so that he could preside over court cases; he was also made a local sub-protector of Aborigines.

Two years later, in 1894, Baldwin Spencer, a young University of Melbourne professor, stayed at the Alice Springs Telegraph Station while on the Horn Scientific Expedition, sent to study the natural history of Central Australia. This was a start of a 17-year exchange of letters between the stationmaster and the professor, who shared an interest in anthropology. Frank Gillen had been recording the Arrernte language and collecting Aboriginal artefacts. Not realising their sacred significance, he had collected churingas; he was devastated when he discovered this was transgressive. But Gillen was greatly trusted by the Arrernte; they called him *akngerrepate*, meaning 'teacher', a title usually given to old men.

In 1896 Spencer returned to Alice Springs, where he and Gillen witnessed a series of sacred ceremonies organised by Gillen's friend, Unchalka, a local lawman and ritual expert. Three years later Baldwin and Gillen's book, *Native Tribes of Central Australia*, was published; it was considered the most significant anthropological field research conducted in 19th-century Australia. It showed that the Aboriginal people had not only a complex social structure but also a well-developed spirituality intrinsically linked to the natural world.

After 25 years in the region, Frank Gillen left Alice Springs to take a position as stationmaster at Moonta, south of Port Augusta on the Yorke Peninsula. He would write to Thomas Bradshaw, who took over as Alice Springs stationmaster, asking about his Aboriginal friends and sending money for them. In 1901 Baldwin Spencer and Frank Gillen were given a year on full pay to do further anthropological research, and three years later their second book, *The Northern Tribes of Central Australia*, was published. Gillen achieved international fame for his anthropological work, but despite his requests he was never promoted by Charles Todd to a position in a telegraph office in Adelaide, which would have enabled him to engage with the academic community. From Moonta he was moved up the coast of Spencer Gulf to Port Pirie, where he died in 1912.

A year earlier his friend Baldwin Spencer had agreed to take up the position of Chief Protector of Aborigines in Darwin for a period of 12 months. Here he began the implementation of the Northern Territory *Aboriginals Ordinance Act 1911*. Spencer divided Aboriginal people into two main groups: 'those living in and out of townships, and employed in the latter; and those living more or less in their wild state'.

Spencer's solution in both cases was to establish reserves, which he believed would protect Aboriginal people from exploitation and abuse. For those Aboriginal people 'living in their wild state', he recommended large reserves with enough natural resources that the people could continue their existence in remote areas, but also with future potential for agriculture or pastoralism. He believed that no mixed race children should be allowed to remain on these reserves and that they should instead be taken to stations, compounds or 'half-caste homes'. The *Aboriginals Ordinance Act* would remain in effect until 1957, having a devastating effect on thousands of Indigenous people.

Not only were their lands taken from them, but also their families were torn apart and in many cases their children forcibly removed. And despite having been here for thousands of years the Aboriginal people were powerless. They had no voice in this democratic country. They were not citizens.

I sit on a rock and watch a willie-wagtail hop across the sandy ground. The black and white bird flits onto a red boulder before flying into a cassia bush. My mind jumps to the two Aboriginal women who travelled from Port Augusta following an age-old songline and stopped here to rest many years before the Overland Telegraph Line wire was slung between 36,000 poles through the heart of Australia. I then imagine what life was like for Alice Todd, after whom the town was named. Having lived in Adelaide for five years, she was desperate to see her family again. She persuaded Charles to purchase tickets for her and their four-year-old daughter, Lizzie, for a trip back to England.

She returned with 12-year-old Fanny Todd, the orphaned daughter of Charles's older brother, Griffith. Fanny's parents had died in India. Later her two younger brothers would also come to live with the Todds in Adelaide.

Alice's father died in the mid-1860s, and the following year, unaware he was ill, Alice received a letter saying that her brother, Alfred, had died. A year later she received a letter informing her that her sister, Sarah, had died. Of her 10 siblings, she now had only one brother. And her mother, Mrs Bell, came to live with Charles and Alice, complaining, as her grandchildren rode their horses and ran wild, that they were unruly.

During the early stages of construction of the Overland Telegraph Line, Charles spent much of his time up and down the line between Port Augusta and The Peake. Then in January 1872 he sailed to the Roper River to help with the northern section of the line and didn't return to Adelaide for 10 months.

Alice, meanwhile, was looking after their five children at the Adelaide Observatory. Lizzie was now 16; Charles Edward, who was born the day after Alice climbed and fell out of an almond tree, was 14; Hedley Lawrence, Barry Todd's grandfather, 12; Maude was seven; and Gwendoline just three. Their youngest daughter, Lorna, wasn't born until 1877. Alice was also responsible for the meteorological observations, which had to be taken at regular intervals throughout the day. In addition, she kept up a social life and did charity work.

As I'm walking back to the hostel my mobile rings. 'Would you like to drive a four-wheel drive campervan from Alice to Darwin?' asks the woman at the other end. She's from the company I contacted a month ago, and she explains that we would leave in a couple of days. I jump at the opportunity, even though we'll have only four days to do the trip. It means one less vehicle driving 1500 kilometres – a significant reduction in CO_2 emissions – not to mention that we'll save on the cost of both car rental and hotel accommodation. I ring Alison and she agrees. So I spend the rest of the afternoon cancelling bookings and finding alternative places to stay in the camper.

On Sunday morning, Lesley offers to drive me to the Old Ghan Railway Museum in the little car she has bought for getting around while she is in Alice. The vehicle looks like it might grind to a halt at any moment, but we reach the museum. It's 10.25 when we walk in and see a sign: 'Ride the Old Ghan train along the original narrow gauge. Departs every Sunday in season at 10.30am.' We run to the old railway station at the far end of the open-air museum.

'Are we too late to get the train?' Lesley splutters to the man at the counter.

'The train hasn't run since 2006,' he replies. 'The line got washed away in a flood.'

We walk out to the empty platform, and sitting on the track is the Old Ghan locomotive with half a dozen carriages attached. Walking through the wood-panelled carriages with their pink curtains and hard, upright chairs, through the dining car with its Formica-topped tables and the kitchen carriage with its huge black iron stove, I imagine the long, slow journey from Adelaide to Alice.

Back in the station building I come across a black-and-white photograph of Gool Mohamed, who married Fleur's cousin, Beth McWilliams. He's a young man wearing a turban, long baggy trousers held up with braces and a long-sleeved white shirt. As Fleur had said, his feet are exceptionally large.

Underneath I see a handwritten note about him. He was the last known cameleer of Afghan descent to live in Alice Springs. His father, Peer Mohamed, arrived in Australia from Peshawar with his string of camels in 1872, and initially carted goods and building material for the workers on the Overland Telegraph Line. One of seven children, Gool was born in 1907 and started working with his father at the age of 12, carting goods up and down the Birdsville and Innamincka tracks. Using between 70 and 75 camels, they transported goods, building materials and fuel to Birdsville and Innamincka and returned with loads of wool. Gool made his first trip from Oodnadatta to Alice Springs in 1922, and he made many after that until the railway was completed in 1929. For 40 years Gool worked on the railways, before he and Beth ran the Mataranka Hotel. He also served as a judge for the annual Alice Springs Camel Cup.

I find press cuttings for the first train to travel from Adelaide to Alice Springs in August 1929, and under the heading 'Prominent Passengers' I see the names of Sidney Kidman's son, Walter, and his wife, Muriel.

Only minutes after Lesley and I get back to the YHA, Alison arrives from the airport. It's wonderful to see her smiling face and receive one of her bear hugs. We've been friends since we sailed together 15 years ago on a timber Swanson yacht called *Patsy*. Nowadays, with a shared passion for fish spotting, we go snorkelling together.

I admire Alison. Born in Glasgow, she left school at 16 and worked in Boots pharmacy before training as a nurse. When we met, she had recently had breast cancer, which had taken her mother's life when Alison was in her early 20s. Her grandmother had also died from it. Alison was diagnosed with breast cancer a second time, and since then she has taken major steps to improve her health. She lives life to the full, always grabbing opportunities to travel, and I'm so grateful to her for coming with me on this final section of the Overland Telegraph Line.

Lesley heads off to feed her beloved joeys and Alison and I go to the Red Dog Cafe for lunch. As we're eating, she confesses she can hardly stay awake, having worked night shifts all week and then getting up early this morning for the flight. Immediately after we've eaten, Alison hops into the bunk below mine and goes to sleep.

I'm sitting in the courtyard, writing my journal, when Jack appears. He brings out his iPad and shows me an orange chat, a red-necked avocet and a spotted crake, all of which he's seen over the last few days. He plays their respective tweets before heading to the river in the hope of adding a few more species to his birding list.

I wake Alison in time for a sausage sizzle in the courtyard. The YHA continues to show films every evening, although on a much smaller screen than the Pioneer Walk-in Theatre's original one, so along with a few others we settle into the old deckchairs to watch *First Citizen*, a film about the life of Albert Namatjira, the brilliant Western Arrernte artist.

When he was three, Albert's parents moved to the Hermannsburg Lutheran Mission in the MacDonnell Ranges, south-west of Alice Springs. As a teenager he was taken by the tribal Elders to ceremonial grounds for his initiation into manhood. He now had to accept tribal laws, and when he was older he would take his place as a leader.

He was in his early 30s and living with his wife and children at Hermannsburg Mission when, in 1934, artists Rex Battarbee and John Gardner held an exhibition there of their watercolour paintings of the MacDonnell Ranges. Seeing these paintings, Albert, who had an aptitude for art, became obsessed with a desire to paint in this style. He persuaded the mission superintendent to buy him paper and a box of watercolours, and he began painting. When Rex Battarbee returned to the mission two years later, Albert received tuition from him in exchange for his services as a camel handler. For eight weeks they travelled together through Western Arrernte land. Battarbee was amazed by Namatjira's progress – his understanding of perspective, the rules of composition and his way of seeing colour.

Albert Namatjira's paintings were celebrations of the land and his deep bonds with Country. He had solo exhibitions in Melbourne, Adelaide and Sydney. But as a full-blooded Aboriginal man, he was a ward of the state, and his application for a grazing lease on a small cattle station was refused. He also applied to buy a block of land in Alice Springs and build a house on it, but his application was rejected on the grounds that Aboriginal people were prohibited from remaining within the town boundaries after dark.

His work, meanwhile, was achieving critical acclaim. In 1953 Albert Namatjira was awarded the Queen's Coronation Medal, and the following year he was presented to Queen Elizabeth and the Duke of Edinburgh at Government House in Canberra. A portrait of Albert Namatjira by William Dargie won the Archibald Prize in 1956 and, in 1957, Albert and his wife, Rubina, were awarded full Australian citizenship.

But with citizenship came crisis. Namatjira could now legally buy alcohol. He started drinking, and white men bought him grog in exchange for paintings. The tax office charged him back tax for his earnings before he became a citizen. He fought with Rubina and she returned to Hermannsburg, where the couple and their children had lived for many years and where Albert had grown up on the mission.

Albert remained at a camp on the outskirts of Alice Springs with fellow tribesmen. He was bound under white man's law not to buy or supply liquor to other Aboriginal people because they were wards of the state. He was also bound by tribal law to share what he had with tribal members. Large amounts of alcohol were consumed in the camp, and Namatjira was believed to be responsible for supplying it. One night in August 1958 a young Pitjantjatjara woman was killed by her husband. That evening Albert had gone with a friend to the pictures. I wonder if he had been sitting in one of these deckchairs at the Pioneer Walk-in Theatre, gazing up at the screen as Alison and I are doing now.

Although he wasn't involved in the murder, alcohol was seen to be an indirect cause of the woman's death, and Albert was charged with supplying it. In October 1958 he was sentenced to six months in prison. His sentence was reduced to three months' imprisonment at Papunya Native Reserve, where he carried out light duties under supervision.

But when he was released, he had lost his will to live. He withdrew from the world and no longer painted. Three months later his heart stopped and he died in August 1959, aged 57, in Alice Springs Hospital.

This heart-wrenching film has me in tears.

CHAPTER 31

Calling Australia Home and Up the Stuart Highway

I get up early and sit on the cold sand beside the dry Todd River, the morning sun warming my face. It was 20 years ago today that I first set foot on Australian soil.

Alison and I walk across town to the Araluen Arts Centre to see Albert Namatjira's paintings. I move from one watercolour to the next, each one capturing this country in a profound way. I'm spellbound by the exquisite painting of a ghost gum and his depiction of Heavitree Gap – Ntaripe – which holds all the mystery and magnificence of this pass through the ranges.

In the evening Alison suggests we walk up Anzac Hill/Atnelkentyarliweke to watch the sunset. A small group of tourists are there with their cameras, catching the sun as it disappears behind the West MacDonnell Ranges. The words 'Lest We Forget' are written in bold letters on the cream-coloured war memorial. As well as being a special place to remember all those who died fighting for Australia, this hill, Atnelkentyarliweke, like Billy Goat Hill/Akeyulerre – has Dreaming associations with the two travelling women, as well as the boys, who journeyed north from here in the direction of the telegraph station along the river.

From the flagpole beside the memorial flies the Australian flag. I think of my Australian citizenship ceremony in 2006, which Alison attended along with Steve. As the three of us walked around the corner to the community centre where the ceremony was to take place, we saw a ring-tailed possum sitting wide-eyed in a tree. I assumed it was a sign that, because I was about to become an Australian, I was being given the duty of looking after these creatures.

Calling Australia Home and Up the Stuart Highway

Seeing the flag fluttering in the breeze, I know MK might consider me a blow-in, but I feel overwhelmingly grateful that Australia is my home.

It's the last evening for Alison and me in Alice Springs, so Lesley drives the two of us and Rose and another New Zealander at the YHA, Brenda, to Tinh and Lan Alice Vietnamese Restaurant. It's out near the airport, and we're driving along dark country roads, wondering if we're heading in the right direction. Eventually, we find ourselves in a little oasis with water features and a walkway adorned in greenery. We pass a large white statue of Kuan Yin and reach the interior decked out with coloured fairy lights, ornate chandeliers and ornaments. The restaurant is on a farm, where most of the vegetables it serves are grown. The owners came as refugees to Alice Springs in 1994 and created this haven. We share servings of spring rolls, bowls of chicken curry and plates of stir-fried vegetables, every dish delicious.

The following morning I pick up the four-wheel drive campervan. I am excited to be embarking on this next leg of the journey, but also feel nervous. We'll be on the Stuart Highway all the way, but there are long stretches between towns, and this endless stretch of bitumen runs through a remote region of the country. Alison, moreover, doesn't drive, so I'll be the one behind the wheel.

The camper is a huge shell on top of a manual Hilux ute. It has a pop-up roof, and inside a sleeping area, a fridge and a two-burner gas stove – all the essentials. But I've never driven a vehicle as large as this, so I head slowly back to the hostel. Alison and Lesley are waiting outside with the bags, which we stow along with the food supplies. As I give Lesley a big hug, I realise how much I'll miss my roommate.

By 10 o'clock we're on our way. I shift into fifth gear and accelerate the Hilux to 100 km/hr. Alice Springs is behind us, and red earth stretches out to the horizon on either side of the long, straight bitumen highway. A wedge-tailed eagle floats on the thermals ahead of us. The camper is heavy, so I sit on 100 kilometres as a stream of sedans and four-wheel drives towing caravans overtake us. Alison sagely reminds me we have only four days to get to Darwin.

An hour and a half later we stop at the Aileron Roadhouse. On a nearby hill stands a 17-metre-high sculpture known as Anmatjere Man. Based on a traditional Anmatjere man of this area, this impressive figure holds a

Whispering Wire

spear and stands on red rocks; near the entrance to the roadhouse is a sculpture of an Anmatjere woman and her child. These magnificent pieces were created by Mark Egan, who made the controversial statue of John McDouall Stuart in Alice Springs.

Inside the roadhouse I follow a sign to the 'Shit House', while Alison buys a Duran Duran CD. She has taken charge of music, and we forge north to the strains of 'Come Undone'. Alison is also organising our food for the journey, and insists we stop when we see a sign advertising mango ice cream. We drive up a dirt track and are astonished to see rows of mango trees with their large green leaves growing in the desert. It turns out that the mango farm was the brainchild of John and Shirley Crayford, who gave up their jobs in Alice Springs to establish it in the late 1980s. Alison rushes into 'Shatto Mango', the wooden hut that is the shop, while I turn the vehicle. She emerges with two ice creams and tells me the mangoes are pesticide-free, there being no fruit flies in the desert.

Back on the highway, as we're savouring every mouthful of the delicious ice cream, we pass a sign that says 'Drive to conditions'. 'That means there's no speed limit,' Alison points out, as I sit steadfastly on 100 km/hr and three trucks whizz past.

I pull up at the Central Mount Stuart Historical Reserve. A cairn erected in 1960 commemorates the pinpointing by John McDouall Stuart of the geographical centre of Australia a century earlier. The exact spot is near a mountain several kilometres north-west of here. Travelling with only William Kekwick and 18-year-old Benjamin Head, Stuart was making his second attempt to reach the north of the continent. He named the mountain Central Mount Sturt, after Charles Sturt, who he had accompanied on their failed expedition to find the centre in 1844. Its name was later changed to Central Mount Stuart.

Stuart and Kekwick climbed the mountain and on the summit built a cairn. In the centre they placed a pole with the Union Jack nailed to it. Stuart wrote in his journal:

We then gave three hearty cheers for the flag, the emblem of civil and religious liberty, and may it be a sign to the natives that the dawn of liberty, civilisation, and Christianity is about to break upon them.

Stuart wrote this with such conviction, but in the next few decades the Aboriginal people of Central Australia would see their loss of liberty and lands.

Three workmen in fluorescent green shirts are positioning another monument near the commemorative cairn. They have just placed a large piece of stone on a concrete base when we arrive. One of them has read Stuart's journals and is a great admirer of the explorer. I ask him what he thinks about the controversial statue in Alice Springs, and he points out that the artwork depicts Stuart very much as he would have looked on his expeditions. As the three men wave us on our way, he suggests we talk to Les Pilton. 'He's been the publican at the Barrow Creek Hotel for 25 years.'

CHAPTER 32

Barrow Creek and a Boulder

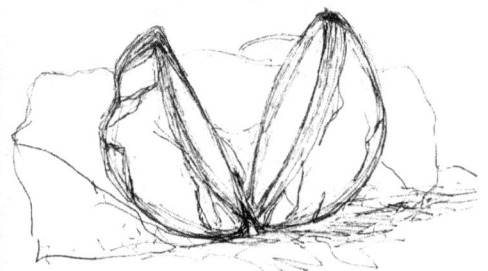

Seventy kilometres on, we reach Barrow Creek, with its pub, service station and now empty telegraph repeater station. We pull up outside the hotel expecting it to be deserted at lunchtime on a Wednesday, but it's doing a roaring trade. About 20 Aboriginal men and women sit outside in the sun, drinking beer.

Behind the bar is Michael Romaro, who tells us Les Pilton has gone to Alice Springs. We sit at the bar. Alison orders a Diet Coke and I have a ginger beer. Every couple of minutes someone pops through the door, or sticks a head through the open window and orders a beer.

'This is our busiest time,' Michael says, explaining that his clientele has come in from a nearby community. He says that between 12.30 and 2.30 pm each person is allowed to drink up to six beers. They have to pay in advance, and Michael keeps a tally of how many beers everybody has had.

Originally from Melbourne, Michael tells us that he was on his way to Darwin but only got as far as Barrow Creek. He used to work on Stirling Station before he got the job in the pub. He has a bald head and grey beard and, despite having no front teeth, he tells us that the locals have been trying to marry him off to their daughters. 'One of the daughters was only 13 at the time, so I explained that I'd be arrested if I took up that proposal.' Many of the older people, he says, now consider him like a son. He has even been given a skin name, which he has forgotten.

Like the ceiling at the William Creek Hotel, the walls around the bar here are covered in banknotes from all over the world. Behind the bar, pinned to a shelf lined with dusty bottles of wine, whisky and liqueurs, we pick out a Scottish one-pound note and an old Irish punt. Les Pilton has initiated what he calls the Barrow Creek Bank, inviting travellers to stick a signed banknote of their native country on the wall so it can be used at a later date when they are passing through and need a beer.

Details of the Peter Falconio 2001 murder case have been pinned on the wall at the other end of the pub. After British tourist Peter Falconio was killed near here, his girlfriend, Joanne Lees, managed to escape from the assailant and hid in bushes for five hours. When the attacker finally gave up searching for Joanne and drove off, she ran out onto the highway, 13 kilometres north of here, and flagged down a truck. The driver unbound her hands and brought her here to the hotel. It's chilling to be in the area where this horrific incident took place.

I'm not reassured by five jars on the mantelpiece each containing a pickled snake. But I'm delighted to see several glass and ceramic insulators, a battered old brown felt hat that belonged to Tom Roberts – known as 'Telecom Tom' – and a portrait of him hanging above a doorway. Like Michael, Tom Roberts said he was 'just passing through' when he first came to Barrow Creek to take up a promotion with the Postmaster General as foreman-linesman in the early 1950s. He stayed for 33 years and all those years he remained married, but his wife never wanted to come to Barrow Creek and Tom didn't want to leave. Considered the unofficial mayor of Barrow Creek, he lived at the telegraph station, and when he retired in 1977 he was made caretaker. He continued to live there until a couple of years before he died.

Alison and I finish our drinks and walk to the telegraph station. A single Oppenheimer pole stands in front the large, eight-roomed, single-storey stone building with its corrugated-iron roof. This repeater station had a continuous association with telecommunication technology from its opening in 1872 until 1980. With the laying of cables across the Indian Ocean in 1901 and the Pacific in 1902, traffic along the Overland Telegraph Line was greatly reduced. But in 1941, because of a need to ensure communication links between Australia's north and south during World War II, a third wire was added to the two existing ones. This new copper wire had a three-channel system: two channels for long-distance telephone calls, the other for telegraph traffic. In 1980 the microwave telecommunications link replaced the telephone carrier, and Barrow

Creek Telegraph Station became redundant. Telecom Tom, though, continued to live here until 1986.

We open the old wood-panelled front door and step into the main room with its flagstone floor and fireplace. A door leads through to the courtyard at the back where we see a large cistern for collecting rainwater. As we walk through the empty whitewashed rooms with bare light bulbs suspended from the ceilings, I sense a place having been lived in not so long ago. I can imagine Telecom Tom sitting in a large armchair in front of the fire.

On our way back to the pub we pass the cemetery where Tom Roberts's ashes are buried. But the inscription on a headstone catches my attention:

In Memory

of

James L. Stapleton

Stationmaster

and

John Franks

Linesman

Killed by Natives

Barrow Creek

23rd February 1874

In early 1874, less than 18 months after the telegraph line was completed, a police station was opened in Barrow Creek in response to the spearing of a horse and some sheep by local Kaytetye people. Eight days later, on a warm Sunday evening, stationmaster John Stapleton, the other telegraph station staff and Constable Samuel Gason of the new police station were sitting outdoors at the side of the building when a shower of spears rained down from behind the telegraph station. On running to the only entrance – a large iron gate at the rear of the building – they encountered a crowd of Kaytetye men who threw spears and boomerangs at them. Linesman John Franks was speared and died almost instantly. Stapleton was hit by four spears as he tried to close the

Barrow Creek and a Boulder

gates, and assistant Ernest Flint was also speared. A telegraph message was sent to Adelaide explaining what had happened to the three men, and saying that Jimmy, 'a civilised native boy', also had three spear wounds.

A doctor was called into the Adelaide Post and Telegraph Office to administer instructions for treatment of the wounded. Realising Stapleton didn't have long to live, Charles Todd sent his carriage to bring Stapleton's wife to the telegraph office. When the dying man heard she was there, he tapped out his final short message, which Todd took down letter by letter: 'God bless you and the children.' He died the following day.

Todd, who personally chose all the repeater stationmasters, was known to alleviate their long, lonely evenings by telling jokes and playing chess with them down the line from Adelaide. Canadian-born James Stapleton had worked on telegraph lines in not only Canada but also the United States and Central America before coming to Australia. Todd organised a concert at the Observatory to raise money for Stapleton's widow and four children.

Several Kaytetye men had come to the station earlier that day asking for flour. They were told it was only given to the aged, the sick and those who worked. Charles Todd had given detailed instructions to the overseers during the building of the Overland Telegraph Line to minimise contact with the Aboriginal people as far as possible. The purpose of this directive was to prevent conflict, and the builders of the line were also to have regard for both the space and possessions of the Aboriginal people. But now that the line was operational and the repeater stations established, the situation was different. The new arrivals and the Kaytetye, who had lived on this country for thousands of years and whose traditional lands included the telegraph station and its acreage, were competing for finite resources, such as water. The telegraph station had been built very close to a significant waterhole, and access to it was now limited.

No arrests were ever made, but over the next two months Constable Samuel Gason, assisted by telegraph staff and a constable from the Peake, rode over the surrounding area and carried out reprisals. In several engagements, it's estimated that around 90 Aboriginal men, women and children were killed. Approximately 50 of these people, who almost certainly had not been involved in the attack on the telegraph station, were killed at what became known as Skull Creek. This group of white men took the law into their own hands and the killings were never reported. I am sickened and sad.

The drinkers have disbanded by the time we return to the hotel, and we climb into the campervan and continue up the highway. It's late afternoon when we reach the extraordinary granite boulders of Karlu Karlu – a place of great cultural significance to the Warlpiri, Warumungu, Kaytetye and Alyawarra people, who traditionally came together here for weeks of dancing and singing to the spirit people to bless them and their land.

John Lewis, a horseman who played an integral part in the Overland Telegraph Line construction, gave an account of having seen Karlu Karlu. He referred to them as 'the Devil's Marbles', the first record of this English-language name by which they are also known.

We are the only people in this sacred place and walk slowly around the giant stones. The huge rounded boulders cast their long shadows across the bed of rock beneath. One is split cleanly down the middle, the two halves creating a huge V; on the edge of another boulder balances a stone sphere.

The stones are alive with life and energy in the evening light. Yellow-flowering cassia grows in a rock crevice. Nearby are two boulders with a third balanced on top. Framed by the deepening blue sky, they remind me of an enormous Celtic dolmen, which minute by minute turns an ever richer red with the setting sun.

In 1953 one of these boulders – weighing eight tonnes – was taken from here to Alice Springs and placed on the grave of Reverend John Flynn, founder of the Royal Flying Doctor Service, who had started his ministerial life in the tiny church Fleur and I visited in Beltana. The boulder was transport 400 kilometres to the gravesite by the Northern Territory Public Work Department. The traditional custodians of Karlu Karlu were not consulted. The people wanting to respect the man, who had realised his dream of providing 'a mantle to safety over the outback', were unaware of the spiritual and cultural significance of these boulders for the Aboriginal men and women of this area.

It was not until the early 1980s, after talks between the Uniting Church and Aboriginal representatives, that the research for a replacement rock

Barrow Creek and a Boulder

began, but there was huge controversy about the plan to swap the rock as such a move was considered by some Australians as a desecration of the grave. It was not until the late 1990s that the Arrernte, the traditional owners of the gravesite, resumed the search for a replacement. In a gesture of reconciliation, the Arrernte selected a boulder from a sacred site in Alice Springs associated with the *yeperenye* – caterpillar-Dreaming, and in 1999 the original boulder was returned to Karlu Karlu.

***

In the fading light we drive 80 kilometres to Tennant Creek. 'This place reminds me of Beverly Hills,' Alison says, as we drive past the Bluestone Motor Inn. Having never been to Los Angeles, I'm struggling to imagine the similarities between the enclave of Hollywood stars and this outback mining town.

'It's the palm trees,' she adds.

We roll into Tennant Creek's Outback Caravan Park just before dark and proudly pop up the roof of the camper in a matter of seconds. Alison warms risotto on the gas stove and we eat it quickly before gathering with a dozen other people for a talk by Jimmy Hooker. This small, wiry man under a scruffy felt hat cooks witchetty grubs while he yarns. He tells us he's from Queensland, was born around 1947, and his mother was a Kalkadoon woman.

'I never learned to read and write,' he says, flipping a grub, 'and when I was 14 my father showed me a swag, gave me a billy and told me to get out.' Having been booted out of home, he found work with a man on a property.

'I thought it was a bit odd that we never used gates and instead always cut the wire in the fence when we moved from paddock to paddock,' Jimmy recounts. One day the police pulled up and his boss took off, leaving young Jimmy to face them alone. Only then did he discover his employer was stealing poddy calves from his neighbour.

He cuts the witchetty grubs into small pieces, places them in a coolamon, which he has carved himself, and hands them around for us to eat. A round, prepubescent boy squirms at the mere idea of eating a grub, and there are giggles and gruff refusals. But I eat the grub – and it's delicious. I wish there were more.

Whispering Wire

Jimmy Hooker was passing through Tennant Creek in the late 1960s, planning to stay for a week on his way back to Queensland. But he never left. He worked for the big gold mines, including Peko and Juno, bought himself a metal detector and started prospecting for gold, living for 15 years in spinifex humpies.

'I always called my camp Gumtree 69,' he says with a grin.

He gives us some acacia pods to rub together with water, and they lather like soap.

'This,' he says, 'is very good for sunburn and mosquito bites.' He hands around a coolamon of mistletoe berries for us to try – another delicious delicacy. Some of us stand around talking afterward, and Jimmy tells me there's a tree in the caravan park that has a blaze cut made during the construction of the Overland Telegraph Line. Another man, Warren Corrick, works at Charles Darwin University, and until recently has been teaching courses in Tennant Creek. He says that while he was working on a drilling rig for a mineral exploration company in the late 1960s, he would frequent the Barrow Creek Hotel.

'We worked 11 days and had three off, so we used to go to Barrow Creek for the long weekend. A well was being dug behind the pub, and invariably one of us would run out of money. So we'd have to go out and do an hour's digging in order to buy another beer.'

Back at the campervan, Alison falls asleep almost immediately, but I lie awake, my mind churning over what happened in 1874 at Barrow Creek.

CHAPTER 33

Nuggets of Gold

Alison and I eat breakfast in the camp kitchen, before I thread my way through the campervans and caravans, searching for the tree that Jimmy Hooker told me about last night. I find the scarred ironwood and a plaque at its foot, claiming that the blaze was most likely made by the survey team for the Overland Telegraph Line. It fills me with a sense of timelessness. I wonder if the men who marked this tree camped here 150 years ago.

We close up the camper, but now feel utterly devoid of camping prowess as despite numerous attempts we're unable to keep the latches of the pop-up roof from unclipping on one side, so I drive slowly back to the centre of town.

I've been given an introduction to Ms P. Phillips Napangardi at the Papulu Apparr-kari Aboriginal Corporation, the language and cultural centre in Tennant Creek. A woman comes to the door and tells us that Ms Phillips has been in hospital all week, adding that anyone else who might have been able to talk to us is unavailable because of sorry business.

'Ten people here have passed away recently,' she tells us.

Despite being unwell, however, Ms Phillips has very kindly given my business card to the Central Land Council across the road and also forwarded my email. Barbara at reception tells us that the person to talk to is Francine McCarthy, but she isn't available for another 45 minutes. So we drive back to the caravan park and pick up a key for the Tennant Creek telegraph repeater station and head there, 11 kilometres north along the Stuart Highway.

Kites wheel in the clear blue sky and a termite mound pushes out of the dry ground beside an Oppenheimer pole. We walk to the collection of stone buildings with their green corrugated-iron roofs and peer into the whitewashed smoke house and the small cellar building before opening the door into what was the telegraph station kitchen.

In the fireplace are an old wood-burning stove and a couple of old pots; three paraffin lamps and three empty longneck beer bottles sit on the mantelpiece above. Against the wall is a dilapidated organ, several of its dusty keys stuck and most of its stops missing. But my eyes are drawn to the table in the middle of the room, and the copies of newspaper headlines from when the line was opened.

On Wednesday 23 October 1872, the *Age* reads: THE NEWS OF THE DAY: 'We are now actually in possession of news from London up to the day before yesterday.'

I read the headline from the *Sydney Morning Herald* for Wednesday 23 October 1872:

> ENGLISH NEWS
>
> TO 21ST INSTANT.
>
> BY CABLE AND OVERLAND LINE.
>
> [ASSOCIATED PRESS TELEGRAMS]

The following message was transmitted from London on the 21st instant, at 16 hours 25 minutes astronomical time [equivalent to 4.25 am of 22nd Sydney time]. It began to come through last night at 12 o'clock, and was completed this morning at 12.46. It will be seen, therefore, that the news has been forwarded with great rapidity, and that there can be no doubt as to the perfection of the telegraphic arrangements or the quality of the line.

This was the dawn of instant communication. Mail sent by ship between England and Australia had taken months to arrive, now it was only a matter of hours for news to travel across the world. It wasn't long before the commercial benefits were realised; prices for crops, wool and minerals sold to England could be negotiated and sales closed in just a few days, instead of products being sent to Britain with no idea of current market prices.

The maintenance track, running beside the line, became a route for travellers. Pastoralists brought cattle and sheep up the track and established stations along the Overland Telegraph Line. The natural springs and waterholes, so important to the Aboriginal people, became watering points for thirsty livestock. As the cattle industry grew, the track became part of a network of government stock routes, attracting people to the new territory. Within two decades of the first telegraph poles being planted, Central Australia had changed significantly.

We walk to the old blacksmith's building. Here, in 1897, the blacksmith made a section of a bicycle pedal for Jerome J. Murif, a 34-year-old Irishman who was the first person to cycle across the continent. In his book, *From Ocean to Ocean*, Murif writes that this blacksmith's work was as neat 'as if one of the most expert of cycle-repairing shop hands had been the craftsman'.

Murif was the subject of many telegraph reports as he cycled from Adelaide to Darwin. Far more intrepid than Fleur and me he carried and dragged his bicycle over sand dunes before contending with the wide, crocodile-infested rivers further north. But like me hunger was an issue. When staying at the telegraph stations en route, he describes being ashamed of his voracious appetite and his 'unnatural-seeming craving for food'. He ate twice as much as everyone else at every meal.

'At Tennant Creek', he wrote, 'during the many days I remained at the telegraph station, I would eat almost continuously. My happiest thoughts were centred around the dinner table and there was a savage delight in the partaking of every meal'.

Old telegraph poles presented unexpected obstacles. As early as 1873 the wooden poles were replaced by Oppenheimer iron ones in the areas most threatened by white ants and fire. By 1875 the repoling had been completed in the Tennant Creek area, but Murif noted the hazards still facing the cross-continental cyclist:

> *Riding over telegraph poles is a feat which the cyclist here is called on frequently to perform. In many places, the track runs alongside the old line of wooden poles; in other places, again, the modern galvanised-iron rods stand just where stood those wooden poles of older days. In each case the old poles, in various stages of decomposition, lie often right across the track; and the rider cannot always see them until after he has felt the bump.*

Not wanting to be late for our appointment, we rush back to the Central Land Council, only to find a notice on the door: 'Office is currently CLOSED staff @ POST OFFICE.' So, we stand outside the yellow-painted brick building and admire the impressive mural on the front wall, depicting the Dreamings of the Warumungu people, until Barbara returns.

Francine McCarthy, Senior Project Officer at the Tennant Creek Central Land Council, takes us into a meeting room. The three of us sit at one end of a long table. Her father, Francine tells us, is from near Gosford in NSW; her mother is Warumungu from Tennant Creek. Francine was born here and grew up in Alice Springs. Over the next hour she quietly explains how that one piece of wire running through the heart of the country affected the Warumungu.

When Stuart travelled through this area in the 1860s and the telegraph station was established in the 1870s, the Warumungu people were a flourishing nation. But by the 1880s pastoralists had moved into this region and procured leases on vast tracts of land. Aboriginal people were still leading a nomadic life. A clause in the South Australian government's pastoral lease agreements stipulated that Aboriginal people be given 'full and free' access to the leased land and its 'springs and surface water', the right to hunt wildlife for food and the right to erect 'wurlies and other dwellings, as if the lease had not been granted'. It was intended that the traditional owners and the pastoralists would coexist on the land. Today, the *Northern Territory's Pastoral Land Act* still has a clause allowing Aboriginal people to access leased areas, enabling them to continue connection to Country to undertake cultural and traditional activities. However, they cannot build permanent structures.

Under the pastoral lease agreements, landholders had three years to comply with a minimum stocking rate. The introduced cattle soon destroyed the pristine waterholes, the rights of the Aboriginal people were ignored, and they were dispossessed of their land. By 1890, the telegraph station had become a ration store distributing flour, sugar, tea and blankets to the local Indigenous people. In 1892 an Aboriginal reserve was established on land to the east of the telegraph station.

Severe droughts came several years later, impelling the Warumungu to camp around the telegraph station, which was near the perennial waterholes along the creek that they traditionally used in drought years.

Nuggets of Gold

'My grandmother and grandfather worked at the telegraph station,' Francine says. 'This was probably in the late 1920s. Their eldest son was born at the telegraph station and he passed away only a few years ago. He used to tell us all these stories about living there. I remember he told us about the droughts in the late 1890s, which forced people to come to the telegraph station to get access to water.'

'My grandfather did woodchopping and general jobs, and my grandmother did washing. Other people lived traditionally and camped close by, because there was a permanent water supply there.'

Then Francine mentions that in 1932 her grandfather, Frank Juppurla, found a nugget of gold. He took it to telegraph operator Woody Woodruffe, who had enlisted local Warumungu in a search for gold. It was a lump of black ironstone in which specks of gold could be seen. Before then, gold had been found only in quartz, but now prospectors started to look at the previously overlooked ironstone caps south of the telegraph station. They found significant gold deposits, precipitating Australia's last great gold rush. When 600 people descended on this remote area, the government gazetted the new township of Tennant Creek.

Ted and Mary Ward, a stockman and his schoolteacher wife, joined the gold rush to Tennant Creek in 1935. They made a temporary camp at the telegraph station, and it must have been then that the Wards met Topsy Nampijinpa, Francine's great-grandmother, and her grandparents, Topsy's daughter Linda Napanangke, and son-in-law Frank Juppurla. Mary Ward accepted a contract to do the laundry for No. 1 Battery, which crushed the ore, and Francine says her grandmother and great-grandmother washed and cleaned for the mining families.

Francine tells me that her grandfather found another gold nugget – this time about 15 kilometres south-east of the telegraph station. He gave it to Ted Ward, and Ted, Mary and her brother, Stuart McIntyre, started mining the site, which they named Blue Moon. Francine's grandfather became known as Blue Moon Frank. He and Linda lived at the mining camp with the Wards, and Linda kept the camp's garden, where she grew fruit and vegetables.

By the 1940s the Blue Moon gold mine was starting to dry up, so the Wards sold up and bought Banka Banka, a station north of Tennant Creek. The Wards, along with Stuart McIntyre, Topsy, Frank and Linda and their two children, moved there. Ted and Mary Ward had no children of their own, but Mary focused her energies on the health and education of the Warumungu children at Banka Banka, where she started a government school. In the 1960s, after her husband had died, Mary bought and renovated six houses in Tennant Creek for her old retainers, which included Francine's grandmother. She also built a large red-brick hostel, known as the Pink Palace, which was used as a bunkhouse for Aboriginal stockmen when they came to Tennant Creek.

Francine tells us that her grandmother spoke six languages: Warumungu, Warlmanpa, Warlpiri, Kaytetye, Mudburra and some English.

'Do you speak Warumungu?' I ask.

'A little bit,' she replies. 'I understand more than I can speak it. I know a few words.'

Francine says that what she is telling us about the telegraph station is anecdotal and that her mother would probably correct her. We sit in silence for a moment, before she admits she's actually very shy.

She talks about the Warumungu land claim, telling us that in December 1976 the federal parliament passed the *Aboriginal Land Rights (Northern Territory) Act*, which enabled Aboriginal people in the Northern Territory to claim right to Land based on their traditional law and connection to Country. Land rights and recognition were further strengthened when the *Native Title Act* was passed in 1993, which can be applied across Australia.

With the gold rush, the Aboriginal reserve to the east of the telegraph station was revoked in 1934 to allow mining in the area. The Warumungu people who were living a traditional way of life on it were moved to a new reserve further east. The new reserve had no permanent water and was about 80% spinifex desert. When it was revoked in 1962, the Warumungu were left with no access to their traditional country.

'The Warumungu land claim, lodged in 1978, was one of the longest and hardest fought in the history of the *Aboriginal Land Rights Act*. It was nearly 20 years before land was eventually handed back to the Warumungu,' she says. At one point the NT government enlarged the town boundaries of Tennant Creek to cover 750 square kilometres, the size of a major city, because land within town boundaries could not be claimed. As she quietly explains what took place it's hard to comprehend the injustice.

Nuggets of Gold

The three of us sit in silence for a moment, then aware that Francine needs to get back to work I thank her profusely for taking time to talk to us. She lets us out a back door of the building into the narrow laneway where I've parked the camper. To my horror, she tells me it's a dead end, so now I have to reverse this enormous camper all the way back to the road. It has side mirrors but no rear-view one, so Alison guides me, while Francine assures me I have plenty of room, as I inch the vehicle slowly back. When I eventually reach the road and promptly hold up the traffic in both directions as I turn this unwieldy machine I vow to never again negotiate it in any direction other than forward.

At a service station on the edge of town we get fuel and address the loose side of the camper roof. Two men see us trying to secure it and come to offer help and advice. One jiggles the latches. The other says we need a shifter, but neither solves the problem. So while Alison buys an INXS CD and a Crowded House CD, I purchase thick tape. We strap the latches down and hope they'll hold.

CHAPTER 34

The Joining of the Line and a Stuart Lookalike

The day is half over and there are 400 kilometres to cover to Daly Waters. Back on the Stuart Highway, a sign warns of road trains over 50 metres long. We pass Banka Banka Station, where Francine's grandparents lived, but we don't stop until Renner Springs. We pull up outside the roadhouse and quickly eat the sandwiches Alison has made for lunch, before driving on. Renner Springs marks the end of the dry centre and the start of the Top End with its monsoonal rains.

In the first few months of 1871, the crews building the northern section of the Overland Telegraph Line felt the full force of the wet season. Sometimes 250 millimetres of rain fell in a day. The tracks became flooded and impassable, construction was impossible, food supplies couldn't reach the camps, and half the workers went on strike. Seeing the low morale of the workers, William McMinn, the government overseer of the northern section, terminated Darwent and Dalwood's contract and accused the contractors of mismanagement.

Work on the southern and central section was going well, so Charles Todd assumed that the northern section was also progressing as planned. Then, on 8 July 1871, the ship *Gulnare* arrived at Port Adelaide, carrying McMinn, the contractors and 50 workers. Charles Todd wasn't in Adelaide at the time, but the government acted quickly, appointing Robert Charles Patterson, an assistant engineer with the railways, to oversee the completion of the work. Three weeks later Patterson left for Port Darwin with six ships loaded with men and supplies.

Robert Burton, McMinn's deputy, was the surveyor left in charge

The Joining of the Line and a Stuart Lookalike

of the northern section at this time, but in the valuable months of the dry season no new poles were planted. And a lack of transport to haul additional wire from Darwin meant that Burton and the 27 men who had remained had managed to run only 48 kilometres of wire.

Patterson sent three working parties to continue constructing the line from where Darwent and Dalwood had stopped, south of Katherine. He also sent the *Gulnare*, loaded with supplies, around to the Gulf of Carpentaria, with instructions to sail the ship as far up the Roper River as possible. But the ship ran aground on a reef at the Vernon Islands, northeast of Darwin, and never reached the river.

Over a third of the 500 bullocks shipped from Adelaide had died on the voyage. And now, because it had been a particularly dry season, Patterson had three construction parties heading southwards whose animals were dying because of a scarcity of water and no supplies to relieve them.

Patterson realised that the line couldn't be completed by 1 January 1872, as stipulated in the South Australia government's contract with the British Australian Telegraph Company (BAT). His main concern was now for the safety of the men. He knew he needed to call on Todd for help. The quickest way to contact Adelaide would have been to send a boat to Batavia, where a message could be telegraphed to Galle in Ceylon – present day Sri Lanka – and picked up by the next mail ship to Adelaide. But his telegram would have been handled by BAT, and although telegraph operators weren't meant to disclose the contents of private messages, he was reluctant to trust that its contents wouldn't be disclosed. He therefore sent a message on a ship sailing to Galle, from where it went on the next mail ship to Adelaide. In the message he explained to Todd that he needed 30 teams of bullocks or horses to be taken up the Roper River in order to complete the line.

Patterson wasn't by nature a cheerful man, but his spirits were dampened further by the arrival in Darwin in October 1871 of the Telegraph Construction and Maintenance Company's cable-laying fleet. The cable was brought ashore, and in early November the ship *Hibernia* started rolling out the undersea cable. On 20 November, Captain Douglas, the Government Resident in Port Darwin, received a telegraph message from Captain Halpin, the commander of the cable-laying expedition:

> *I have the honour to announce to you, in the name of the Telegraphic Construction and Maintenance Company, that we yesterday completed perfect submarine cable communications with your colonies, and with Java, the mother-country, and the Western World. May it long speak words of peace and reiterate 'Advance Australia!'*

Now Port Darwin could communicate with London – but not with Adelaide or the rest of Australia.

When the wet season set in again in November 1871, not one pole had been put up since McMinn had cancelled the contract. Patterson sent another message to Todd, saying the situation was worse than he had previously thought and that he needed further reinforcements. Poling began again in December, but by the end of the year the continually bogged working parties were making slow progress.

By the end of 1871 the southern and central sections of the Overland Telegraph Line – from Port Augusta to Tennant Creek – had been completed, and from Darwin the wire ran to south of Katherine. There was, however, a gap of 618 kilometres. It was raining heavily and workers' lives were endangered because of a lack of supplies. When Patterson saw in the new year while camped with 40 men on the Roper River, they had only two days of food left.

Four black cockatoos fly ahead of us as we come over a ridge. It's four o'clock when we reach the small town of Elliott.

'I thought Powell Creek Telegraph Station was before Elliott,' I say.

'There's nothing on the map,' Alison replies.

I slow down and stop beside the road. She hands me the map, which shows that there's nothing marked between Renner Springs and Elliott. It then occurs to us that when we were planning our journey we weren't looking at this map – which we picked up from the tourist information centre in Alice Springs – but the Hema one instead. Alison now unfolds the Hema map and there it is – 'Powell Creek', clearly marked, 61 kilometres back down the highway. Powell Creek is the next telegraph repeater station along the line. I was keen to look around its abandoned buildings, but there isn't time to turn back. I'm still upset at having missed it when we reach the turning to Newcastle Waters.

We cross a causeway over the large lagoon where Stuart and his party bathed and fished when they found it in 1861. It truly is an oasis.

The Joining of the Line and a Stuart Lookalike

Long-legged grey brolgas wade in the shallows and straw-necked ibis scour the muddy water with their long, curved bills. On the bank stands a great egret and nearby a yellow-billed spoonbill, while little coots scoot back and forth across the still, silvery surface.

At the top of the hill is the entrance to Newcastle Waters Station and the nearby ghost town, doomed by the end of long-distance droving. We peer into a deserted building and see a wall made of brown longneck bottles and mud. This was the Junction Hotel, established by local storekeeper Jack Sergeant and built out of scrap materials, including old windmills, by people who owed him money. Once it was completed he considered his debtors' slates were clean. The Junction Hotel quickly became a favourite drinking hole for drovers.

We explore the nearby empty corrugated-iron buildings. I'm wondering how to find out which of them was the telegraph station, given there's no one around, when a handsome man in his 20s wearing a wide-brimmed hat pulls up in a truck.

'Could you tell me where the telegraph station is?' I ask. He looks puzzled, then says, 'These guys should know,' as a ute appears from the opposite direction and stops. 'They're from Telstra.'

'There's an awful lot of traffic in Newcastle Waters,' Alison says.

The Telstra men appear delighted to find someone interested in communication wires in this dusty, deserted township. 'There's a new repeater station,' one tells us. He says they're from Brisbane and are currently installing optic fibres into said station. None of them, however, knows of an old telegraph station, and they drive off.

Newcastle Waters marks the end of the 250-kilometre Murranji stock route, which starts from Victoria River, north-west of here. The Mudburra people guided Nat Buchanan, who pioneered the route, to the two major waterholes along it. It reduced the east-west droving route via Katherine by 600 kilometres. But without permanent water it was an unreliable and dangerous route, taking the lives of cattle and men and earning it a notorious alternative name – the Ghost Road of the Drovers.

In 1904, Blake Miller, one of Sidney Kidman's drovers, brought 1000 head of cattle from Victoria River Downs Station down this track and into South West Queensland. The cattle king became so excited when he received a telegram saying the droving had been successful that he rushed into the glasshouse at Eringa to tell Isabel – and sent both his wife and her pelargoniums flying. Several years later Kidman bought a quarter share in Newcastle Waters Station.

While researching the Overland Telegraph Line I came across a piece of writing by Arthur Beau Palmer, an ethnographer who was head of Land Claims for the Northern Land Council in the late 1970s. Over a number of years he mapped Mudburra names on the Country around Montejinni at the Victoria River end of the Murranji Track with an elderly Mudburra stockman, Albert Laika Crowson, and two of his brothers. Albert had grown up living traditionally before he became a stockman, and sitting around a campfire in the evening told stories to educate this 'white boy'.

Albert Laika Crowson talked about the early contact days between white settlers and his family, Arthur Palmer explains, relating how initially Albert's mother and father could not even conceptually differentiate between rider and horse – that 'the first explorers and drovers seen riding through the scrub were perceived as one being, a centaur-like supernatural form'. Albert's family group were wary of these Europeans because they always travelled as groups of men without women.

Albert Laika Crowson told Arthur Palmer that his father's traditional Country had been much further south in the Mudburra estate and the reason for the move was the building of the Overland Telegraph Line.

Albert said that his father thought the telegraph line must be a fence, and being 15 foot high, presumably for a tall animal not agile enough to duck underneath it or climb over it. As all the other introduced animals were fairly harmless herbivores, Albert's father's group were not too concerned.

But when stone buildings were constructed with gun slits facing in all directions they deduced that the animal to be introduced must be extremely large, probably also carnivorous and fierce, if the whites needed these fortresses for protection. Perhaps it ate the newly introduced cattle, they thought, and if the white men were afraid of it, maybe it would also eat blackfellas.

The tricky question was on which side of the fence, which stretched to the horizon in both directions, was this beast going to be kept. Because there was a 50:50 chance of being on the wrong side of the fence the group decided to quickly and permanently locate as far away as possible.

The Joining of the Line and a Stuart Lookalike

'The embellished stories told by this group to their Northern cousins justifying this move took a lot of living down in later years when the telegraph line monster failed to materialise,' Arthur Palmer concluded. He reflected on Albert's wonderful humour when I spoke to him on the telephone. And later he emailed me a photograph of a collection of superbly crafted spear points, including one made from a white porcelain insulator. Many business communications between London and Australia he said 'were to be rudely interrupted by somebody taking advantage of this newly, evenly distributed, welcome and valuable resource'.

The Telstra men drive back down the road and point out a corrugated-iron house with an air-conditioning unit protruding from one side just beyond the deserted general store and hotel. They say it used to be the telegraph station. I knock on the door, and a boy stares at me from behind the flyscreen, until his mother, Tash Barlow, appears. She tells me her son is one of the 10 pupils at the local school. She knows nothing of the history of the building, but I discover later that it was built in 1942 when the line was upgraded in World War II.

It is late afternoon when, 50 kilometres up the Stuart Highway, I turn off the road again. 'What are you doing?' Alison asks.

'We have to stop here. This is where the line was joined,' I reply, leaping out of the cab. A couple of Oppenheimer poles and an unimpressive small stone obelisk mark the point, 1.6 kilometres west of here at Frew Ponds, where Robert Patterson made the final join of the telegraph line.

For over three months, from late December 1871 to April 1872, no work was done on the telegraph line because of the wet season. The three working parties were camped in different spots, each marooned by high floodwaters. Two of the teams were reduced to a diet of nothing but biscuits. But when the flooding eventually subsided, work steamed ahead to complete the last sections of the line.

Now what was urgently needed was a pony express to carry telegrams across the several gaps in the wire. Patterson, though, didn't want to slow the completion of the line by using horses currently deployed on its construction. Then in May 1872, John Lewis and his brother Jim arrived at Barrow Creek with 40 horses, having travelled from Adelaide with plans to start a stud in Port Darwin. The South Australian government leased the horses and employed the brothers and their four stockmen until the line was completed.

With the equine express covering the gaps in the line, messages from Adelaide could now reach London in eight to 10 days. On 24 June 1872, John Lewis and one of his men rode south from Daly Waters to Tennant Creek with the first-ever private cables from England. The same day another message was sent down the line from Darwin, saying communication had been lost with Batavia because the undersea cable was dead.

There were mixed feelings when the South Australian government received the news in Adelaide, because they had just learned that BAT now intended to lay a cable from Port Darwin to the mouth of the Norman River in the Gulf of Carpentaria. That would mean that all communications could go via Queensland, leaving South Australian's long and expensive Overland Telegraph Line unused. It was six months after the contracted completion time of 1 January 1872, so the South Australian government was very much on the back foot. But now, with the undersea cable not operational, BAT was on the defensive.

Charles Todd had arrived in the Top End at the beginning of the year to support Patterson and his men. Now Todd was travelling south, checking the line, while Patterson supervised the final stages of the construction. The last remaining gap was south of Newcastle Waters, but Patterson came down with a fever and was unable to travel that far to make the join. When the final gap was closed, the line was cut at Frew Ponds so that Patterson could have the glory of making the final connection.

On Thursday 22 August, Patterson wrote in his diary:

Half the party seized hold of me and the wire, and the other half of the other end, and stretched with all might and main to bring the two ends together. All our force could not do this. I then attached some binding wire to one end. The moment I brought it to the other end the current passed through my body from all the batteries on the line. I had to yell and let go. Next time I proceeded more cautiously, and used my handkerchief to seize the wire. In about five minutes I had the join made complete, and Adelaide was in communication with Port Darwin. It could have been with England had not the cable broken down.

The Joining of the Line and a Stuart Lookalike

John Lewis also witnessed the event: 'Twenty-one shots were fired from our revolvers, and a bottle of "supposed" brandy was broken over the last post. I think it was tea.'

I stand in the orange evening light and look at the Oppenheimer pole with its wooden crossbar rising out of the red earth, imagining that moment when this great engineering feat was completed and Adelaide could communicate with Darwin. In Adelaide a red ensign was hoisted from the post office tower, the bells of the town hall rang, and the city celebrated the success. Charles Todd, meanwhile, was camped at the foot of Central Mount Stuart, where he attached his pocket relay to the line.

Messages from politicians, ambassadors, dignitaries and friends were relayed down the line, including from Alice, who went with the Todd children to the GPO to send congratulations. Charles Todd responded long into the night until – feeling bitterly cold – he couldn't tap another reply.

'Thus the great work, notwithstanding all our disasters and mishaps was successfully accomplished within two years', Charles Todd wrote in his diary. This man, who had left school at 15, had finally realised his long-held dream.

The tall stringybarks and woollybutts beside the highway cast long shadows over the bitumen. A wedge-tailed eagle stands beside the road. We're still driving when the sun sets, and it's nearly dark by the time we turn off the Stuart Highway to Daly Waters. We motor down the township's one street and pull up outside the hotel. My heart sinks when I see the 'ANGLE PARKING' sign. I'm contemplating how to position this beast of a vehicle, until I read the line underneath: 'Any angle mate!'

We walk into the bar, where we are told that Steve rang earlier. The place is noisy and filled with people. I've got mobile reception here, so I go back outside to ring him. I'm busily assuring him that we're fine, that it's only just got dark here and we haven't been negotiating the wilds of the Northern Territory in the dead of night, when a bearded man on a bicycle appears out of the darkness,

'Are you Ros?' he asks in a strong Scottish accent.

'I am.'

'Follow me,' he says, climbing onto his bicycle.

Alison and I get back in the van and drive slowly behind him to our designated camping spot, which is directly opposite his tent.

When he stops we notice a brown, fluffy toy horse attached to the handlebars of his bicycle. With his broad hat and long bushy beard, this is a reincarnation of John McDouall Stuart, riding his beloved mare, Polly.

The claim to fame of the Daly Waters Pub is that it's the oldest pub in the Territory. Inside it's festooned with memorabilia. Next to a wind-up telephone is a large bovine bone. Colourful bras and underpants hang from beams, banknotes cover every vertical surface, and thongs dangle like ferns from wooden posts in the beer garden.

We are joined at the bar by the John McDouall Stuart lookalike. This Scotsman, Ed Granville, comes from near where Alison grew up, north of Glasgow. The old bushy has been in Australia for 47 years, and he tells us over a beer that he used to be a psychiatric and disabilities nurse in Melbourne. A need for some time out from that world led him to Daly Waters, and for several years he worked here on a station. This is the first year he has worked at the hotel's campsite. He has his first-aid equipment in his tent, and his medical knowledge, he says, has already proven useful when one of the backpackers working at the pub had appendicitis. Alison and he talk about Scotland, prattling faster and faster with thickening accents, and interspersed with whoops of delight that they both know the same places.

Later in the evening we meet Lindsay Carmichael and his partner, Robyn Webster, owners of the pub for the last 15 years. Robyn shows us a picture of Stuart on his mare, Polly, crossing the Katherine River. It was painted by Kevin Rogers, one of the 23 residents of Daly Waters. Downing his beer, Ed Granville describes his Stuart persona as 'a bit of fun for the tourists', but I can't help seeing the similarities between these two Scotsmen, who have both found solace in the vast Australian outback.

CHAPTER 35

Floating and Flooding

'Definitely a day for swimming,' announces Alison. She studies the map and calculates that we can drive to the thermal springs in Mataranka in less than two hours.

But before we get onto the highway, we drive down a dirt track to the Stuart Tree, which Ed Granville was adamant we visit. Surrounded by a metal fence, this is the tree trunk on which it's thought that Stuart, or one of his party, carved a large 'S'. After peering at it from several angles we eventually make out the faint marking. Even with my love of history, it's a monumental anticlimax.

Even more disappointing are the set of stone steps and part of a rusty telegraph pole in the nearby undergrowth, which are all that remains of the telegraph repeater station. Ed Granville told us this building was made of lancewood, a hardwood of the region that termites don't eat. But, for whatever reason, there's no sign of the building now.

When the telegraph repeater station at Daly Waters opened in June 1872, John Lewis's pony express operated between here and Tennant Creek until the line was finally completed in August. In the early years, stores for the telegraph station came every six months by ship from Adelaide to Roper Bar, about 300 kilometres away, and the staff rode there to collect them.

In June 1875, the stationmaster, Charles Johnston, with two members of his staff, Abram Daer and Charles Rickards, and two Aboriginal men travelled from Daly Waters to Roper Bar. They were looking for lost horses they thought might have strayed back to that area. Along the way they were joined by more Aboriginal men, including a number of Mangarrayi men from Mole Hill, 75 kilometres upstream of Roper Bar. Arriving at the bar, Johnston went for a swim in the river with one of the Aboriginal men from Daly Waters. Daer, meanwhile, went to get water, and Rickards remained at the camp. Daer heard a noise and saw Rickards being speared. He ran to Johnston to raise the alarm, only to find that Johnston had been speared several times. Daer was wounded as he tried to assist Johnston, but he then drew the stationmaster's revolver and drove off the aggressor. One of the Aboriginal men from Daly Waters was beaten by the attackers, some of whom were the Mangarrayi men who had joined the telegraph party earlier. Eventually, he and the other Aboriginal man from Daly Waters were persuaded to flee with these men.

Johnston died the next day, but Daer and Rickards managed to make their way back, despite the long distance, to Daly Waters telegraph station. Daer died from his wounds five weeks later.

The *Northern Territory Times and Gazette* reported on 17 July 1875:

There is some little satisfaction in knowing that the perpetrators of this murder will be punished, and the promptness with which the Government have dispatched a party to the scene of the occurrence is worthy of all praise.

A party of police officers and volunteers, who were either telegraph or ex-telegraph staff and would have known Johnston and his men personally, set out for Roper Bar. Over a four-week period in August they killed Aboriginal people up and down a 200-kilometre stretch of the Roper River. There were reports of serious disagreements between the volunteers and the police over what occurred along the Roper River. Some of the men were troubled by the indiscriminate approach of this punitive expedition. In one instance, men who had worked at the Roper depot objected to the murder of two Ngalakan Elders they knew to be both innocent and harmless. As at Barrow Creek, it was not an execution of justice but a massacre – and another atrocity which leaves me yearning for healing for this place and its people.

By 8.30 am we're back on the Stuart Highway. Stringybarks and woollybutts grow on both sides of the road, and among them we occasionally see the pink trunks of salmon gums or bean trees with their red pods. A great white egret stands motionless beside the bitumen, and lorikeets flit through the green canopy.

Floating and Flooding

We see a group of people ahead, but when we get closer we find two cyclists stopped beside a group of termite mounds, which someone has dressed in purple, red and green T-shirts. A wallaby bounces across the highway and, soon after, with a loud honk, a road train overtakes us.

We are halfway to Mataranka when we find ourselves behind another road train. It's creeping along at 80 km/h.

'You could overtake it,' Alison tentatively suggests, as I slow down and sit on its tail.

'Do you realise how long it is? It could be longer than an Olympic swimming pool,' I reply, sticking resolutely behind it. But when it slows to 70 kilometres an hour, I decide I have to pass it. Another vehicle hasn't driven past in either direction for the last 10 minutes, and we're on a straight stretch of road, so now is as good a time as any. The process seems interminable as we move slowly pass the first long trailer, then the second and third, before passing the driver in his high cab.

'That wasn't as long as an Olympic swimming pool,' Alison observes as we whizz northwards.

Just before Mataranka we turn off to the thermal pool. The parking area at the Mataranka Homestead resort is packed with caravans. There is a replica of the Elsey Station homestead from the 1982 film adaptation of Jeannie Gunn's novel *We of the Never Never*, and in the resort shop we're told that the movie is shown daily in Maluka's Bar at noon. A boardwalk through the tall cabbage tree palms leads to the Mataranka thermal pool. A far cry from a peaceful oasis, it is filled with grey nomads, backpackers and young families with children. The clear water, which gushes in from the nearby Rainbow Springs, is the temperature of a warm bath. This mineral-enhanced liquid is so relaxing that we bob about with everyone else until our fingers are wrinkled like prunes. Then we decide to take another dip at Bitter Springs on the other side of Mataranka.

We stop in the town, where I marvel at the enormous termite mound and expound to Alison about what an extraordinary feat of nature it is. But as we get closer, we notice that it's made of concrete – and it talks. One press of a button and out pours information about the nearby tourist attractions. Also studying this local icon is one of the cyclists we passed on the highway this morning. From Wollongong, south of Sydney, he tells us his seven-week cycling holiday isn't the adventure he anticipated but instead a long and painful haul. He's now in dire need of rest and relaxation. We give him a banana and wave him on his way to the thermal pool.

Bitter Springs is a couple of kilometres out of the town. The high mineral content of the water here imparts a bitter taste to it, which prompted Stephen King, a surveyor on the Overland Telegraph Line, to give the place its name in 1871. The local Yangman and Mangarrayi people, who call the springs Korran, believe they were created by the spirits of the red-tailed black cockatoo.

We walk through the paperbark trees and cabbage tree palms to a crystal-clear blue water pool fringed with pandanus and bulrushes. The current carries us a couple of hundred metres down a stream, past the reeds and overhanging palms, to a second pool. A ladder here leads up to a path, so we climb out, walk back up the path and float down several more times. Tiny fish swim below us and dragonflies dance just above the surface.

This spring water flows into the Little Roper, which joins the mighty Roper River about 20 kilometres from here. In 2009, Steve and I crossed the legendary Roper Bar, the natural rock shelf across the wide river, 180 kilometres east of Mataranka. It was near here that Patterson and 40 men were marooned in the pouring rain and rising flood waters – with only two days' food supply – on 1 January 1872, the day on which the Overland Telegraph Line should have been completed.

They made a raft out of one of the wagons, strapping kegs underneath it to improve its buoyancy. Patterson and four men set off down the fast-flowing, flooded Roper River on 2 January, in search of the *Bengal*, the ship bringing their supplies. The raft was unstable, and the strong current meant this was a one-way trip – they couldn't row back. Not wanting to risk their craft being upturned during the night, they tied up to the bank when darkness fell. With rain pouring all night, it was miserable for the men. They set off again the following morning and, that afternoon, having travelled 48 kilometres, they saw the masts of the *Bengal* around a river bend. They boarded the ship and were given a substantial meal and dry bunks.

The following day two longboats, each with four oarsmen, set off up the river. They were loaded with stores for the rest of the men. Meanwhile

Floating and Flooding

the *Bengal*, hampered by the strong current and little wind, continued its slow journey upstream after them.

Patterson remained on the ship, and a small cutter named *Larrakeeyah* came up the river with the news that on 3 January the ship *Omeo* had set sail from Adelaide for the Roper River. Carrying not only the extra men, stock and stores that Patterson had requested, the *Omeo* was also transporting Charles Todd himself. Patterson was furious when he heard that Todd was leading the relief party. To this pessimistic man, it meant that his career and reputation were further ruined. With reinforcements, he planned to finish the line as quickly as possible, believing that would restore his reputation and make the government recognise the valuable job he had done, despite the adverse circumstances. Now it appeared to Patterson that Todd was coming to accomplish what he hadn't been able to do. He therefore decided to resign. He went down the Roper River on the *Larrakeeyah* and camped on Maria Island at the mouth of the river, waiting for Todd.

The *Omeo* arrived at Maria Island in the Gulf of Carpentaria on 27 January. Patterson declared his intention to resign, but Todd said he didn't want his resignation and was there only to lend weight to what Patterson was doing.

Now the two men faced another problem: the *Omeo* was at the mouth of the Roper River, but stock couldn't be unloaded and were dying. A smaller ship, the paddle-wheel steam tug *Young Australian*, was supposed to assist in moving cargo, but she hadn't arrived. The only option was to take the *Omeo*, this large, ocean-going steamer, up the river.

Todd assured the captain that the South Australian government would compensate him for any mishap. So, on a rising tide, the *Omeo* crossed the bar. The crew constantly took depth soundings as the steamer slowly made her way up the river. The *Larrakeeyah*, meanwhile, went back to the mouth of the Roper to find the *Young Australian*.

The extreme flooding of that wet season enabled both the *Omeo* and the *Bengal* to travel 145 kilometres up the river to the depot, where the men had built a jetty. Captain Sweet of the *Bengal* took photographs of these large ships in this temporary river port. Not only were the stock, stores and equipment of the *Omeo* unloaded, but so were the passengers, who included women and children. The *Omeo* was meant to take them to Darwin, but now it was returning directly to Adelaide. Ravaged by mosquitoes, the passengers and the line construction workers camped at the depot for two months. The river rose, the rain continued to fall and the areas surrounding the camp became more flooded.

The rain eventually stopped in March. Todd returned on the *Young Australian* to Port Darwin, from where he planned to follow the telegraph line to Adelaide, inspecting it as he went. But when he arrived in Port Darwin he found there were not enough horses for him to make the trip to Adelaide. So, having checked a few kilometres of line built by Darwent and Dalwood, he returned to the Roper depot and started his journey south from there.

***

Mid-afternoon we eventually emerge from the crystal-clear water. It's only 100 kilometres to Katherine, so just over an hour later we reach our campsite. It's near the river, which John McDouall Stuart, with his propensity for bestowing names on places, called the Katherine River after one of James Chambers' daughters. As it is only a short walk from here to the town's springs, Alison takes herself off for another swim while I go in search of the telegraph repeater station.

From the information centre at the southern end of the town I'm directed along Gorge Road. On a quiet side road near the hospital I find an information sign that indicates the site of the original Katherine settlement. It was here that the telegraph station stood, and later the Sportsman's Hotel and a store were built nearby.

I follow the road less than a kilometre down the hill to the river. The settlement was above what was known as the Katherine Crossing, until Fred and Kate Knott took over the Gallon Licence Store in the 1920s, when it became known as Knotts Crossing. I park the vehicle and am walking down to the crossing when I see a sign:

Floating and Flooding

WARNING

Estuarine / Saltwater Crocodile attacks can cause injury or death. These animals are known to move in this area undetected. Freshwater Crocodiles inhabit this area. They can become aggressive and cause injury if disturbed.

A picture on the sign shows a saltwater croc with its long jaws open, ready to snap, and below is depicted a freshwater croc lurking under the water's surface. Faced with these sobering facts, and given that I'm the only person here, I walk gingerly across the sand to look at the natural causeway. It's a serene spot but, wary of skulking salties, I don't linger and soon scurry back to the safety of the camper.

Further down Gorge Road, on a fence made of old Oppenheimer poles, I see a 'Private Property' notice and, behind it, a large green National Trust sign: 'Overland Telegraph Line 1871. Original Crossing Point at Katherine River.'

Private property or not, I have to explore this place. I walk down a short concrete path to find a nine-metre-tall stone pylon on top of which are two 15-metre Oppenheimer poles. A similar pylon stands 400 metres from this one on the far bank of the river. They were constructed in 1899 to solve the problem of floodwaters damaging the telegraph line.

Standing here in the dry season, I find it hard to imagine that the poles would need to be so high. But the ground between the pylon and the river is piled with flood debris – leaves and branches of palm trees – validation of how high the river rises in the wet season. I later learn that the river can rise over 20 metres, and crocodiles have been seen floating down the main street of town.

Back at the campsite I find Alison basking in the sunshine, blissfully content after her latest submersion. 'Why don't you go down for a swim?' she suggests. It's the ideal end to the day. I walk along the path beside the river down to the thermal springs and drop into the warm water. I swim down a channel to the main pool, where palms overhang the blue water and a group of Aboriginal children splash about, jumping from the bank into the water. I swim slowly, savouring every moment here in this idyllic spa as I try to envisage what it must be like to have this oasis as the local swimming pool.

I shower and change into a cotton skirt and top. It's hard to believe on this warm evening that only three nights ago in Alice Springs I was wearing multiple jumpers and a beanie. Alison is in the camp kitchen, putting together a risotto and salad for dinner. While eating we decide to get up very early tomorrow to have a dip at Edith Falls. The last repeater station between here and Darwin is at Yam Creek. I scour our Hema map of the Top End, but I can't find it.

CHAPTER 36

Pools and Poles

We eat breakfast under a scarlet sky, and by the time the sun comes up we're on the Stuart Highway, belting out 'There is freedom within, there is freedom without' at the top of our voices to Crowded House's 'Don't Dream It's Over'.

Forty kilometres north of Katherine I take the turning to Leliyn. It was the government overseer William McMinn, during the construction of the Overland Telegraph Line, who named the river Edith after the South Australian governor's wife, and Leliyn became known as Edith Falls. We drive down a hill into a blue morning haze that sits in the trees. It's a short walk from the car park to the falls. A wallaby sits up on its hind legs and watches us. An orange-flowered fern-leaved grevillea grows on the bank of the huge freshwater pool fringed by pandanus and paperbarks, and at the far end water cascades over the rocks.

A couple are just leaving as we arrive. We have this magnificent basin of water to ourselves. After the thermal springs in Mataranka and Katherine, initially the water feels cool, but I swim out to the middle and quickly warm up, while Alison floats on her back with her arms outstretched and a huge smile on her face. I kick my feet in sheer joy and swim to the waterfall.

We're standing on the bank drying ourselves half an hour later when a couple of grey nomads appear.

'I definitely wouldn't swim there,' the man says.

'Why?' Alison and I ask.

'There's a large crocodile trap further downstream.'

'That's only for after the wet,' I snap. But still can't help feeling uneasy at the thought of what might lurk in the depths of this enormous pool.

The camper has to be at the car rental place by 2.30, so we decide to have a final swim at Berry Springs, about an hour's drive from Darwin. We stop at Pine Creek, which became a thriving mining town after members of the Overland Telegraph Line construction party discovered gold in this area. Now it's a small and sleepy place. We buy bread for lunch at the general store. No one there can tell us the location of Yam Creek, let alone the repeater station. And the National Trust Museum, which has an Overland Telegraph Line display, isn't open. So we continue north, whizzing past another telegraph station. Later, I learn that it's just off the Stuart Highway not far north of here. There is little evidence of the telegraph buildings today, but it was at Yam Creek that the telegraph workers, while digging holes for the poles, hit gold.

On both sides of the highway are tall, sandy-coloured termite mounds and yellow-flowered kapok trees. Kites feeding off a dead kangaroo take to the air as we approach.

Driving into the town of Adelaide River, I see a sign for an Overland Telegraph Line exhibition at the old railway station. 'We have to stop,' I say, pressing my foot to the brake. Outside a large corrugated-iron shed are 10 varieties of telegraph pole, including six different types of Oppenheimer pole and 'Dog-Bone 80 lbs rail' railway line used by the military during World War II for the line upgrade.

Inside, the shed is filled with telegraph line artefacts, all meticulously labelled – timber bearers, original insulators similar to the ones Fleur and I found at Merna Mora, and the smaller thinner insulators like the one I found at Oodnadatta. In a cabinet are metal straps, which were fitted around the top of the timber telegraph poles to prevent splitting. There's also a length of the original galvanised-iron line, a section of the line installed in 1889, and a segment of the copper wire added in 1899. I feel as if I have fallen on a treasure trove as I peer into the glass cabinets and study each display.

I come across a fiercely worded notice from the Commonwealth of Australia in 1907. Titled 'Damaging Telegraph or Telephone Insulators', it states that 'any person who unlawfully or maliciously breaks, injures, or removes any insulator or any post or apparatus connected therewith, is liable to imprisonment with or without hard labour'. I think of the photograph of the spear point carved from an insulator sent to me by Arthur Palmer.

Pools and Poles

There is no one else in this shed, so I search the rest of the museum in the hope of finding an Overland Telegraph Line expert who can direct us to Yam Creek. But the place is deserted, so we keep going north. A glossy ibis flies over the Adelaide River as we cross the bridge.

At Berry Springs we pull into the only available space in the car park. It's Saturday, so the pools are packed. Couples and families splash about in the water as music blasts from a radio. People perch on rocks beneath the shade of the pandanus around the water's edge. We swim to the waterfall in the upper pool and sit where the warm water pummels our backs. We then float down the narrow channel to the main pool to find further throngs.

Alison grabs ingredients from the fridge and makes us sandwiches, and I put my foot to the floor. With Crowded House's 'Weather with You' on full volume, we set off on the final 50 kilometres to Darwin. We pass the turning to Point Stuart, the exact spot on the north coast that John McDouall Stuart and his party reached in 1862.

Stuart was heralded a hero when he returned to Adelaide, having finally, after all his attempts, crossed the continent. Initially he stayed at Montefiore House with James Chambers' widow and their children, and then moved to rooms in the Freemasons' Tavern. He was unwell and drinking heavily and without family or an income. His eyesight was bad, his damaged hand was immobile, he had severe stomach pains – and word was spreading around the city about his constant drunkenness.

He asked the South Australian government for the £2000 reward for his transcontinental crossing. But he was no longer thought capable of handling his own affairs, so rather than the principal sum itself, he received only the interest of £162 a year. He was considered for a knighthood but didn't received one; Governor Daly, after whom Stuart had named Daly Waters, said he couldn't recommend him because of his 'unfortunate habits of intemperance'.

His companions from his final expedition went their own ways, back to families and on to other activities. Stuart got his surveyor's licence again, but bush surveying was now too much for him because of ill health. He paid the government £500 to extend his lease on the 1000 square miles at Chambers Creek, but seven months later he sold it at a loss to James Chambers' brother John.

Stuart's other benefactor, William Finke, died in January 1864, and in April that year Stuart returned to Britain. He lived initially with his widowed sister in Glasgow, then with his older sister and her husband in London. His journals were published, and Stuart presented a copy to Queen Victoria. His supporters at the Royal Geographical Society approached the South Australian parliament for a pension for him, which led to him being given the yearly interest on £1000.

In June 1866, Alexander Hay, a prosperous South Australian pastoralist who was visiting London, opened a copy of *The Times* and saw the death notice for 50-year-old John McDouall Stuart. A couple of days later he attended the funeral of the explorer. Two members of the Royal Geographical Society, four of Stuart's relations and Hay – just seven people – were the only mourners for the man who only three years earlier had been heralded a hero by huge crowds in Adelaide.

We drop the camper off at the car rental place on the outskirts of Darwin, pile our belongings into a taxi and head to the YHA on Mitchell Street in the city centre. The Darwin hostel is smaller than the Alice Springs one, and it's full of backpackers, most of whom are preparing for a big Saturday night on the town.

I'm standing in the hallway, overwhelmed by the list of dos and don'ts we've been given by the woman at reception, but Alison, always pragmatic, is greeting everyone left, right and centre as she navigates us to our allocated dormitory. The bottom three beds are occupied, so we make up two top bunks. The heat is stifling, making it impossible to hurry, so we slowly sort out our food and clothes and head to a nearby café. Its comfortable seats and air conditioning provide great relief, so we linger here. But being used to the perpetual search for poles and wires, I am keen to get out and explore the city.

Three attempts were made to establish settlements on the north coast of Australia in the 1820s and '30s, all of them unsuccessful. Then in 1864, a year after the Northern Territory was annexed to South Australia, Boyle Travers Finniss, a former premier of South Australia, was given command of an expedition and instructed to establish a settlement at the mouth of the Adelaide River. He left Adelaide with livestock, supplies and 40 men, two of whom – Pat Auld and Stephen King – had been on Stuart's sixth expedition. The men landed at Escape Cliffs, where they began measuring

Pools and Poles

out town plots, and Finniss sent parties to search for suitable grazing and farmland. But due to poor leadership, a bad choice of location and conflicts with the local Wulna people, the settlement was abandoned by the end of 1866.

Three years later, Surveyor General of South Australia George Goyder established a settlement at Port Darwin and called it Palmerston, after the British prime minister. While surveying the land, Goyder was invited to a corroboree by the local Larrakia people, who performed word-perfect renditions of 'John Brown's Body' and the 'Glory Hallelujah' chorus. The Larrakia had learned the words from the Wulna, who had memorised the tunes while observing the surveyors working near Adelaide River.

***

Back at the hostel we fall into conversation with Andy, a Scotsman, and Indy, an Estonian. After working in Perth as a civil engineer, Andy is now taking eight months to ride his motorbike around Australia. Indy is about to return to his home country to start a masters in diplomacy and international relations. He tells us he has spent the last three months working on a pearling boat in Western Australia. Every day three of them would leave the main boat on a smaller vessel to retrieve pearls from long lines in the ocean. He fell overboard three times in rough seas, but he was really shaken when he saw a five-metre tiger shark in the spot he had fallen in only minutes earlier.

In the early evening Alison and I walk up Mitchell Street. In the park near the Darwin Civic Centre we find the huge old banyan tree with its pole-like aerial roots. Known as the Tree of Knowledge, it was where the Chinese elders taught their young. On the waterfront we spot the Wave Lagoon. Being free of crocodiles and sharks, Alison decides it's the perfect place for a swim tomorrow – despite my disparaging remarks about man-made waves.

At a Mexican restaurant, where we eat spicy chicken and tortillas, a toddler in a high chair at the next table flings her meal piece by piece onto the floor. Her oblivious parents sit deep in conversation. We toast having reached Darwin but the journey is not over. I need to find where the undersea cable came ashore.

CHAPTER 37

The Undersea Cable and the Telegraph Station

It's only half past seven, and already it's hot and sticky. Alison and I are sitting beside the pool, devouring Weet-Bix doused in cold milk, when Andy appears from the kitchen with a bowl of steaming hot porridge, his staple energy-giving breakfast, regardless of the heat.

I've found an article by Bev Phelps of the Historical Society of the Northern Territory about the Overland Telegraph Line featuring photographs of people looking at remnants of the cable. So Alison and I walk to Damoe-Ra Park on the Esplanade, where native vine thicket clings to the rock, and a tiny peaceful dove struts across the grass. At one end is the Deckchair Cinema; at the other Alison finds a sign about the cable.

The black-and-white photograph of the beach, crowded with people as the submarine cable was landed, has faded and disintegrated. But we can make out the words from Trooper Catchlove's diary on 7 November 1871:

> The steamers Hibernia and Edinburgh sailed [in], the former laying the cable as she went ... the great cable was laid at 11 am. Great excitement met with about 300 present ... when the cables reached the shore; salutes were fired by the Hibernia and Edinburgh in honor of the great event.

And written underneath it says, 'at a point about 200 metres north of this spot the cable was brought ashore and taken up the cliff for connection to the line to southern Australia'.

We clamber over the rocks and walk down the beach to find the cable. Half a kilometre offshore, a grey naval frigate is anchored, and a masked lapwing with its distinctive yellow face perches on a rock, gazing at the

The Undersea Cable and the Telegraph Station

calm turquoise water. I stand among the sprouting mangroves, scanning the shoreline for the cable.

Attached to a pole covered in oyster shells is what looks like a cable, but on closer inspection I find it's a thick piece of rope. Further out I spot another possible cable, arching up out of the water and encrusted in mud and oysters. I then find a piece of twisted old wire near the concrete blocks of the seawall. But in Bev Phelps's photographs there was what looked like a clear line of cable going straight out from the beach.

It's so hot that Alison retreats to the shade of the park, but I keep looking. Further up the beach I find two pieces of grooved concrete, and among the ochre, pink and white porcellanite rocks I discover more. I suspect they had nothing to do with the Overland Telegraph Line, but were rather part of a World War II fortification. Despite my increasing confusion, there's something magical about this beach, so I continue scrambling round the rocks looking for clues – until Alison rings me.

'Are you all right down there?' she asks.

'I can't find the cable,' I wail. I scour the beach again, before deciding I need to draw on local expertise and return.

Slowly we sweat back up the hill. On the Esplanade, near the manicured lawns and white picket fence of Government House, we find a short Oppenheimer pole standing in a flowerbed. This is the site of the first telegraph pole, erected on 15 September 1870, and there's a photograph of its planting. Among those present were Captain Douglas, the Government Resident of the Northern Territory, and his family; William Dalwood, one of the contractors, and his wife and son, who had sailed to Darwin with the expedition on the *Omeo* to see the start of the work; W.A. Paqualin, who was in charge of the construction; surveyor Stephen King, who had been in Stuart's overland party; and the government overseer, William McMinn.

Captain Douglas's daughter, Harriet, performed the ceremony, pounding the soil around the pole with a rammer made especially for the occasion. She also spoke: 'In the name of Her Most Gracious Majesty Queen Victoria I declare this pole well and truly fixed; and I wish Mr Paqualin and the expedition every success.' Everyone sang the national anthem and the *Omeo* fired a royal salute.

As I prance around the pole Alison declares that she's going to Wave

Lagoon for a dip. But I am eager to find the telegraph station and see if I can discover more about the cable at the Northern Territory Library. So we arrange to meet later at the YHA. I walk to the Parliament House building, but discover the library doesn't open until 1 o'clock.

I wander along the Esplanade looking at 1880s buildings constructed from local porcellanite stone and reach the Bombing of Darwin Memorial commemorating the fateful day in 1942 when so many lives were lost. A family friend, 99-year-old Margie Ewart, then in her 20s, was stationed as an army nurse in Darwin at the time. Back in Sydney, I visited her at the RSL Anzac Village. Margie was working at the 119th Australian General Hospital which, she explained, was in the grounds of the Bagot Aboriginal Reserve, its inhabitants having been evacuated.

In February 1942 she got dengue fever. She fluctuated between being confined to bed with a very high temperature and feeling moderately well.

'On the 19th of February,' she recounted, 'I felt reasonably well, so I decided I'd go and have a shower and wash my hair. I was coming back and the sky was covered with these planes flying so high. They looked like little silver moths. I counted up to 128, and then I felt I'd fall backwards if I didn't stop, and, as I was getting a bit dizzy, thought I'd better go and lie down.

'We thought they must be American planes, because every time the Americans lost an area their planes came to Darwin. Anyhow, I went back to bed, and the next thing the doctor is calling out, "Quick, get the patients out! It's the Japanese! Get your patients out into the trenches or into the bush!" The trenches weren't big enough to take all the patients, so those who could walk went into the bush. With those who couldn't be moved, they just lifted the whole mattress and put it under the bed, then took the mattresses from other beds and put them around as protection, and an orderly or trained nurse stayed with each patient.

'I was in a trench. And it was so hot I got dizzy and passed out a few times. Two fighter planes came so low we could see the pilots with their goggles and this *rat-a-tat-tat* of machine guns just above our heads. I've never been so frightened.

'One patient who remained in the hospital was killed when a bullet ricocheted off something and hit him. There was broken glass everywhere, and the mattresses were on fire. It was such a shocking mess. There were

The Undersea Cable and the Telegraph Station

two major air raids that day, and we kept getting smaller ones all through the day, and from then on every night.'

Margie asked if she could go on duty, but she was told by the matron that she could not, because she'd 'faint and be a nuisance'. Instead Margie was given the role of Home Sister. It was thought that any women who hadn't been evacuated from Darwin would come out to the hospital, and she was to look after them.

The first air raid was at 10 o'clock in the morning on Darwin's General Hospital. The first women to arrive were the sisters from there, and Margie had to find beds for them. Then came the nursing sisters from the RAAF camp, which had been bombed to the ground.

'All the oil tanks had been bombed and the harbour was ablaze, and we could see clouds of black smoke. In the early hours of the morning this woman arrived with a six-year-old boy. It was Mrs Jones, the wife of the doctor who was running a leper station on Channel Island, just off Darwin. By this time I'd run out of beds, so I put her in Pat's bed, because Pat was on duty. It was the early hours of the morning before she came off. We had three beds in each room, and I was in the middle one.

'"Shh," I said, when Pat came in.

'"Who's in my bed?" she asked.

'"Mrs Jones from the leper station."

'"What?" she exclaimed. "A bloody leper in the bed?"'

A force of 188 Japanese planes attacked Darwin on the morning of 19 February 1942. Twenty-one ships were sunk or disabled, the waterfront area and much of the town was destroyed, and two hours later a second force attacked the RAAF base. This memorial on the Esplanade states that 292 people were killed in the two raids that day. Hundreds more were injured. In the immediate aftermath, military headquarters, including the army hospital, moved to Adelaide River, and the civilian administration was moved to Alice Springs. There were another 62 air raids on Darwin by the Japanese over the next 18 months, but none of them were as destructive as these first two.

Margie opened an old leather-bound photograph album and showed me a faded black-and-white photograph of her, the other nurses and two doctors in Darwin. The nurses are wearing white caps, capes and identical black shoes. And with her slim figure and jet-black hair, the most glamorous of them all is Margie, kneeling at the front.

Further along the Esplanade, in front of Parliament House, is the Overland Telegraph Memorial, constructed in the 1970s to commemorate the centenary of the completion of the line. Although Patterson had made the final join to the Overland Telegraph Line in August 1872, it was another two months before the underwater cable between Java and Darwin was finally fixed, and on 22 October the first message was transmitted from London to Adelaide. Todd was still travelling down the line and had reached Beltana by this time. He continued south to Burra, and from there travelled by train, arriving weather-worn and sunburnt in Adelaide at the end of October.

Patterson and his men came by ship from the Roper River, reaching Adelaide on 10 November. Five days later there was a huge celebration in the city. All the men who had worked on the line met Todd at the impressive new General Post Office building and marched down King William Street, concluding the celebrations with a banquet at the town hall. Governor Fergusson announced that Charles Todd had been made a Companion of the Order of St Michael and St George. Todd said it was the proudest day of his life. As the men leapt to their feet and cheered, Todd added that the honour was as much theirs as his and the line could not have been built without every one of them. Conspicuously absent from the celebrations was Patterson, apparently because of illness.

A couple of weeks later an MP stood up in the South Australian House of Assembly and proclaimed that the line was insubstantial and shoddily built. Todd didn't know the source of the MP's claim until he read the 8 November edition of Brisbane's *Telegraph*: 'From information obtained from Mr Patterson we learn that the makeshift line at present in use is so badly "built" that there is no possibility of relying on it for any lengthy period.' The article claimed that the line was temporary and that if an area was flooded there would be 'no possibility whatever of effecting repairs'. It concluded: 'Whatever the petty jealousy of the other colonies may have evinced towards Queensland should not prevent our Government from using every endeavour to secure an alternative line of communication.'

Patterson claimed to Todd that he had been incorrectly quoted in the newspaper, but it transpired that he had also been talking critically of

The Undersea Cable and the Telegraph Station

the line to people in Adelaide and had been seen in conversation with the MP who stood up in the House of Assembly. The government refused to give Patterson his bonus until he withdrew his claims. Eventually, as he became increasingly humble, he received his £500.

Patterson said that Todd did not reveal to the government the threat that white ants posed to the wooden poles. Todd insisted that the replacement of wooden poles with metal ones was a maintenance issue rather than a matter of immediate urgency. In 1873 the Overland Telegraph Line handled nearly 9000 messages, even though the minimum cost of a telegram to London was £10, an enormous sum of money at the time.

Meanwhile, Queensland continued to call for a cable from Normanton to Java, and there was also talk of a cable from Western Australia to Ceylon. And while all this discussion was going on, wooden poles along the Overland Telegraph Line continued to be replaced with Oppenheimer ones.

By mid-1875 all discussions about a second cable to Normanton has ceased. But Todd was only too aware of the need to ensure efficiency of the Overland Telegraph Line – South Australia's valuable monopoly.

While continuing as Postmaster General and Superintendent of Telegraphs, Todd also turned his attention to his astronomical and meteorological interests. In 1885 he travelled to Europe, accompanied by his daughter Lizzie. Despite his efforts to matchmake his daughter with his wealthy middle-aged bachelor friend Joseph Oppenheimer – manufacturer of the galvanised-iron poles used on the telegraph line – Lizzie fell in love with solicitor Charles Squires. Todd was elected a Fellow of the Royal Society, and over 20 years after the completion of the Overland Telegraph Line he finally received a knighthood.

At the time of Federation in 1901, his was the only Post and Telegraph department in the country showing a profit; all the others were under the control of a minister rather than a public servant. As Australia could have only one postmaster-general, Todd's title was changed to deputy-postmaster-general. The South Australian government delayed introducing legislation that would make it compulsory for public servants to retire at 70 so that Todd could remain in office, which he did until 1905. He was 78 when he retired. Five years later he died and was buried beside Alice, who had died in 1898, and their son Hedley.

I walk around to the entrance of the Parliament House building, where a security guard puts my bag through a scanner and directs me to the library. I ask librarian Margaret Curry about the Darwin Telegraph Station, adding that I've followed the Overland Telegraph Line from Adelaide. She leads me back to the library entrance and a piece of porcellanite stone wall. I read the adjacent plaque:

> *This portion of the wall left in its original state, is all that remains of the Darwin Telegraph Station built in 1872 when the Overland Telegraph Line was opened. The building was destroyed in an enemy air raid on the 19th February 1942, when ten officers of the Australian Post Office lost their lives very close to this spot.*

Inlaid in the polished granite floor of the main hall is an oval brass plaque that indicates the exact spot where the fatal 450-kilogram bomb fell. On the wall are biographies and photographs of the post and telegraph workers, including two sisters, Eileen and Jean Mullen, and Archibald Thomas Roy Hills, who had joined the Postmaster-General's Department in 1907, aged 15. He had started working in Darwin only five days before the attack.

In charge of the telegraph station on 19 February 1942 was Hurtle Bald. His wife, Alice, was working on the telephone exchange. Because of the high volume of traffic that day, plus her experience as a telephonist in Adelaide, their daughter, Iris, had come down to the telegraph office 15 minutes earlier to help out. The only member of the Bald family to survive that day was Iris's younger brother, Peter, who was at boarding school at the time.

Margie told me that she went back to Darwin 25 years after the bombing with a couple of her nursing colleagues. 'There was a commemorative service, and then everyone went into the Darwin Hotel to have a cooler. We couldn't find anywhere to sit, until some people at a table said, "Come and sit here. We can make room." We sat down and were introduced to Peter Bald and the relatives who he had stayed with when his family were wiped out. He'd grown up, of course. After the dreadful experience of losing his family, he said that his uncle and aunt and cousins had been like family to him.'

I walk back into the library, not quite able to believe what happened to

The Undersea Cable and the Telegraph Station

the telegraph station and how these people lost their lives. Margaret gets up from behind the desk.

'I want to show you something else,' she says. She leads me across the room to a large black-and-white aerial photograph of Darwin on the wall. She points out a faint line that stretches from the beach below Damoe-Ra Park out into the sea.

'That's the telegraph cable,' she says, and I decide to return to the beach tomorrow to continue my search.

By the time I get back to the hostel mid-afternoon, Alison has befriended our roommates – English Kate, Polish Patrice and French Adeline – and she's arranged for us all to go together to the Mindil Beach Sunset Market this evening. As we walk slowly to the market in the stifling heat, Kate, who's in her mid-20s and has been working as an au pair, talks disparagingly about the increasing reliance on the internet for communication. She believes that people are losing the ability to read one another – to pick up on sarcasm, humour, feelings in their interactions. I think of the undersea cables and overland lines in the 1870s stretching from here to Banjoewangi, Batavia, Singapore, Penang, Madras, Bombay, Aden, Suez, Alexandria, Malta, Gibraltar, Falmouth, and then London. Between Adelaide and London was over 20,000 kilometres of line and the Morse code messages transmitted on it were the start of the instant communication that evolved into the digital world we live in today.

We stroll through the rows of market stalls selling everything from Indigenous art to broad-brimmed hats and stockwhips. I buy myself a colourful floral dress and a pair of pearl earrings to celebrate reaching Darwin. Food stalls offer baked potatoes, handmade popsicles, old-fashioned lemonade and pickled octopus, but it's the delicious waft of Thai curries that wins over Alison and me. We join our roommates on the beach and watch the sun transform into a brilliant red ball and slowly disappear below the waterline.

Back at the hostel we open the door of our dormitory to find a woman in a short black dress with a plunging neckline. She is dragging a comb through her long, dark hair.

'I am Mika,' she announces. She goes in and out of the bathroom while applying her make-up, telling us that she's been working for three months as a housekeeper at the Heartbreak Hotel in Cape Crawford.

'Tonight, I'm going to Monsoons to get drunk and party,' she says in her thick Russian accent. She straps on her high heels. 'I bought these from Target for four dollars,' she adds, flicking back her hair. 'I am looking beautiful, so I'll only have to buy one drink and then the men will buy them for me.'

CHAPTER 38

The Mills Family

At 2 am Mika crashes through the door and climbs into her bunk. She doesn't stir when Alison and I get up at seven o'clock. When we return to the dormitory after breakfast, she is sitting up in bed in her black bra looking sultry and hungover. Her evening did not come off as planned, and she didn't want to talk to any of the men who offered to buy her drinks.

Alison is going on an ecotour to Litchfield National Park today while I continue my telegraph investigations. I have arranged to see Lyons Cottage. Peter Van Roden, from the Museum and Art Gallery of the Northern Territory that manages the building, is waiting for me when I arrive. He tells me he was 'made in Holland'; his parents came here in 1952 and he was born soon after.

Situated on the Esplanade overlooking Darwin Harbour, this stone cottage with its blue-painted timber doors and windows was built in 1925 as accommodation for staff of the British Australian Telegraph, operators of the undersea cable. Having survived the Japanese bombings and Cyclone Tracy in 1974, it's the only remaining example of colonial bungalow-style architecture in Darwin.

Peter opens the front door. A light sea breeze this morning flows through the louvred windows as we walk into the empty, high-ceilinged rooms with their picture rails and narrow doorways. A covered walkway leads to the smaller building at the back. In one room there's a copper washtub and two big stone sinks, and Peter tells me that in the second room there would have been a wood-burning stove. On the exterior of the building he shows me tiny native bees buzzing in and out of a hole in the rock.

I walk up to the bus exchange and catch a number 10 to Casuarina, a suburb in the city's north, to meet Patj Patj Janama Robert Mills. The Mills family are a well-known Larrakia family, and Patj Patj owns Batji Tours, which operates guided walking tours of Darwin. This tall, powerful-looking man arrives at the shopping centre with his son, Jaxon, second youngest of nine children. He's not at school today because no one could find his shoes.

I climb into Patj Patj's Landcruiser, the windows wound down and hot air flowing through the vehicle. 'Darwin city is my father's homeland, and I'm a traditional owner,' he says. He tells me that one of his grandfathers, a Malak Malak/Kungarakan man called Ablak, had walked at least twice from Darwin to Mparntwe – Alice Springs – and back. He traversed the boundaries of many Aboriginal groups, learning their culture and sharing his.

'He was respected as a "clever man",' Patj Patj says. 'He had an enormous influence on my life, teaching me the importance of roots, language and culture.'

I'm utterly intrigued at the thought of that journey, and as I ply Patj Patj for details, he tells me he's taking me to meet his mother, Muradup Kathy Nampbitjina McGinness Mills. She is a Gurindji/Kungarakan woman and her homeland, he explains, encompasses country surrounding what is known as Litchfield National Park.

Kathy Mills is a mother of eight children and grandmother of 38. She started campaigning for the rights of Indigenous Australians at the age of 15, and was the first woman to be elected to the Northern Land Council. In the 1960s she and her sister, Vai Stanton, got the idea for an alcohol 'drying out' facility for Aboriginal people, and along with Betty Pearce, Veronica McClintic and Barbara Cummings, founded FORWAARD, the Foundation of Rehabilitation with Aboriginal Alcohol Related Difficulties. On a shoestring budget, they provided shelter and food until 1978, when FORWAARD became government funded.

As well as driving initiatives for the preservation of Aboriginal languages, particularly in Darwin's schools, she was the co-commissioner for the Northern Territory Inquiry into the Stolen Generations in the mid-1990s.

'She's a political fighter and a strong activist,' Patj Patj says. 'She was

The Mills Family

at Parliament House in Canberra when the then prime minister, Kevin Rudd, made the National Apology to the Stolen Generations.'

We pull up outside his mother's home. Patj Patj calls out to her and she opens the flyscreen door, pushing her walking frame into the front porch barefooted. Her face, framed by white hair, suggests a strong engagement with life and also great joy. She sits and indicates for me to sit near her. Patj Patj sits on a chair opposite; Jaxon remains in the Landcruiser.

Kathy Mills grew up in Katherine, where her father worked on the railways. She says she can distinctly remember walking under the counter in the Knotts' shop as a child. 'People used Knotts Crossing when they were going to Darwin,' she says. 'That was the only crossing on the Katherine River that they could negotiate. And that's where the telegraph went through.'

I tell her I saw the tall telegraph poles across the Katherine River. She's recently been talking to a man about the early surveyors and remarks how accurate they were, because every bridge built over the creeks and rivers was situated above the flood level.

'The only one that would catch them would be the 100-year flood. And that's true. It came up 50 metres back in the 1950s.'

She talks about founding KARU in the 1970s, a child-care agency that recruited Indigenous foster parents for Indigenous children and also reunited Indigenous children and their families. 'My mum was a Gurindji woman from Wave Hill and, being of mixed descent, she was taken as a child to the Kahlin Compound.' Her grandmother, on her father's side, a Kungarakan woman, was also sent there after her Irish husband died.

The Kahlin Compound opened in 1913, two years after the implementation of the *Aboriginals Ordinance Act 1911*, in accordance with the policies of Professor Baldwin Spencer, anthropologist and Alice Springs stationmaster Frank Gillen's friend.

The Aboriginal people living in and around Darwin, Spencer believed, had lost their traditional culture and way of living. So together with people of mixed descent, they were placed in the Kahlin Compound. Spencer planned for the compound to be self-sufficient, provide schooling and housing with a vegetable garden for each Aboriginal family, and arranged for inmates be trained in domestic duties so they could work for white people, for which they would be paid minimum wages.

Whispering Wire

The 2003 Human Rights and Equal Opportunity Commission publication *Bringing Them Home – The Report: Learning About the National Inquiry into the Separation of Aboriginal and Torres Strait Islander Children from Their Families*, describes the effect of the *Aboriginals Ordinance Act 1911*:

> *Aboriginal females were under the total control of the Chief Protector from the moment they were born until they died, unless married and living with a husband 'who is substantially of European origin' … They could be taken from their families at any age and placed in an institution. They could be sent out to work at a young age and never receive wages. They had no right of guardianship over their own children who could be similarly taken from them. Male Aborigines fared little better except that they could be released from guardianship at 18.*

The Kahlin Compound operated through the 1920s and 1930s, despite criticism of its living conditions. In early 1937 a cyclone hit Darwin and damaged many of the Kahlin Compound's buildings, causing living conditions to deteriorate further. So in 1938 the residents of the Kahlin Compound were moved to a new reserve, a 369-acre property in the Darwin suburb of Ludmilla, which became known as the Bagot Aboriginal Reserve. But in August 1940 the buildings at Bagot were handed over to the army to be used as a hospital and military camp; this was where Margie Ewart was based when Darwin was bombed in 1942.

'Recognition of prior ownership has always been on the agenda for Aboriginal people,' Kathy Mills says. 'For the First Nations People to be recognised as having full rights. Because with that we are a people and we have our dignity. Until that happens, there'll be no justice for Aboriginal people, and "sorry" doesn't mean anything.

'We've weathered the storm, but we still can't beat the legislation, which is a foreign set of laws. It's a different set of governance to our Aboriginal laws, and it doesn't look at Aboriginal spirituality and how that spirituality controls life and the environment.'

Jaxon leans out of the window of the Landcruiser. 'Hello Jaxon,' his grandmother calls out. 'Would you like a biscuit? Give him a biscuit, Rob, from the tin in the kitchen.' She turns to me and asks if I'd like a cup of tea.

The Mills Family

I can think of nothing better than to sit and drink tea with her for the next several hours, but Patj Patj is eager to go.

'You people have to learn we go on universal time, not Greenwich Mean Time,' she says. I respond that it's her son who is the busy man, and now was the only time he could see me.

'I know,' she replies, 'he goes at this pace because he has to, we are governed by Greenwich, but universal time is best. When the time is right.'

At her mention of Greenwich Mean Time, I can't help thinking that Charles Todd has a lot to answer for. Much of his early working life in England was spent perfecting the science of time measurement. And it was the telegraph that ensured the British population operated on Greenwich Mean Time, enabling post office and town hall clocks across the country to be set to the second. Later in life, Todd became involved in keeping this continent up to the minute with the 1890s movement for standard time in Australia.

'*Mamak*,' says Kathy, as I stand to go, 'It means "goodbye" in Kungarakan.'

'*Mamak*,' I reply.

'*Kemek*,' she replies, 'that means "good".'

'How do I say "thank you"?' I ask.

'We have no words for "please" or "thank you".' Patj Patj explains there is no concept of individual ownership. 'We share what we have.'

'*Kemek, kemek*,' I say.

'That's very good,' Kathy replies. 'And it means "very good".'

Driving back to the city, Patj Patj tells me that his mother has never drunk alcohol or smoked. 'She was always busy,' he adds. 'And there was no television, just radio, when we were growing up. But we had our instruments and would get together and have a singsong, and that's when the stories would come out.'

CHAPTER 39

Connection

Patj Patj pulls up on Smith Street at the site of the first telegraph pole, where he talks about its planting in 1870.

'My people didn't understand the telegraph at all. The government officials tried to explain it, but they still couldn't work it out. "Are they trying to tell us that the voice travels through a piece of wire?" my old people said. They couldn't fathom it. They reckoned it was white man's magic.

'But when they heard the sound of the Morse code, they registered. It was like us singing – telling our story through song. It had a rhythm to it. It was like music or knowledge through song. Once they heard the rhythm, they understood. They realised it was a form of communication.'

On the Esplanade, he stops at Lyons Cottage. 'My father's mother worked here in 1935. She was a domestic. She worked in that outhouse, which was the kitchen and the washhouse,' he says, pointing out the small building at the back. He explains that, being of mixed descent, she was another relative sent to the Kahlin Compound. 'She babysat, as well as cleaned, and she ran errands, including taking the mail up to the post and telegraph office. She was a bit of a rouseabout. Her English name was Alice and her cultural name was Ebinjakbah. She was from the Mataranka area and identified as a Yangman woman.'

He walks across the road and leans against the stone wall. Behind him is the brilliant blue harbour, and eight brown kites sit above him on the branches of a dead tree.

'Darwin is only 150 years old,' he says. 'In that short space of time non-Aboriginal people have destroyed my homeland. They've polluted

Connection

the waters. They've fished out the sea and destroyed my land. Whether they meant to or didn't mean to, they have. Aboriginal people looked after this land for at least 60,000 years, because we lived in harmony with nature. Mainstream civilisation doesn't live in harmony with nature, and it has to find a way to do so.

'Governments have turned a blind eye to the fact that two-thirds of Australia is desert. If they continue to destroy all the greenery on the coastline, we've got nothing but desert and salt water surrounding us.

'So governments need to start thinking how they can accommodate populations without destroying rivers and native wildlife. Having national parks doesn't solve the problem. There has to be conservation across the board, and it's probably our most pressing issue. People aren't aware of it, because you don't miss water until your well runs dry.'

Jaxon, who has been so patient throughout the day, is hungry. Patj Patj says he needs to give him a feed. As he leaves, he says: 'I recognise the people you spoke of in South Australia and in Alice Springs. We all know each other. With the Aboriginal names, including my mother's, and finishing off with mine, it kind of resembles an old Dreaming track, an old songline that connected us people.'

'We're all connected, you know,' he says as he drives off.

I walk down to Damoe-Ra Park and clamber over the rocks to look again for the cable. It's low tide, and a black bittern stands in the shallows. Mud squelches between my toes as I wade towards short rusty metal posts. Beside them, curling up into the air, is what looks like a thick wire cable covered in barnacles. Could this be this the undersea cable? But as the tide recedes I see it is surrounded by bits of concrete, and I wonder if it's a remnant of a later era.

Driving back from his mother's place, Patj Patj told me that Damoe-Ra is a sacred women's site. 'My great-grandmother, my father's grandmother, was a custodian of the area,' he explained. 'It's an ancient meeting ground.' I said this beach felt like a very special place and that I was drawn to spend time there.

'That's a good thing,' he replied.

Mangroves dot the shoreline and the roots of a large fig tree spread tendril-like over the rock. I am mesmerised by the ochre, white and deep-pink rocks and their different shapes. It's as if an artist had dabbed

Whispering Wire

colours here and there in a fervour of inspiration and yet with a hypnotic perfection only nature can create. My eyes move slowly from rock to stone, captured by the brilliance and beauty, and then back to water that gently laps the shore.

I climb back to the park above the beach. I look at the entrance to the Deckchair Cinema with its red-and-white painted corrugated-iron roof and peer over the fence, where the deckchairs are lined up. On the noticeboard is an acknowledgement by the Darwin Film Society of the Larrakia people as the Traditional Owners of Darwin, and a quote from Patj Patj's sister, Elder June Mills Gubiling:

> *We, the Larrakia, call this place 'Damaro' (Damaroa). It is part of a much larger area, which includes Lameroo Beach, the Esplanade and further down towards Doctors Gully. This place was an area filled with freshwater springs. We would come here to fish barramundi, mullet, salmon, prawn, whiting, snapper, bream, shellfish and crab.*
>
> *We would stay as long as we wanted, fishing, swimming and enjoying the area, as fresh water was always available. We would gather bush tucker, which was in abundance throughout this area.*

At the base of the cliffs, near the entrance to a World War II oil storage tunnel, I find a metal telegraph pole. It has four porcelain insulators on one cross bearer and five on the other. It looks to me as if it's an upgrade from the World War II era. I walk across the grass to the information sign about the landing of the cable and read it again: '… 200 metres north of this spot the cable was brought ashore and taken up the cliff for connection to the line to southern Australia.'

My path blocked by a fence in front of the seawall, I am unable to walk out to sea from the sign. So I climb down the seawall near the Deckchair Cinema and walk back along the beach. When I reach the seawall in front of the sign, I walk directly out to sea. There, among old bricks and pieces of concrete, I see a piece of cable, about an inch in diameter, protruding out of the pebbly beach. About a metre long, it's covered in mud and oyster shells.

I've been scouring the mud flats, never looking much higher up the beach, nearer the seawall. But this is it. I've found it. From Adelaide's

Connection

grand General Post and Telegraph Office on King William Street, the telegraph line ran through the heart of Australia to connect with this cable.

I follow the line of the cable down this small, deserted beach and gaze out at the still blue water.

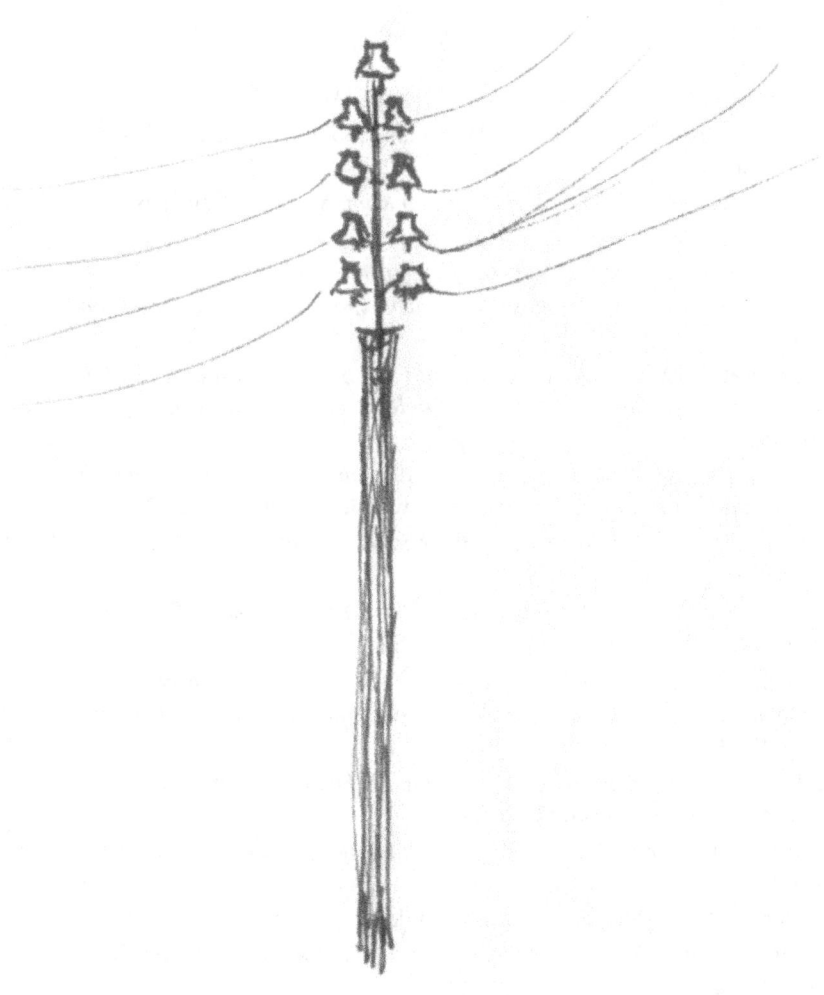

Selected Bibliography and Further Reading

Bailey, John (2006) *Mr Stuart's Track*, Pan MacMillan
Blackwell, Doris and Lockwood, Douglas (1965) *Alice on the Line*, Rigby Publishers
Bowen, Jill (1987) *Kidman: The Forgotten King*, Angus & Robertson
Brooks, David for Mparntwe People (2003) *A Town Like Mparntwe: A Guide to the Dreaming Tracks and Sites of Alice Springs,* IAD Press
Cryle, Denis (2017) *Behind the Legend: The Many Worlds of Charles Todd*, Australian Scholarly Publishing
Clune, Frank (1955) *Overland Telegraph: The Story of A Great Australian Achievement and the Link Between Adelaide and Port Darwin*, Angus & Robertson
Dodd, Reg and McKinnon, Malcolm (2019) *Talking Sideways: Stories and Conversations from Finniss Springs*, University of Queensland Press
Forrest, Peter and Sheila (2011) *In the Middle of Everywhere: A History of Elliott and District*, Shady Tree
Gammage, Bill (2011) *The Biggest Estate on Earth: How Aborigines Made Australia*, Allen & Unwin
Januschka, H.D. and V.J. (1968) *A Stroll in History down the Roper River*
Lockyer, Paul (2012) *Lake Eyre: A Journey through the Heart of the Continent*, ABC Books
McGinness, Joe (1991) *Son of Alyandabu: My Fight for Aboriginal Rights*, University of Queensland Press
Moore, Philip (2005) *A Guide to Plants of Inland Australia*, New Holland Publishers
Moriarty, John (2000) *Saltwater Fella*, Viking
Mudie, Ian (1968) *The Heroic Journey of John McDouall Stuart*, Angus & Robertson

Murif, Jerome J. (1897) *From Ocean to Ocean,* George Robertson and Co.

Northern Territory Government, Heritage Branch (2009) *Kahlin Compound: Background Historical Information*

Pugh, Derek (2022) *Twenty to the Mile: The Overland Telegraph Line*, self-published

Read, John L. (2003) *Red Sand, Green Heart: Ecological Adventures in the Outback*, Lothian Books, reprinted by Wakefield Press 2020

Roberts, Tony (2005) *Frontier Justice: A History of the Gulf Country to 1900*, University of Queensland Press

Roberts, Tony (November 2009) 'The Brutal Truth: What happened in the Gulf Country', *The Monthly*

Simpson, Ken and Day, Nicholas (1989) *Field Guide to the Birds of Australia*, Penguin Books

Stuart, John McDouall (1864) *Explorations in Australia: The Journals of John McDouall Stuart*, Saunders, Otley and Co.

Taylor, Peter (1980) *An End to Silence: The Building of the Overland Telegraph Line from Adelaide to Darwin*, Methuen Australia

Thomson, Alice (1999) *The Singing Line*, Random House UK

Traynor, Stuart (2016) *Alice Springs: From Singing Wire to Iconic Outback Town*, Wakefield Press

Turner, Margaret Kemarre, OAM (2010) *Iwenhe Tyerrtye: What It Means to Be an Aboriginal Person*, IAD Press

Uluru Statement From the Heart www.ulurustatement.org

Urban, Anne (1990) *Wildflowers and Plants of Inland Australia*, Portside Editions

Webster, Mona Stuart (1958) *John McDouall Stuart*, Melbourne University Press

White, Mary E. (1994) *After the Greening: The Browning of Australia*, Kangaroo Press

Author's Note

Geoff Tiller sold The Barbed Wire Hotel in 2017. It is now known as The Spalding Hotel. The barbed-wired collection is now at the Daly Waters Pub in the Northern Territory.

William Creek now has a desalination plant, Optus and Telstra mobile coverage, and Trevor Wright owns the hotel freehold.

Margie Ewart died in 2016 aged 101.

In 2019, Kathy Mills was awarded a Member of the Order of Australia, and sadly passed away in May 2022.

Acknowledgements

So many people have played a part in making *Whispering Wire* a reality. Thank you to everyone mentioned in the book. I am very grateful to Rosemary Wanganeen, Reg Dodd, Bobby Hunter, John Moriarty, M.K. Turner, Frank Ansell, Francine MacCarthy and Kathy and Patj Patj Mills for sharing their stories. Many thanks to Bev Phelts, Historical Society of the Northern Territory; Samantha Wells, Northern Territory Library; Margaret McCallum, Melrose Museum; Associate Professor Gavin Mudd, RMIT University; Maria Stewart, Dunjiba Community Council; Tim Dickson, National Trust Museum, Pine Creek; Dan Fitzgerald, Alice Springs Telegraph Station; Eric Brace, The Australian Literacy and Numeracy Foundation; Rick Moore, John McDouall Stuart Society, and Trevor Horman, Deb Danks, Karen Williams and Jo Oakes. Also, the generosity of Barry, Ola and Julian Todd in providing information about Charles Todd and the Overland Telegraph Line.

I so appreciate Dervla Murphy's advice to just get on and write the book, Jan Cornall's mentoring to help me to find the bones of the story, the inspired guidance of writers Maggie Hamilton and Walter Mason, and the enthusiasm of Sharon Klingler.

Many thanks to Penny Campbell for her research and ideas, and to Philippa Clayton for saving my bottom with a pair of padded cycling pants. Jenny Danks's reading of and feedback on an early draft was invaluable, Tim Graham's beady eye for detail was crucial, and thank you to Jo Butler, Benny Agius and Kathy Mossop for their generous advice.

I would never have finished the book without the gentle goading of Lani Foulger, Caro Williams and Melissa McLeod, and the encouragement of Helen Leslie and all my family.

My utmost thanks to Wakefield Press, to Michael Bollen for believing in *Whispering Wire* and publishing it, to Julia Beaven for her wonderful editing skills, to Michael Deves for bringing the manuscript to life with his layout and text design, and to Stacey Zass for a cover design which truly captures the essence of the book. I so appreciate the great work of Poppy

Nwosu and Polly Grant Butler in promoting *Whispering Wire*, and all that Jonny Inverarity, Milly Bollen and Maddy Sexton have done to get it out to the world.

Thank you so much to Denise Miller for having Fleur Dare and me to stay. I am enormously grateful to Fleur for not only coaxing me up the Adelaide Hills and our wonderful weeks of cycling, but also for her divine drawings for the book. I so appreciate Alison Martin accompanying me from Alice Springs to Darwin and her insistence on all our delectable swims.

And thank you to my soulmate, Steve Leslie, for not only driving me along the off-road section of the Overland Telegraph Line, but for his love and support, and belief in this book, despite the years it has taken to write.

Wakefield Press is an independent publishing and
distribution company based in Adelaide, South Australia.
We love good stories and publish beautiful books.
To see our full range of books, please visit our website at
www.wakefieldpress.com.au
where all titles are available for purchase.
To keep up with our latest releases, news and events,
subscribe to our monthly newsletter.

Find us!

Facebook: www.facebook.com/wakefield.press
Twitter: www.twitter.com/wakefieldpress
Instagram: www.instagram.com/wakefieldpress

www.ingramcontent.com/pod-product-compliance
Lightning Source LLC
Chambersburg PA
CBHW050347230426
43663CB00010B/2023